PENGUIN BOOKS

PLAYING THE SELECTIVE COLLEGE
ADMISSIONS GAME

Richard Moll has spent most of his professional life in college admissions: first at Yale, then at Harvard (as Director of the African Scholarship Program of American Universities), then as Dean of Admissions at Bowdoin, at Vassar, and at the University of California at Santa Cruz. He has written extensively on "getting in": articles in *Harper's*, *The New York Times*, *Saturday Review*, *The Washington Post*, *The Wall Street Journal*, *College Board Review*, and *The Journal of the National Association of College Admissions Directors*, and two books—*Playing the Private College Admissions Game* and *The Public Ivys*. Moll is a frequent talk-show visitor on the subject of selective college admissions, having appeared on the Public Broadcasting System, "Nightline," "Today," "Good Morning America," and "CBS Morning News." Richard Moll also wrote *The Lure of the Law: Why People Become Lawyers and What the Profession Does to Them*. He now lives in Boston, is a consultant to colleges on matters related to enrollment health, and lectures widely to student and parent audiences on selective college admissions.

Playing the Selective College Admissions Game

Richard Moll

PENGUIN BOOKS

PENGUIN BOOKS
Published by the Penguin Group
Penguin Books USA Inc., 375 Hudson Street,
New York, New York 10014, U.S.A.
Penguin Books Ltd, 27 Wrights Lane,
London W8 5TZ, England
Penguin Books Australia Ltd, Ringwood,
Victoria, Australia
Penguin Books Canada Ltd, 10 Alcorn Avenue,
Toronto, Ontario, Canada M4V 3B2
Penguin Books (N.Z.) Ltd, 182–190 Wairau Road,
Auckland 10, New Zealand

Penguin Books Ltd, Registered Offices:
Harmondsworth, Middlesex, England

Playing the Private College Admissions Game first
published in the United States of America by
Times Books, a division of Quadrangle/The New York
Times Book Co., Inc., 1979
Published in Penguin Books 1980
Revised edition published 1986
This second revised edition published 1994

10 9 8 7 6 5 4 3 2 1

Copyright © Richard W. Moll, 1979, 1986, 1994
All rights reserved

LIBRARY OF CONGRESS CATALOGING IN PUBLICATION DATA
Moll, Richard.
Playing the selective college admissions game, revised edition.
ISBN 0 14 05.1303 5
1. Universities and colleges—United States—Admission. I. Title.
[LB2351.M64 1980]   378'.1056   80–12987

Printed in the United States of America
Set in Caledonia and Times Roman

Except in the United States of America, this book
is sold subject to the condition that it shall
not, by way of trade or otherwise, be lent, re-sold,
hired out, or otherwise circulated without the
publisher's prior consent in any form of binding
or cover other than that in which it is published
and without a similar condition including this
condition being imposed on the subsequent purchaser.

To

the family—especially Mom and Dad, whose
encouragement to the young I have attempted
to emulate in these pages—

and to Joe and Peaches and Katherine,

and to all those teenagers who have more
to offer than they know
or perhaps are willing to admit

Acknowledgments

Where does one begin in acknowledging the scores of dedicated high school counselors? They are overworked and underpaid, and are so often more effective then their audiences know or acknowledge. My thanks to them all.

My thanks also to the host of savvy and sensitive college admission and financial aid officers nationwide who, despite difficult economic and demographic hurdles, more often than not elevate the well-being of young people above institutional gain. In recent years, I have been particularly grateful for the examples (and so often, the advice) of Joe Allen, Andre Bell, Gail Berson, Carl Bewig, John Blackburn, Bill Elliott, Jean Fetter, David Finney, Bill Fitzsimmons, Dan Hall, Fred Hargadon, Zina Jacques, Linda and John Maguire, Robin Mamlet, Joan Isaac Mohr, Jim Montoya, Walter Moulton, Bill Munsey, Duncan Murdoch, Ted O'Neill, Paul Ranslow, Gary Ripple, Jim Scannell, Chuck Schuler, Mary Anne Schwalbe, Rick Shaw, Cliff Sjogren, Rae Lee Siporin, Dick Stabell, Dick Steele, Susan Tree, Ed Wall, Ann Wright, and Kris Zavoli.

This book would not have happened without the incentive and/or counsel of my agent, Molly Friedrich, my patient editor, Nicole Guisto, and Gerry Friedman, Lewis Lapham of *Har-*

per's, Professor William Gifford of Vassar, Susan Connolly Eckert, David Levy of Caltech, Bart Astor of *College Planning Quarterly*, the officers and publications of several professional organizations—College Board, the National Association of College Admissions Counselors and the National Association of Student Financial Aid Administrators—and the following students, who agreed to share their college application essays: Carlos Griffith, Jade Jeng, Wade Komisar, and Jessica Miller.

Very special thanks go to Pat Henning and Katherine Kendall, good friends and exemplary college counselors in California, who spent hours of research, writing, and editing for this edition of *Playing the Selective College Admissions Game*.

Contents

ACKNOWLEDGMENTS ix

INTRODUCTION xiii

1. **PLAYING THE GAME FOR PRACTICE** 1

2. **THE CANDIDATE LOOKS AT THE COLLEGE** 85

Myth I, NAME: "The More Prestigious the College, the Better the College" 85

Myth II, LOCATION: "To Retire to the Ocean or the Woods with My Books—or If Not, to Boston—Would Be Utopia" 89

Myth III, SIZE: "The Smaller the College, the More Personal the Education" 92

Myth IV, MAJOR: "Any Prominent College Will Be Good in My Field" 94

Myth V, SOCIAL TYPE: "Single-Sex Colleges Are Dead" 97

Myth VI, COST: "The Ivy-Type Colleges Are Now for the Rich and the Poor: The Middle Class Has Been Squeezed Out" 100

In Summary 108

3. **THE COLLEGE LOOKS AT THE CANDIDATE** 117

Structuring the Classful of Differences 117

Juggling the Specific Factors 123

The Academic Evaluation 124

The Personal Evaluation 151

4. **SELL, SELL, SELL: WHY COLLEGES *AND* STUDENTS MUST FLAUNT THEMSELVES** 187

The College 187

The Student 193

APPENDIX I
WHEN EVALUATING AN INDEPENDENT COUNSELOR 199

APPENDIX II
FINANCIAL AID GUIDE: CALTECH, 1993-94 201

APPENDIX III
REPRESENTATIVE RESPONSES TO MOLL'S *HARPER'S* ARTICLE, "THE COLLEGE ADMISSIONS GAME" 221

APPENDIX IV
STATEMENT OF PRINCIPLES OF GOOD PRACTICE 225

APPENDIX V
THE LIGHTER SIDE 229

Introduction

The envelope in my mailbox on April 17 was a thin one. Without opening it, I knew: I was a Princeton reject.

Correction: I am a Princeton reject. Somehow we never quite forget that introductory hour of judgment when a selective college announces that our first major Here-Am-I Statement has "passed" or "failed." The college admissions office plays a heavy and quick hand in adolescent flirtation with self-worth.

Around the family dinner table that evening there were tears, then anger . . . then a quiet, slightly resentful withdrawal to take stock.

Maybe Princeton just couldn't bear to include my Hoosier trappings on their freshman roster? I was graduating from Broad Ripple High School ("The Ripple Rockets") and had prepped for Broad Ripple at John Strange Elementary School. To top all, the Strange School had a principal named Mr. Quear (I swear to God: Check Ripley's roster of wonders, late forties). And it didn't seem to matter to Princeton that Ripple's colors were orange and black.

It *did* matter to Princeton that my academic involvements had been rather thoroughly displaced in favor of running every schoolboy organization in sight—that is, when incessant schoolboy song-and-dance performances provided intermission for more serious activity. But tough courses and disciplined study? No.

In short, Princeton was right.

Looking back, how was it that my family and I avoided arranging a session—just one—with the guidance counselor? How did she avoid getting to me for a little tough talk regarding objectivity in college planning? And what right did the Princeton alumni rep (everyone's favorite local clergyman/sportsman) have to assure my family that I was a "clear admit"? (The Reverend's nod of approval caused us to hop to New Jersey during high school spring vacation to see which dorm might be nicest for fall. As I recall, we even made a deposit on a black-with-a-touch-of-orange tweed couch at the local Tigertown mart.)

This book is being written with the knowledge that there are too many Broad Ripples (some called St. So-and-So), too many how-did-she-avoid-me counselors, too many families who mistake local-turf fame for Ivy suitability, and, alas, too few Princetons who (most abruptly at times) issue forth a judgment that is, more often than not, sound.

We in admissions are inherently garrulous. We talk a lot not only to candidates, parents, and counselors, but also to one another. In fact, we talk candidly *mostly* to one another, and say far too little beyond Why-My-College? to all you others.

This book is an attempt to share insider talk on selective college admissions, public and private, with outsiders.

And this is, essentially, a how-to book. But before the tips can be implied or spelled out, several basic concepts must be understood:

1. Many prestigious colleges in America today are *not* highly selective; if they feel you can survive their program, you'll be admitted. High price, a declining number of college-age Americans, and apprehension regarding the worth of a bachelor's degree in the job marketplace have created this phenomenon.
2. Unfortunately, many colleges and universities pose as be-

ing more selective than they really are. They feel good students will not be attracted to them if they do not create an aura of selectivity at the front gate. But as a result of the hidden anxiety that the upcoming class may not be filled with the quantity and quality of students hoped for, the admissions office tends to *over*state the qualities of the institution. So students and families must analyze a private college as carefully as they would analyze an automobile before buying it. Probing questions must be asked to confirm what is advertised and to check tone, performance, and justification of price. "Test rides" must be made by visiting classes, libraries, Union buildings, campus art galleries, athletic facilities, laboratories, and dorms. Hunches must be confirmed by talking with those who earlier decided in favor of the product.

3. A *few* public and private undergraduate institutions in America today are as highly selective as they ever have been, and a handful are even more selective. But it is rare that a college enjoys the luxury of admitting one out of two of their candidates, and not more than a half dozen colleges nationwide admit one out of five applicants. Aspiring kids and parents flock in droves to the latter little inner circle, hoping to get a bit of the juicy and seemingly irresistible prestige. Even though fame-of-a-name is not always consistent with an elite college's quality, the hordes keep applying, not realizing (or caring?) that the academic program may be as good or better at a place considerably more accessible.

4. Nothing speaks louder than a strong high school record in the college admissions game. "Other considerations" are almost always secondary in importance to the degree of difficulty of a candidate's courseload, grades, class rank, recommendations from teachers and school officials, standardized test scores, and the depth of extracurricular involvement.

5. Given the (rare) highly selective college situation, and given an average candidate in that college's admissions

competition, "other considerations" can indeed enter the picture, some of which the candidate can capitalize on. Who is admitted from the muddy middle of a selective college's applicant pool is partly a matter of chance, and the applicant has some control over "positioning" himself. (Also, alas, one applicant's ability to pay the full cost without financial aid may well be relevant when two candidates seem equally attractive.)

It might be most helpful to concentrate on the end of the admissions process first, and to reserve our discussion of the beginning of the process for later. Thus, the first section of this book speaks to where the average reader probably aspires to be: on the borderline of being admitted—and consequently the subject of debate by the Admissions Committee—to a college we'll call "quite selective" (for the sake of realism, not one of the tiny few "highly selective"). One might substitute a Colby or Colorado College or University of California at San Diego or Barnard or Boston College or Lafayette or Hamilton or Johns Hopkins or Sarah Lawrence or University of Pennsylvania or NYU or Occidental or Howard or University of Richmond or University of Vermont for what I'm calling "Oldebrick." Such a college is prestigious, has a strong undergraduate program, and admits approximately half of its applicants; the applicants are, overall, of quite sound quality because Oldebrick has always been known as one of "the fine, demanding schools" and has traditionally been able to attract bright, interesting (and often affluent) young people.

My hope is that when the reader sees what happens at the end of the line in the college admissions game, he or she will know how to make wiser starting moves: how to search for the right universities and college(s) amidst a barrage of rumors from friends and family and a barrage of professional marketing techniques by the institutions; how to recognize which elements of the secondary school record are most important and which elements of *self* should be dramatized; and how to understand how and why selective colleges structure a "classful of differences."

First, a simulated Admissions Committee meeting that draws heavily on actual cases, committee personalities, moods, and processes of the meetings I've attended or commandeered during my three decades in undergraduate college admissions.

Playing the Selective College Admissions Game

1.

Playing the Game for Practice

> Note: Although "Oldebrick" is a private college, it should be noted as we begin this mock admissions committee exercise that the most selective public institutions ("The Public Ivys") often pass through a similar "subjective" process to admit undergraduates, particularly for the precious *out*-of-state slots in the class (usually fewer than 10 percent of the freshman openings at the University of California campuses, but as many as 35 percent of the class at superselective University of Virginia or nearby William and Mary). Often the public institutions admit *in*-state students largely by formula, including grade-point average in the substantial courses and standardized test scores (ACTs or SATs) related to the proposed academic major.

Benson was late again.

The Mathematics, Political Science, Art History, and Classics faculty reps to the Admissions Committee had shown up on time as expected, and were now on their second round of coffee in the sparse and functional President's Conference Room, Main Building. But the Dean of Admissions knew he'd have to wait for Professor Truman Benson of the English Department.

The appearance of the conference room was less than grand. Amidst the clutter of cardboard file boxes holding 3,700 tired manila folders was a huge coffeepot surrounded by colorful hot-and-cold dixie cups, two stacks of ashtrays, rubber-banded cylinders of yellow pencils, and computerized printouts of the entire applicant pool. The paraphernalia so necessary to this committee's mission did nothing to enhance the appearance of an already sterile setting.

In two's and three's, faculty members were simulating serious conversation with members of the admissions staff, so often perceived as "extras" to the faculty, and slightly distrusted. ("After all, you've moved into heavy marketing and recruiting now," a faculty member said to the Dean of Admissions at the Student Union recently.)

It was spring break at Oldebrick, and "representative" faculty consultants to the Admissions Committee had been called upon to give precious vacation time to augment the admissions staff's votes in deciding which candidates would be admitted from the final muddy-middle group of the applicant pool. The assignment: Vote in half of the 125 applicants whose folders would be reviewed in an intense five-day period. The rules: 1. No vote and no discussion until *all* members were present (six admissions staff, five faculty) so that every vote would be uniform; 2. Committee members were urged to vote in favor of only those candidates who seemed truly desirable—those with the most votes would win in the end, and all others would fall to the waiting list (or be rejected, if something unusual was afloat).

Professor Benson finally blustered forth, in uniform: horn-rims, yellow striped shirt, rumpled gray suit, pink polka dot hanky flopping from the pocket. He thought he could warm up the cool reception by springing his oft-published flip: "I know we're here to sweat over College Board scores, absurd hairline differences between A– and B+ averages, and Miss Tillihofer's credibility when she says, 'This is the best student I've taught in twenty years at Central High.' But I say to hell with it. This year I'm going to sit dispassionately outside your rantings over seventeen-year-old accomplishment, and vote with one consideration in mind: *Whom* do I want in the bow of my canoe?"

Drawing a guffaw from Butch Lassiter of Classics (also volunteer assistant line coach of football), no response from Harry Chin of Mathematics, only the hint of a forced smile from Nora

Taylor of Political Science, and an outright hostile stare from Rita Dorsett of Art History, he retreated to a serious posture.

"Whom do I want in the bow of my canoe? I mean it! That's the hurdle each kid must jump. And which of you will prove to me before we begin that my number-one criterion is less reliable than yours?" Benson skipped the coffee, grabbed a Danish, and slumped in the one remaining black-with-Oldebrick-seal chair at the large oval table.

While Ms. Dorsett fidgeted with her handkerchief, mustering courage to snap back at Benson, the Dean started the meeting, twenty minutes late. This was an 8:00 P.M. orientation session on the eve of the five-day voting marathon.

"A few of you have been through this exercise before, but most of you are new. Thanks to you all for giving up five days of vacation time. As you know, I've consulted with the Dean of the Faculty to structure a balanced group of representatives to this Committee, hoping the entire faculty will feel indirectly involved in selecting the new class. We in the Admissions Office too often feel like an island at the College, and I struggle to find lines of communication to the faculty. This is one.

"You're here to help us decide whether Jane Jones should be admitted before John James, and why. Frankly, I'm a bit weary of those friendly locker-room-after-squash conversations when you earnestly query why our College Board averages aren't as high as Yale's, how so-and-so got into the class when he can't quite seem to put a sentence together, and why we can't attract more who want to major in Physics or Classics."

"Jesus, that's all we need to lure some of our disenchanted alums to cough up extra endowment capital: more drones for Physics and wimps for Classics," sputtered Benson.

Scowling at the representative from English, the Dean began again hurriedly:

"This will be a tight five days, reviewing twenty-five candidates per day. We won't begin until everyone is in his or her seat—hopefully, at nine each morning. I'll read the comments of teachers and guidance counselors from applicants' folders aloud while you check out the students' statistics in the computerized docket in front of you. We'll break one hour for lunch (I'll jog, and would enjoy your company), and we'll disband promptly at five. If we can hold down editorial and emotional chatter and limit discussion to clarification of the kids' credentials or honest talk about what a specific candidate symbolizes in terms of overall admissions policy, we can finish the job on time. Actually, we *must* finish on time: Our secretaries need over two weeks to prepare the decision letters, all of which will be mailed to applicants during the first week of April. As always, we and twenty or so of our colleague colleges will mail on the same day."

Nora Taylor of Political Science shook her head. "This already sounds tedious to me. Can I smoke in here?"

"Sitting next to a smoker for *five days?*" gasped Rita Dorsett of Art. "Oh please, Nora. Why don't we take a five-minute break every hour on the hour for the smokers to leave the room?" The Dean nodded quick approval, and continued.

"Before we get into the line-up of candidates, let me tell you where the admissions staff has brought us to date. You might want to jot these numbers down for reference during the next few days. We have 3,707 completed applications this year, up 3 percent over last year—a comforting sign in this era of fewer seventeen-year-olds and declining interest in private colleges (the latter probably related more to cost than to any other factor). The target number for next fall's class is 600, down a little from last year as we seem to have fewer students transferring out, so less room for entering freshmen. To get a class of 600 we must admit approximately 1,275 kids, anticipating a yield of 47 percent. In other words, slightly fewer than half of those we admit will choose us on May 1, the National Candidate's Reply Date."

Mr. Chin adjusted his glasses. "Excuse me. Less than half of those we admit actually choose us?"

"I know it's disappointing," replied the Dean, settling somewhat more comfortably into his chair now. "But don't be discouraged by our 47 percent yield: Columbia's yield last year was 44 percent; MIT's 52 percent; Duke's 44 percent; UCLA's

38 percent; Carleton's 33 percent, and Swarthmore's 34 percent. Most secondary school seniors apply to five or six places now, and can obviously attend only one. Harvard/Radcliffe is the only college in America with a consistently high yield, around 75 percent year after year. Even Yale normally lands only about 55 percent of those they admit, losing hundreds of admittees to Harvard alone each year.

"But back to us. Each folder has been read by three different admissions officers. And each reader has rated the candidate on a one-to-five scale in three categories: academic, personal, and overall evaluation. Prior to this evening we on the staff admitted 1,212 applicants, rejected approximately 2,130, proposed 240 for the waiting list, and sent 125 to this Committee for final deliberation."

Adam McDermott of the admissions staff started circling the table with coffee refills. The faculty delegation looked as though they were taking an examination, busily scribbling notes and numbers on paper provided.

The Dean moved on. "You will note in your computerized docket of candidates, arranged by state and then alphabetically by secondary school, that there are some inconsistencies in our decisions, at least in terms of straight statistics such as GPAs (Grade Point Average) or class rank. If you spot any proposed decision that seems out of line, question me after one of these meetings and I'll pull the folder from the file for you to see— all folders are here in these boxes. If you feel the entire Committee should review the case, we'll add it on at the end."

"Oh, my," said Mr. Chin softly. "I'm leaving for a mathematics conference two hours after our sessions are over on Sunday, so I certainly hope we do not add many cases to our deliberations."

The Dean stood to stretch. "We can finish up on time, but I don't want to close off discussion on any candidate you spot on the docket—particularly a reject—whose proposed action you cannot understand. Remember, though, that stats alone do not tell the whole story. We're interested in an appraisal of motivation. We must analyze whether one school's grading system is as tough as the next. And we also have to pay attention to the forest as well as to the trees: will the class have adequate minority representation? decent football and hockey squads? enough students who can pay their own way so our scholarship resources are not overdrawn? an adequate showing of alumni children? a spread of proposed academic majors so the entire class won't end up in the pre-med or pre-law hoppers?"

Nora Taylor of Political Science interrupted. "Well, I'm not going to overlook the cold statistics with ease. I'm really concerned about the gradual decline in SATs over the last several years at Oldebrick and I'm here, quite frankly, with the intent of being score-conscious. Those who were on this Committee last year have led me to believe that we're going to second-guess socioeconomic advantage or disadvantage, the influence of an alcoholic mother on a teenager's in-school performance, how important it is to throw a ball well, and how much better a student's record might have been if only she had been able to attend a more demanding high school.

"Law schools look at test scores! One of my responsibilities here is to slip kids into law school as a reward for their $100,000 investment in Oldebrick. Law schools seem to use standardized test scores as an initial screening, and do not even move to appraise a student's four-year undergraduate record if the Law Boards aren't above a certain fairly high cut-off level. Certainly, some students will be spliced into the class on the basis of somewhat different and imaginative standards. But for the mainstream applicant, the standardized tests seem to stand supreme in importance. In other words, there is no substitute for brains!

"My informal studies at Oldebrick show that, on the whole, a high performer on the SATs will be a high performer on the Law Boards four years later, regardless of what happens in the four intervening years of undergraduate study.

"Now, if this theory is correct—and I'm rather certain it is, probably as much for the medical school as for the law school aspirants—I'm voting for the highest College Board scores I can find in the pack. I can only enjoy my summer canoe, Truman, if my graduate school placements have gone well in the spring."

The Dean sat patiently and watched Taylor as she made her statement. It seemed the Dean welcomed basic questions at this stage in the proceedings. There was a short silence.

"Perhaps you'll all be surprised that I'm the one most eager to disagree with what Dr. Taylor said," Mr. Chin of Mathematics said suddenly. "When I look around the table, I think that my department must seem the most cut-and-dried, perhaps the most confining in terms of a student's ultimate vocational choice. I'll save the speech refuting that for later. But right now I would like to say just one thing. This is a liberal arts college. We are here to teach students to broaden their horizons. Much as I, too, would like to improve our graduate school placement record, *for* the record, I would like to remind you that it is not the business of this institution to be career-oriented. The pressure has clearly increased to become so, but I want no part of it. A person spends only one-fifth of his or her life on the job, if my calculations are correct, and I'm more interested in educating toward the *other* four-fifths, when one is confronted with priorities and the values of decision-making. We in Mathematics have stumbled upon such wonderful human surprises at this college that to chart success by means of our own statistics would be subterfuge."

Truman Benson stirred. "I'm moved, but I'm staying with my canoe." He prepared to take the floor once again, but Rita Dorsett of Art, a fiftyish, prime fixture at Oldebrick, broke in.

"I'm moved too; in fact, I've just been quietly jolted to become a fan of the Math Department. To think I have been fooled all along about what was going on over there!" Ms. Dorsett and Mr. Chin exchanged formal, nodding smiles, looking somewhat like peace ambassadors at a conference table.

"Of course this is a liberal arts college, and the strength of my department is a symbol of its remaining so. Students often don't find something like Art History until the sophomore or junior year of college. Worrying about students' job preference would inhibit the intellectual expansion our less visible departments can provide. Give the students time to stumble upon us, off the track of job myopia."

Ms. Dorsett stiffened in her chair and reached to adjust the bun she wore as a crown. "I am prompted to say something else before our candidate review begins. I'm just wondering how on earth we are supposed to spot 'motivation and thirst'? The attitude in my classroom is beginning to remind me of the fifties, and I don't particularly like it. As our tuition soars, I fear we're attracting more of the very rich who are not at all nervous about the important step of college, do not even give much thought to it, and who seem considerably more intrigued by the next party than by the next reference book or social issue.

"I serve on the Records Committee, where we are noting a pattern among those who fail which is strangely reminiscent of a bygone era. Yes, there were a few students in difficulty whose advisers had not cautioned them that they were over their heads in a heavy pre-med curriculum, or who just had not had satisfactory preparation in secondary school to cope—and we were sympathetic in their cases. But there were too many bright students whose SATs were above the class average and who just plain disappointed us—they didn't work hard because they didn't care. Most of them, judging from their schools, were affluent. Cyclical patterns scare me a little."

"You mean, is it a matter of money?" the Dean asked, obviously interested in Rita's statement. "Do we *have* to take the rich? Well, nothing contributes more to class diversity than scholarship resources. We're in a reasonably good position here but not as good as some of the competition. Rice, Wellesley, Cooper Union, Harvard, and Duke are examples of institutions which can comfortably fund all admitted students who have proved financial need. We can't. We're more in a league with Bowdoin, Brown, and Wesleyan in having the money to give scholarship assistance to approximately 40 percent of the entering class: We'd be strained to move beyond that proportion. (Almost all of our scholarships, remember, are on the basis of financial need. A good many colleges have moved to awarding scholarships on the basis of merit rather than need—they call them 'no-need awards' or 'merits,' but I would call them 'bribes.')

"The fact remains that my admissions staff must find nearly two-thirds of a freshman class (or 400 bodies) who can pay their own way. What this does to the general motivation level of the class, I don't know."

The financial aid topic was obviously falling on a few deaf ears around the table, but the Dean was earnest in pursuing it, with Mr. Chin, Rita Dorsett, and the younger members of the admissions staff listening intently.

"Now, let me anticipate one of your questions: Does the need of financial aid handicap a student in the admissions process? Somewhat, it seems to me, although you will be in a position to decide that as we vote on a few of these cases. I had a rather embarrassing public spat with a Director of Admissions from one of the Seven Sister colleges not long ago on this very topic. She was pontificating that she would leave the admissions field if ever 'ability to pay' were to become an admissions criterion at her college. So be it. But if an institution does not have the financial aid endowment of a Wellesley, and cannot possibly fund all candidates who are 'muddy-middle' in the applicant pool, I'm not convinced it is so evil to tip the scales toward a candidate who can pay his or her own way. After all, even Wellesley probably tips the scales now and then in favor of Utah over Massachusetts, or a candidate with a Wellesley mother rather than a Bryn Mawr mother. The admissions process is, and perhaps has to be, sprinkled with inequities."

Rita Dorsett straightened in her chair again. "Wellesley does so many things so well. Let's not be critical of them, Dean."

"I'm less critical than envious of institutions like Wellesley, which have more extensive financial resources than Oldebrick. Most selective private colleges do have the resources to fund all *outstanding* candidates, however, as do we. But well down the scale, when we have a broad choice of above-average but not thoroughly outstanding candidates to complete the class, we may favor the student, all else being rather equal, who can pay. Now, whether the consequence of accepting one more who can pay means less motivation in the classroom or not—who knows? Maybe we can talk about this again as individual candidates' cases beg the issue."

Butch Lassiter of Classics, who did not appear to have quite tuned in to the discussion yet, rose to open a window. Looking out on the freshman yard, he executed three quick knee-bends and four touch-your-toes.

"I think it is time to get to the first case," said the Dean, noting Lassiter's impatience. "Policy talk is easier when we're not discussing specific candidates. Let's let the applicants suggest policy decisions as we go."

"Hold it," said Butch Lassiter, jumping back to his seat with a broad grin. "I won't make a speech, but I just wanted to say one thing."

Lassiter was a thirtyish alumnus of Oldebrick with a boyish face and the ability to skirt offensive topics. "I just want to say that I'm in favor of school spirit, and in my experience, that means good athletics. There is a growing apathy and me-centeredness here at Oldebrick that may also mean a declining loyalty to the college. This careerist era has simply exhausted us and we're in a period of catching our breath, but I see no need to retrench altogether. I hear this mood is everywhere—at other colleges and in secondary schools, too. But one special ingredient at Oldebrick has been its spirit and sense of community, and I am beginning to miss it."

Now Nora Taylor rose to view the freshman yard as Lassiter continued.

"Oldebrick *needs* a rallying point or two right now, and I think that a winning athletic team or two can do the trick. We don't have to compromise academic stature for athletic strength—Michigan, Harvard, Stanford, and Berkeley are pretty good at winning games while pumping out more than their share of Rhodes Scholars. A good team or two in highly visible sports like football and basketball wouldn't hurt us one bit and might help us muster a little more enthusiasm throughout all levels of the college family."

Rita Dorsett smiled politely. "Now, Butch, that *is* a flashback.

I don't mind the presence of a few superb ballplayers here, providing we see some of them on the *female* team rosters also. What I do hate is spotting the goof-offs on campus who probably were admitted to help a team win, but who end up playing cards for four years at the Sig House. And if their ability on the field doesn't pan out, they're lost and rather pathetic souls, and we are the losers, too."

The Dean, missing an attempt to hit the wastebasket halfway across the room with his empty dixie cup, responded. "Well, you're certainly going to find others besides ballplayers failing to fulfill the potential you thought you had spotted at this table. You'll be charmed during the coming days by math potential, leadership potential, journalistic potential, et cetera. But who can predict which students, experiencing at age seventeen and a half a total change of environment and perhaps their first real freedom ever, will work and produce? So we're back to motivation and how to spot it."

"Let's go!" blurted Truman Benson, sharing his prolific doodlings with admissions staff members on either side of him (whose expressions seemed to suggest "How did *this* guy get appointed to the Committee?").

"Yes, Truman, let's go," nodded the Dean with a somewhat apologetic smile. "The seven candidates picked for discussion at this evening's orientation session seem to me almost to represent a microcosm of the entire applicant pool. At least they suggest why some of the central policy guidelines have no clear applicability once we come down to the choice of one candidate over another.

"The first candidate on your docket is TRUDI JAMESON." Suddenly everyone at the table straightened up, as though a starting gun had been fired.

"Trudi attends a superb country day school, one we'd like to do more business with. Note also that Trudi is from the Midwest, the area of the nation most underrepresented on many eastern private college campuses, partly because of the superb state university system out there, and partly because the area is just plain provincial. Anyway, Trudi is a Midwesterner, and we need more of them *if* you feel geographical diversity is important at the College. Your predecessors on this Committee felt that we will only be as lively as we are different, and splicing a little Orange County together with the Bronx can assure it.

"Let's look first at Trudi's transcript." *(See pages 13–14.)*

"What do we look at first?" Taylor asked, puzzled. This was her first year on the Committee.

"Well, look at the actual course listings to appraise the degree of difficulty of the courseload. Then you'll probably want to look at grades to see level of performance and whether she has performed consistently. Then, notice her class rank based on six semesters to the right of the transcript.

"Frankly, I find the quality of Trudi's courseload to be mixed, although I know this is a no-nonsense school. Trudi appears to have bailed out of Science and Foreign Language after the junior year, and her courses in those areas during junior year are weak. Her lowest grades throughout were in Math, so I can understand why she chose the least competitive senior math course. But why this good school also let her leave Science and Foreign Language is unclear. Her senior courseload appears on the surface to be adequate, although it is obviously centered in areas of key interest to her."

Around the table there was subdued chatter as faculty members checked transcript impressions with the admissions staff. And the Dean continued:

"Although the 'core curriculum' has returned to most secondary schools, we cannot presuppose that the best high schools and prep schools give kids a sound enough training in basic disciplines. A few of those avant-garde electives are still left over from the seventies. Trudi is probably happy that she was able to develop specific interests in the Humanities and the Arts, and thereby improve her overall record. But was she shortchanged in not being forced into a more balanced secondary education? I think so.

"Trudi's record improved with time, and she now ranks twentieth in their class of sixty-seven. By the way, a profile from the school in Trudi's folder indicates they had eighteen National

YEAR	CLASS RECORD *Include Subjects Failed or Repeated* SUBJECTS	IDENTIFY LAB TV SEMINAR SUMMER	IDENTIFY HONORS ACCEL AD. PL. ETC.	MARKS 1ST. SEM.	FINAL OR 2ND. SEM.	CRED OR UNIT	STATE EXAM. SCORES
9	English I - Genre			C+	C+	1	
	Math I - Algebra			D	C	1	
	Earth Science			C-	B-	1	
	Latin II			C+	C	1	
	French II			B-	B+	1	
	Studio Art			A	A	n/c	
10	English II - Creative Writing			A	A	1	
	Math II - Geometry			C+	B-	1	
	Modern World History			B-	B-	1	
	Biology I			B-	B	1	
	French III			B	B	1	
	Studio Art			A-	A-	n/c	
11	Studio Art			B+	B+	n/c	
	French IV			P	-	½	
	English III - Am Lit			B+	-	½	
	English III - Shakespeare			-	B+	½	
	Math III - Adv Alg			B-	C+	1	
	Physics - (Electricity), non-lab			B	B	½	
	American History			B-	B-	1	
	African Studies			-	A	½	
	Ind Study - Theater			-	P	n/c	
12	(mid-year: 7th semester)						
	Studio Art A P			A			
	English IV - Alienation & Affirmation			B+			
	Math IV - Prob & Stat			P			
	Journalism			A-			
	Senior Seminar: Int'l Rel			B+			
	Creative Reading (Ind Study)			B			
	Phy Ed			P			

Passing Mark	Honors Mark (if any)	LOWEST NUMERICAL EQUIVALENT			
		A	B	C	D
D-	B				

EXPLANATION OF HONORS COURSES

RANK IN CLASS BASED ON __6__ SEMESTERS

☑ EXACTLY 20   ☐ APPROX. _____ IN CLASS OF __67__

FINAL RANK _____

Check Appropriate Rank Information

☑ ALL SUBJECTS GIVEN CREDIT   ☑ ALL STUDENTS
☐ MAJOR SUBJECTS ONLY   ☑ COLL. PREP. STUDENTS ONLY

Explain Weighting of Marks in Determining Rank

Merit Semifinalists or Commended students last year in a class of sixty-five. Their own SAT medians for last year's seniors were 530 Verbal, 580 Math. Trudi's best SAT Verbal is a 580; her best Math score is 510; her College Board Achievements were 490 in English Composition; 560 in Math I; and 530 in American History. To put all this in context, remember that Oldebrick's median Verbal for last fall's entering freshman class was 580; our median SAT Math was 600."

"Oh, God, let's work on that," said Nora Taylor with her eyes still glued to the docket in front of her.

"I'll read bits and pieces from Trudi's folder now," said the Dean. "She had two sisters who graduated from here three and four years ago, so this is a family who knows Oldebrick well. Trudi's father is a bank executive with an M.B.A., and her mother is a housewife with a B.A. She does not need financial aid."

Mr. Chin squirmed. "Is it really necessary for you to tell us whether her mother and father went to college, and what they do for a living? Why is that important?" Mr. Chin was an understated and highly regarded professor who, as the son of a waiter and waitress, had gone to a public high school for the "gifted" in New York City prior to winning a full scholarship to NYU.

"Well, I think it is important," said Al Hodges, the precise and bow-tied Director of Financial Aid, who was annually invited to attend these meetings so his office, too, would feel more in communication with Admissions. "Has this candidate benefited from informed discussion night after night at the dinner table? Whether Mom and Dad and brothers and sisters went to college can give us a feel for the type of household the applicant has been exposed to. If we're talking about a noncollege taxi driver's or construction laborer's kid, there is a strong likelihood that we may be talking about an applicant who did not have certain advantages and encouragements that most other Oldebrick candidates did have."

As Mr. Chin nodded courteously, the Dean said, "Unless anyone strongly objects, I'll continue to comment on the education and employments of parents and siblings, where listed. But back to Trudi. When asked about her main academic interests, she says:

> My main interest at Oldebrick will be in the Fine Arts. I feel that communications is a very new and developing field, and that one of the best ways to communicate is through fine arts such as theater, dance, and film. I am interested in performing, directing, writing, designing, business, or any other of the many facets these fields offer.

Trudi has obviously had advantages, and she seems to have used them well. In the application slot designated for out-of-classroom activities, she says:

> During the last four years I have acted in 14 plays, and have also taken part in other aspects of the theater such as costuming, props, set construction, and student directing. My participation has been at school, community theater, and with the American Repertory Theater in Europe. Other activities at school have been in chorus, and student government. I am the Editor of the school's literary magazine, and Advertising Editor of the school's news magazine. Outside of school I have tutored for OEO, and studied piano. This past summer I performed with The American Repertory Theater Company in Europe. There were four classes every morning in voice, acting, Mime, and movement. There were six hours of rehearsal in the afternoon and evening. We rehearsed for five weeks on two plays, *Medea* and *The Birds*.
>
> When rehearsals ended, we left Lugano, Switzerland for Taormina, Sicily. After Sicily we performed in Pompeii and Fiesole, Italy. All the places in which we performed were old Greek and Roman outdoor theatres.

"The essay our candidates were assigned this year is intentionally wide open. We're one of over a hundred private colleges using what is called the Common Application. A candidate fills out the original, and mails photocopies to several colleges, and the schools do likewise with their forms. To get so many colleges to agree on a common form was obviously a minor

Playing the Game for Practice

miracle. Our greatest argument came over the choice of a common essay topic, and the result is a rather sweeping assignment:

> This personal statement helps us become acquainted with you in ways different from courses, grades, test scores, and other objective data. *It enables you to demonstrate your ability to organize thoughts and express yourself. Please write an essay about one of the topics listed below.*
>
> 1. Evaluate a significant experience or achievement that has special meaning to you.
> 2. Discuss some issue of personal, local, or national concern and its importance to you.
> 3. If you could interview a prominent person (past or present) in the arts, politics, religion, or science, for example, whom would you choose and why?

I'll read you snatches of Trudi's essay:

> I am I!/ And I may not know why/ But I know that I like it./ Three cheers! I am I.
>
> The above quotation from Dr. Seuss is what I think is important about me, 'I am I.' Being yourself and recognizing what is your 'self' is necessary for all people, so that they can live their lives fully. For if you do not understand yourself, how can you begin to understand others?"

"Spare us the pain," groaned Truman Benson. "My *God*, how do you Admissions people read 2,800 of these dreadful things? Please, good Dean, telescope the essay reading the next few days."

"Well, Trudi goes on to say, down the page here:

> If I sound like Hermann Hesse there is a reason, for he has played a part, as many authors have, and will, with how I see myself. . . . Through literature I have found a piece of myself which will help me endure life with others. But reading is a mental activity, and many physical ones contribute to form one's 'self.' I tend to think of art, the fine arts, and how they have expanded me personally.

> Each theater production was an awakening to new characters, new behaviors, etc., etc.

Trudi ends by saying:

> I have begun to understand myself, and by taking that step I have also begun to understand others. As for the future, not just mine, but anyone's, I have to agree with the Moody Blues: 'Just what you want to be, you'll be in the end.'"

"At least she can put a sentence together most of the time," Ms. Dorsett injected. "But I'm very tired of drama aspirants, not to mention the let-me-be-me syndrome, at least when presented in such shallow terms. I keep forgetting, however, that she's only seventeen, and from the sounds of it, one who has viewed the world from a very limited, carefully screened, perspective."

"Now we come to the School Report," continued the Dean. "You'll find as we move along that prep schools on the whole report more thoroughly, and perhaps even more sensitively, than the large public schools. Public school counselors just have too huge a student load to know kids well, and they also seem somewhat intimidated by the Buckley Amendment, or Family Educational Rights and Privacy Act. But there are only 67 seniors in Trudi's class, so this school knows its kids well. I'll read from the Headmaster's report:

> Trudi is a truly unique person who lives life to the full and enjoys it. Her philosophy is that one gets out of life exactly what one puts into it. Her standardized testing is not impressive, but she has a working ability as a student and as a person that far exceeds her numerical scores. In spite of the fact that she has always carried a remarkable schedule of activities, she has usually earned honor grades and certainly observes well-ordered priorities. She thrives on overinvolvement. From a purely traditional academic viewpoint she is not deeply intellectual, and her reading and writing skills are adequate for serious college study but not outstanding. But in self-confidence, self-discipline, willingness to work, and interest, she is

outstanding. Her driving interests are in the creative communication arts as well as the humanities.

She is truly one of the most vivacious, lively, and interesting members of her class, if not the entire student body. She is most respected for her honesty, self-confidence, and energy. Always easy to communicate with, she is a delightful friend and companion with her peers, and she also has highly successful, informal relations with the adults she knows. One teacher said recently, 'All the world *is* a stage for Trudi and she turns in an excellent performance in all of life's roles.' Yet, there is nothing 'stagey' or insincere in her approach to people or responsibilities.

The Headmaster continues his raves about Trudi's energies, the fact that she wishes there were 25 hours in every day, and concludes by saying:

I believe that the college in which Trudi enrolls will be fortunate to have her and I think she is ideal for Oldebrick in spite of test scores obviously below your average (and ours). She is thoroughly familiar with Oldebrick, which was attended by two older sisters. In short, we enthusiastically recommend her for admission."

"Was all that verbiage necessary?" queried Political Science's matter-of-fact Nora Taylor, already impatient with 124 candidates yet to be read. "All that the Headmaster said can be narrowed down to: 'Here is an energetic, involved, artistically inclined, affluent girl with middling abilities whom we'd like to slip into Oldebrick. You took her sisters, so why not Trudi?' "

As Butch Lassiter resumed his position at the window, the Dean continued after a cool glance at Taylor. "The verbiage does get a bit long-winded, Nora. But so often counselors and teachers truly capture a candidate in these characterizations. Let's hear what Trudi's Senior Seminar teacher has to say. By the way, we ask each candidate to submit at least one teacher's recommendation. We find that teachers are often less cautious than guidance counselors or principals, not to mention the fact that they know the kids better, having seen their ups and downs in the classroom. Someday we should consider eliminating everything in the candidate's folder except the kid's own application, a transcript, and comments from the English teacher. We might learn just as much as we do with today's fat folders that include comments from everyone around the schoolyard. Anyway, Trudi's African History teacher says:

> During the last several years, Trudi has taken every opportunity to diversify and take control of her own learning. She has studied education, politics and mountain climbing in East Africa. She has traveled in Europe with a repertory company. She took practical electricity as a junior and thoroughly enjoyed it. She has also designed independent study projects in costume design, contemporary literature, and grassroots politics. She is independent, sophisticated, well-traveled, strong-willed, sometimes intolerant, always proud, and an extremely confident girl. She has grace under pressure, at 15,000 feet on Mt. Kilimanjaro, or in a difficult dance sequence in a school play.
>
> As a reader, she is quick and critical. As a writer, she is straightforward and to the point. She can use dramatic analogies very effectively in both writing and speech. Her sense of balance and proportion is always true, both at the seminar table and in the art studio.

"Note that everyone thus far seems in unison regarding Trudi. Finally, here is a summary paragraph from the interview report in our office. Kelly Darby saw Trudi back in November:

> A very good prospect: strong-willed, very involved, innovative in approach to a sedate school setting, and obviously intelligent. She seems to have the combination of discipline and imagination needed."

Benson reached for his third Danish. "Now, how can anyone be *that* profoundly convinced of another's qualities in a twenty-minute interview?"

Kelly Darby, a bubbly 26-year-old Assistant Director of Admissions, spoke up, breaking the silence of the admissions staff who always found it a bit difficult to speak with confidence in the presence of faculty.

"I remember this girl well. Her energy, her composure, her willingness to try different things, her articulation: all were obvious. Granted, the interview—which is, by the way, usually considerably longer than twenty minutes, Professor Benson—often allows us to notice just the very obvious. If an applicant is particularly high-strung, particularly jolly, particularly shy, particularly intense about his or her studies, it sticks out. Regrettably, some of the subtle characteristics of the candidate don't show in this staged situation. But we *can* sight the obvious, often factors not indicated (for good or for bad) by teachers or by the candidates themselves in the folders. In Trudi's case, the interview confirmed all of the qualities mentioned by her school." Kelly bowed her head slightly, and smiled broadly.

"That, Ms. Darby, was a fine response to a sharp query. I'm going to believe everything you say about a candidate from now on," quipped Benson with an inviting glance.

"Well, that's all we know about Trudi Jameson," said the Dean. "Let me add that there are four candidates from her school this year. There is a brilliant all-everything boy who is second in the class and who probably applied here because his mother went here—perhaps in deference to her, perhaps because he thinks he's a sure bet to get in because he's a legacy. Anyway, we're admitting him but I'll wager he'll end up at one of the Ivies. We're also admitting a girl who is fourteenth in the class, high Board scores, and a bit of an underachiever, but she has spent all her time playing tennis and is currently ranked third in her age group in the state. She, according to a phone call from the guidance counselor last week, is torn between Carleton and Oldebrick: We may get her. Trudi is next in line in class rank. And we're rejecting another Oldebrick legacy who is in the bottom fifth of the class and dull, dull, dull."

Mr. Chin adjusted his glasses once again. "What does it mean today in admissions to be the son or daughter of one of our alumni?"

"This is a favorite question of the alums who return to campus," Butch Lassiter said in turning from the window. "What can we tell them?"

"Last year we admitted 68 percent of our legacies," the Dean said. "We define legacies as sons or daughters of alumni, *not* sisters or brothers or grandsons or nieces. We seem to end up admitting roughly the same percentage each year, somewhat coincidentally. Our legacies are often above-average candidates. But also, we're kind to them in the admissions process. I'm not saying we'll sell out to take a legacy, but all things being rather similar between two applicants, we'll tip toward the legacy. After all, our own alumni must support this place, and admitting their kids seems to *them* the most visible symbol of Alma Mater's caring in return."

"What do the Ivies, public and private, do—and the rest of our competition?" asked Butch Lassiter, his interest obviously piqued.

The Dean lifted his hands to his head and started a slow twisting exercise. "Oh, most of our colleagues in the private sector respond similarly. Some are extraordinarily generous with offspring of alums; it is not uncommon to admit *twice* the percentage of legacies that are admitted from the applicant pool overall. For example, last year Amherst admitted only 22 percent of all its candidates, but 49 percent of its legacies. Some colleges check with the Development Office before rejecting legacies."

Adam McDermott, a handsome, well-spoken 22-year-old and the latest in a string of admissions fellows hired at graduation from Oldebrick for a two-year term ("to get out and hustle where Oldebrick doesn't seem to be getting to first base in recruitment—Michigan and Indiana, for example"), nervously entered the conversation.

"Granted, I'm a newcomer and don't know all the ropes—and don't think I'm ungrateful, as I was on scholarship and know it was alumni who made it possible for me to graduate from this place. But after seeing dozens of deserving, well-qualified, and naive kids throughout the nation this year who would benefit so much from attending Oldebrick if just given the chance, it irks me to see us giving *any* favoritism to the 'old families' of the college, with the cash register ringing in our ears. If we're concerned about loyalty and dollars and future, what's wrong with attracting *new* families?"

Adam paused for a moment to catch his breath, and then said in an apologetic tone, "Sorry to interrupt, but having met some of our stuffy alums on the road, and having had my fill of their expectations of favoritism in the admissions process as some sort of payoff, I just had to say something."

For several moments no one spoke. Then the Dean said, "Thanks for your thoughts, Adam. Continue to speak up. That's the sort of thing we need to hear. In defense of the legacies, however, I should add that their record of performance at the College, once admitted, is strong. But it is also relevant to add, I think, that the admission or rejection of a legacy—after all the shouting is over—seems to make little difference in the giving pattern of the parents to Alma Mater. Studies here and elsewhere confirm that."

"Look, let's vote on Miss Jameson," said Benson. "Aside from her tweedy enthusiasm, I think she's dull as beans."

"Give her greater exposure, and she may develop nicely," responded Mr. Chin. "It seems to me that her basic instincts are quite good, and she has made the most of her aptitude and her manifold opportunities. What, exactly, is her flaw, except the absence of 750 Verbal and Math scores? I think she suffers here from being the first in line."

"She *does* suffer because she's first," Rita Dorsett agreed. "Since we know this is a 'control group' tonight, and since we're just getting our feet wet, why don't we hear and discuss each candidate, then vote on all seven at the end of the evening? That way we'll be able to put them all in context, at least with one another. Tomorrow morning we can go to the regular procedure, voting after each applicant is read. We'll have an educated base of reference then. I can see this is going to be draining." She frowned and glanced about, but there were no receivers.

"Unless there is strenuous objection, I find that a good suggestion to follow," said the Dean. With even Benson quiet at this point, the group proceeded to the next case.

"Our next candidate also attends a private day school, or rather did attend one. (I've put our private school candidates together tonight just for the ease of comparison.) PATRICIA MURPHY graduated a semester early and is now working in New York City for several months before entering college in the fall. Her school would be considered fairly decent, but not nearly as strong at Trudi Jameson's. You have Patricia's transcript in front of you." *(See page 25.)*

Butch Lassiter interrupted: "I notice you always seem to start with a comment about the candidate's school. What benefit does a kid actually have coming from a private school?" Butch had taught and coached at a boarding school prior to being hired by Oldebrick.

"The benefit of being a prime candidate for our Records Committee," Ms. Dorsett snapped back tartly and uncharacteristically. "Some of the prep school products are spoiled children, regardless of what advantage they might have had in academics. So what if they read *Catcher in the Rye* one or two years early? At most of the boarding schools they learn social values by cold rules and regulations. Is that right for a fifteen-year-old? Once they get to college, they flounder in pretentious emancipation, while their public school colleagues earnestly, apprehensively, intelligently, and quietly dig right in because the comfort level isn't quite as high."

Rita Dorsett often twisted her handkerchief or poked her bun. At this point, she twisted, then poked.

Others around the table appeared unmoved.

"Rita, that indictment strikes me as a little heavy," replied the Dean. "It is true that some of the prep school products, particularly the boarding school kids, may fly a little high on their newfound freedom—and with a coterie of last summer's friends transplanted here from Cape Cod or the Hamptons. But maybe part of the problem is that we offer too much choice and freedom to our freshmen, particularly those who were part of a rather tight situation such a short time before, be it a school or a family. True, the home may provide a more flexible hit-or-miss social laboratory than the boarding school, but let's look

3. STUDENT'S ACADEMIC HISTORY

MINIMUM PASSING MARK		OTHER PASSING MARKS USED (AND NUMERICAL EQUIVALENT)	
GRADE & YRS.	COURSES TAKEN (AND SPECIAL LEVEL WHERE APPROPRIATE)	MARKS	CREDITS
9th	English 1	B	
	French 1	A	
	Geometry	A	
	Biology	B	
	Civics	A	
10th	English 2	A	
	French 2	B	
	Algebra 2	A	
	Physics 1	A	
	European History	A	
11th	English 3	A	
	French 3	A	
	Analytic Geometry	A	
	Physics 2	A	
	Art Major	A	
	U.S. History A.P.	A+	
12th (one sem.)	Humanities (Eng. 12)	A	
	Literature Tutorial	A	
	Philosophy	A	
	French 4	A	
	Greek 1	A	
	World History A.P.	A	
	SAT: V = 730; M = 700		
	ACH: En = 640; Ml = 560; Fr = 580		
	AP : AH = 4		

at how the prep school product ultimately fares here rather than just judge the entering student with his cool, sophisticated facade."

Butch persisted. "I just want to know if prep school kids are somewhat advantaged in our admissions situation."

"Well, Butch, I like to think we're looking at kids more than at schools," said the Dean. "Not long ago, some boarding schools served essentially as farm clubs for the most sought-after colleges. No longer. College admissions has democratized on one side, and the schools have broadened their college counseling on the other. Also, remember that a good many boarding schools were more selective in their admissions some years ago than they are now. St. Grottlesex today is probably not helping us with the one-out-of-three screening in *their* admissions process that used to be rather automatic. The high price of education and charges of elitism have hurt them, too. Their popularity will return, however, if the quality of the public schools continues to be perceived as on the decline.

"But we get some fine kids from the prep schools, particularly the private *day* schools. Some of our prep school products, often with a lackadaisical start here, flourish to become our most accomplished. Actually, we're like a good many colleges in our league today, enrolling approximately 35 percent from private schools (including parochials) and 65 percent from public high schools.

"Back to Patricia, whose private school, I repeat, strikes us as middling in quality. Interestingly, her home area has some outstanding public high schools, so I don't know why her family decided she should go to private school. But she obviously has done well—only three B's flaw her otherwise perfect record. Note also that she has taken a fairly 'straight' courseload, though she bailed out of science and math in the senior year. Her SAT scores are superb—far above our averages here. Interestingly, her Achievements, or 'SAT II's,' as they're now called, are good but not consistent with her SATs: one wonders, as a result, how tough it is to get an A at this school, or whether she just had a 'bad afternoon' with the tests, which could well be. And note her '4' in AP History—a '5' is the top score, so she did very well.

"Let's see what else is here." He shuffled the folder.

"Patricia was born in Seattle and moved to North Carolina before secondary school. Her father is a college-educated senior engineer, her mother a part-time secretary. She is one of seven children and all the older ones have gone to or are going to college. She will need scholarship aid of approximately $8,000. Patricia obviously charts her own course, and is allowed to by the family. Her application reads:

> I just moved to NYC three months ago, found myself an apartment and a job, and commenced to live on my own. In my most recent memory, these 3 months have been the biggest event ever; I have never had to support myself *completely* before, and I have never lived in New York. In between work and sleeping, there is not much time for real consideration of what I am doing, but when there is a little quiet time to think, I can see how much more aware of myself, my strengths and my weaknesses, I have become. In short, I'm enjoying my freedom.

"Forgive me if I stumble over some of this," the Dean said. "She's written her application in longhand. It's hard to read." He twisted and held the paper toward the light:

> "Right now I want to become a doctor, which means a required set of courses probably, but I also want to learn something about Philosophy and Art. The medical interest has come as a result of my youngest brother's learning disability, which may be either organic or emotional, if not both.

Regarding her extracurricular involvements, Patricia says:

> Right now there is not much time for anything beyond work. Almost every free second is spent at a potter's, 2 blocks from my teeny apartment. However, when I was in school, I played lots of volleyball, began my interest in pottery, tutored and did bits and pieces of substitute teaching, belonged to a woman's group, had major and minor parts in many plays, as well as doing lots of makeup and

costume work, did a short stint with the Young Democrats, etc. For the largest part of my senior year I tutored for an hour every morning in the second grade of my school. It was the first thing I did every morning and I greatly relished it. My kids were all very loud and precocious, but also often lonely and in need of a lap.

For two winters, I worked weekends in a bakery. And for more years than I care to remember, I have done baby-sitting.

"I won't read all of Patricia's essay. She did a clever thing, though. To document her interest in art, she sent what might be called a maze-essay. She drew and painted high points of her life on a huge, unfolding piece of paper. Here it is. But what it says doesn't really add much to what I've already read from other parts of her application. Although this was a clever idea and she executed it well, it strikes me as a bit gimmicky.

"The headmaster from Patricia's school sends us raves on the school report:

> It isn't just that Patricia is in the top of her class, because we do not stress such things very much. It isn't that she has come so far and yet is still so young. We think she is really a strong person who is able and sensitive in a number of very important ways. Whether this comes of her being raised in a large family or whether it is inborn, we have found Patricia to be a most remarkable person who is peculiarly fitted to do more than usual in college.
>
> As a student Patricia is gifted both in class under guidance and also on her own with the loosest of reins. I do not think that I have ever seen quite such a balance of receptive skill and forward self-start in one person.
>
> Even though Patricia is not clear on her specialty as yet, I see her as the kind of person who will need the opportunity to specialize early. In the second place, she has the natural talent for concentration when she needs it. I do not need to say more to indicate that we think she is a very unusual student. Her independent work this year has been marked by a very fine approach.
>
> In addition, Patricia has a good many artistic sensitivities. Last year she did very well in her art work and this year she is going on with ceramics in such a way that I am quite surprised to see. Only a beginner, she seems to show a natural feel for what she does. She has the grace to pick up the job by the right handle.

Playing the Game for Practice

I can think of no one in the past ten years that I would recommend more highly. She is an excellent student but she is outstanding in any number of other ways."

Mr. Chin was pressing his hands together as though in prayer. "I hate to be critical and cut you short, but it strikes me that the candidate is probably more precise in telling us about herself than this headmaster. Do you have any teachers' comments?"

"Yes," the Dean continued, smiling.

"I have taught Patty English for three years. She is one of the best writers I have met in my teaching career. Her capacity for clear, precise, and subtle expression is great. In her present development, she writes more subtly than clearly, more clearly than precisely. She first exercised her writing powers in flowery expressions, puns, exotic and delicious words. Control came late, and is still coming. Last year her sentences grew more lucid—one could find the thought more easily and the thought had greater force as a result. She does not always manage to express the right thought, the very thought she had in mind. Few writers do. Precision is the hardest of the accomplishments on the list you have provided me for comment.

As to her speech—well, I can only say she always improved any class she entered. And she is not merely a good student, but her citizenship in my classes has benefited others. She has to a noticeable degree the public virtues helpful in a community of learning."

"Oh my God," exclaimed Nora Taylor. "Are *all* these kids going to be paragons of virtue? That's what I mean about tests: We ought to stick with test scores rather than this glib mush. I must say, however, that after hearing all this, I'd like to meet Patty."

"Let me add our campus interviewer's comments. Adam McDermott interviewed Patricia in January," said the Dean.

"A free and gentle spirit with an inquiring mind, a stripe of daring, but above all, enormous personal charm. She's looking at Radcliffe and Yale, so we may have to kiss her goodbye, but I *quit* if she's not admitted! Her family was somewhat dismayed that she chose to spend a year in the Big Apple, but she pinned down the job and the apartment and then they fell in line. Still wallowing in self-discovery, perhaps, but with a sense of joy and awareness. Probably pre-med, though this is probably a romantic notion grounded in her kid brother's medical problems. Also vitally interested in ceramics and philosophy—has read quite a bit in the latter field in her spare time. Trying out Kierkegaard, and admits to being lost but intrigued. In short, this one has all the ingredients. Of course we want her—but will she want us?"

"Well, sounds as though someone is making our decisions for us," Ms. Dorsett said, a bit haughtily. "Nonetheless, this young woman does have spunk and grace and intelligence and all other good things going for her. She is even more intriguing because of the semester off, and the way she has handled it. Friends of mine have a son who wants to take the year off before college and work on a kibbutz in Israel. The parents are leery. . . ."

Sid Goldstein of the admissions staff suddenly sat up. "Right! I headed off to Israel to work on a kibbutz after high school nine years ago, before entering Berkeley. I know that was a trendy thing to do. It still is. At first, the trip and the orientation week on the kibbutz gave me a new sense of my Jewish heritage, and I was elated. But then my assignment! They stuck me out in the hills picking olives. I was almost alone out there. After several weeks, I was so damned tired of picking olives that I didn't know what to do! I wrote Berkeley and asked if I could enroll at midyear, and happily they said, 'Come on.' I haven't eaten an olive since."

There were a few chuckles, and then a silence while the group returned to Patricia Murphy. But the Dean added, "We've seen some disastrous years off. I guess it all comes down to good planning—and Patty's venture in New York strikes me as a worthwhile example of that. But for an affluent kid just to go travel in Europe for a year—I have questions about that sort of thing. I remember one boy recently, however, who went to Montreal to work as an apprentice for a violinmaker. He was himself an aspiring concert violinist, so this was a great experience for him. But most kids who are seventeen or eighteen can't get a decent job, and the year is of little value as a true learning experience. I wish some of them would wait and take off the year between the sophomore and junior years of college—go work in a hospital, for example, if they're on the threshold of serious premedical training."

The Dean snapped back to the matter at hand, glancing at his watch. "Any other questions about Patricia? She is a strong candidate, and I'm almost spoiling you by introducing a student of her credentials at this orientation session. Remember, most of our time will be spent with truly borderline candidates. Patricia has been thrown in to demonstrate balance within the applicant pool. Let's move on."

Butch Lassiter circulated with coffee refills as the Dean changed folders.

"We're about to look at SOPHIE WILSON, an African American applicant. Before we go into Sophie's record, let me pause and discuss Oldebrick's affirmative-action status with you *briefly*. I realize you have heard a great deal on this topic already at faculty meetings but I'd like to attempt to summarize.

"You surely know that Oldebrick announced in a very fuzzy statement some years ago that, in an attempt to help African Americans and other students of color catch up in education nationally, and in an attempt to make due reparations for Oldebrick's less than noteworthy record in accommodating minority students through the years, we would now strive to get a 'representative number' of students of color—which everyone read as actually meaning blacks—into each incoming freshman class. Frankly, I'm irked that our mandate was not made more clear at that time, or since. Our Trustees have said intermittently that because Oldebrick cannot 'be all things to all people,' preference would be given to African American students over other minorities, since we are better prepared to accommodate them with the Black Studies Program, the Crispus Attucks Cultural House, et cetera.

"Although we've put aside considerable monies each year in our Admissions budget for black-oriented recruitment activities, and lately for programs targeting other minority groups, we've never actually succeeded in drawing a freshman class with a 'representative number' of students of color. I'm inferring the Trustees meant 11 percent by that phrase 'representative number,' or the approximate percentage of blacks in the national population. We have been enrolling 5 to 7 percent, which is, frankly, somewhat better than most of our colleague colleges. Wellesley, the University of Virginia, and Stanford, however, are examples of colleges that have been more consistently successful in this area—not just in attracting a larger number of blacks than the rest of us but in attracting particularly well-qualified African American students.

"In all honesty, we have had to 'stretch' some to reach our 5 to 7 percent at Oldebrick. By 'stretch' I mean we have had to dip somewhat lower on the scale of traditional indices, particularly College Board scores. I would quickly add, however, that we have always 'stretched' around here—as you might also vote to do during the next few days—for a few exceptional athletes (even for a few extraordinary violinists!), for a few who live far away, for a few wealthy alumni children, and for some candidates who, although not promising scholars, have extraordinary promise as leaders and seem absolutely irresistible as human beings."

"I resist that term 'stretch,' Dean," said Lois Ruffin, the attractive, young, and outspoken African American admissions counselor who had been with Oldebrick two years now after graduating from the University of Chicago. "Yes, we may indeed 'stretch' to take some dumb jock from one of the nation's best prep schools (which itself probably took him as a one-year postgraduate student in order to win more games), but don't use that word regarding the majority of our black applicants who are stuck in the pits of the nation's secondary schools and who have no idea in hell how to get themselves out. *They've* 'stretched' to get an education in those sewers, amidst teachers who, by default, spend most of their time keeping order, amidst facilities that are shamefully underbudgeted by racist school boards, and among kids who would rather do drugs than write."

Playing the Game for Practice

Ms. Ruffin's voice grew intense and loud as she reached into her purse for notes.

"Let me remind you of what's happening in the big world out there: over half of the black folks are stuck, just plain stuck, in central cities; nearly half of 17-year-old blacks are functionally illiterate; there are *more* blacks below the poverty level than there were five years ago; and only a handful of the kids who score over 1000 on the SATs are black kids. Now don't tell me you have to 'stretch' to accommodate a group that this nation and this college have abused for so long. It is not the *privilege* of black kids to work into Oldebrick's freshman class next fall —it is their *right*."

Silence. Everyone seemed to have his eyes on the docket in front of him until Truman Benson said calmly, "I and all my colleagues read *The New York Times*, Miss Ruffin. We may be more aware of the plight of your people than you give us credit for. We may also be more aware of the manifold missions of Oldebrick College than you, since you are new here. We can learn from one another at these meetings, Miss Ruffin. I will listen to you if you will listen to me. We are intelligent people, open to issues of the day, but I for one am not willing to be consumed by any single issue. And to my knowledge, none of us is hard of hearing."

With Lois Ruffin's eyes ablaze, the Dean suggested abruptly that Sophie Wilson's credentials be reviewed.

As the Dean read on, the tension in the room subsided.

"Sophie, who was born in Illinois but now lives in California, attends one of the nation's most prestigious boarding schools. Sophie's school, although famous, leaves some questions now and then in our minds regarding rigorous academic demands. It went through a rather flaky period of curricular change some years ago, but seems to have swung back to a fairly straight and basic program once again.

"Sophie's family is complicated, and we don't know all the dimensions. On the surface, she seems a rather advantaged young lady; her mother and father attended predominantly black colleges, and both are employed in white-collar jobs. Her father is an industrial psychologist, her mother a part-time teacher. However, something is awry, because there appears to be little or no money in the family. Sophie was given a fee waiver (we and many other colleges will waive the application fee if the candidate's school confirms that he or she needs significant scholarship assistance to attend college), and she is sponsored at her prep school by ABC, 'A Better Chance' program, which places disadvantaged kids, particularly blacks, at good secondary schools in order to give them added educational and vocational incentive. ABC strikes us as a worthy and responsible program, and we trust they rather thoroughly analyzed Sophie's economic background before picking her.

"By the way, Sophie has filled out her application in pencil, so it is a little difficult to decipher. But here goes:

> I have found my involvement in student government here to be the most important of my extra-curricular activities. As president of the student body, I find my attendance at all meetings of student concern to be quite important. During these meetings I introduce new reforms in school policies to benefit my peers, and I attempt to appeal unfair decisions made about a student's conduct, if I believe she is innocent.
>
> This position is important to me because the best of my abilities is demanded, which I feel is a service to others. As a leader I have learned one important lesson in how to remain objective, yet sensitive in my evaluation of the needs of my constituency—my peers.

"Sophie goes on to tell us that she has worked as a salaried library aide for two hours per day at the school. During summers she says she reads a lot—last summer, books on political philosophy by Fanon, Malcolm X, and Hitler. Also, she sews many of her own clothes, and informally enjoys modern dance. Perhaps the biggest event in her life was being chosen as a summer exchange student to Japan. She writes her application essay on that experience:

Playing the Game for Practice

As an observer of the Japanese culture, I gained insight into another society and I acquired a better understanding of myself. During my exchange summer to Japan, I became a member of an upper-echelon Japanese family.

My first lesson in Japan was to have respect for my fellow man. I was expected to bow to all my elders and to refrain from familial discord. At first, I was reluctant to comply with the bowing ritual, but I learned to adjust to it. Familial discord was frowned upon, so before I became angry with someone, I learned to find the source of my anger, and many times discovered it to be quite shallow. I thus learned to control my emotions and to carry myself as a more civil, in turn, noble person.

The next tradition from which I extracted a valuable lesson was male supremacy. Male supremacy was exemplified for me in two ways. I was told to serve my Japanese father at any time, and to allow him or any other male to dominate any conversation that dealt with controversial, political, social, or economic issues. I was not accustomed to total intellectual subserviency to a member of the opposite sex. As a member of the female sex, I was considered a second-class citizen in Japan. I felt that the Japanese society suffered as a whole because women were not permitted to acquire key positions in the intellectual world.

I learned from this experience that women must play an equal role in a society, in order that society may benefit from women's contributions.

My blackness was difficult for many Japanese to accept. At one time during my stay, I was called a 'nigger' by a young Japanese man. It was not a new experience for me, but I found a new meaning in the experience. I learned to find peace and worth in myself as a young African American, barring the opinions and beliefs of others about my kind.

In this transition to another mode of living and thinking, I strengthened my weaknesses as a young adult. I learned lessons of life in Japan that will help me make positive contributions to humanity and the world.

"You have Sophie's transcript in front of you. *(See page 36.)* A phone call yesterday resulted in our getting the following first-semester, senior-year grades: C− in Poetry, C+ in French, C+ in Biology, and D in History. Note that she is taking Ad-

YEAR	CLASS RECORD *Include Subjects Failed or Repeated* SUBJECTS	IDENTIFY LAB TV SEMINAR SUMMER	IDENTIFY HONORS ACCEL AD. PL. ETC.	MARKS 1ST. SEM.	FINAL OR 2ND. SEM.	CRED OR UNIT
9	English 100				B-	1
	French 200				C+	1
	German 100				B+	1
	Math 100: Algebra I				B-	1
	Hist 100: Anc-Med.				B+	1
	Music 100: Intro.				B	1/2
	French I (8th Grade)				93	1
10	English 200		H		C+	1
	French 300				B-	1
	German 200				B-	1
	Math 200: Geometry				C+	1
	Hist 200: U.S.				C+	1
	Mus 160: Afro-Amer.				B-	1/2
11	English 300		H		B-	1
	French 400				C+	1
	German 300				C+	1
	Math 300: Alg. II & Trig.				D+	1
	Journalism				C	1/2
12	English 402: Poetry*					1
	French 450*		AP			1
	Sci 300: Biology*					1
	History 410: Am.Pol.Inst.*					1/3
	*Courses in progress					

	DATE	NAME OF TEST	RAW OR STD SCORE	PERCENTILE SCORE	NORM GROUP
TEST RECORD		CEEB PSAT V 47; M 47			
		SAT V 460; M 440			
		ACH EN 460; FR 560			

vanced Placement French and doing reasonably well; it is fair to say, however, that Sophie's overall record has not been consistent. Naturally, we would like to have seen a swing up this last year. In her favor, however, it seems to me that she has taken a decent courseload with the exception of avoiding science until now. And C's from this school should not put her out of the running.

"This is a school that knows its kids well, knows Oldebrick well, and has fed us honest and comprehensive reports in the past. So let's hear what the Headmaster has to say about Sophie:

Sophie is a very complex young woman who has been a boarding student here throughout all four years of her secondary school career. She has been the chief hope of her father, who expects great things of her and is a stern task-master. The expectations of her father have created a perpetual tension for Sophie as she tries to reconcile his plans for her with her own abilities and inclinations.

Sophie is a student who, because of continual strain, has had more than her share of academic ups and downs. She has tended to work in spurts corresponding to moods of self-confident 'new starts,' then receive a series of disappointing setbacks and go into a depression, producing little until her sense of shame drives her to a new effort to succeed. Family problems and personal insecurities have prevented Sophie from remaining on an even keel for long. When she attains a balance, she will be on her way.

Sophie's chief academic difficulty is her tendency to generalize without mastering all the details of a complex situation. Thus she is often unable to sustain an argument or have a meaningful discussion. She is stronger when dealing with factual material to be applied within a given context. She is currently drawn to the field of politics and international relations, perhaps because she admires certain legislators and identifies her student marshalship with their mandate, but she will need to realize that success in this field will not come as easily to her as she thinks. Sophie has yet to make a realistic evaluation of her academic potential. She can be a good average student with consistent effort; she will never set the academic world on fire, no matter how hard she tries. She must come to terms with that reality before she can attain the equilibrium she requires for her best work.

The heart of her pride and self-esteem is her election as president of the student body. She had long been popular as an advocate for various student causes and she felt she could exercise a meaningful leadership if given the chance. She is now discovering the disappointing depths of student apathy; the need for tact, patience, and compromise in attempting to cut through procedural red tape; the burdensome obligations of her office; and the difficult expectations of a marshal as a moral exemplar. Once again, she had not grasped all the ramifications of a complex situation, and coming to terms with the difficulties of this position has again put Sophie under a strain this fall.

To her credit, Sophie has never given up her struggle to become the best possible student and person she could be. A lesser individual would have taken the line of least resistance. Sophie deserves the opportunity to develop her mind and her personality in an atmosphere of challenge and vitality. She has much to give and will make a fine contribution to the academic community she joins. I recommend her for college admission."

Sophie's folder obviously intrigued the full committee. Everyone listened earnestly as the Dean continued.

"The profile of last year's senior class, sent along with Sophie's transcript, indicates that the mean grade there was a B. Although the school does not provide us with a class rank—which we regret, but now find common among the better prep schools—it is obvious that Sophie's record would place her well into the bottom half of the class. Actually, her CEEB scores seem to me rather consistent with her in-school performance, emotional ups and downs notwithstanding. As a postscript on the school, their profile indicates that of last year's class of 275, 12 went to Harvard/Radcliffe, 16 to Tufts, 7 to Yale, 10 to Duke. In other words, we're talking about a high-powered group of kids that Sophie had to compete with academically, and remember, they chose her as student body president. Finally, let's hear what her Advanced Placement French teacher says:

Being Sophie's Fourth Year Honors French teacher, I feel well-qualified to evaluate her academic potential. She may not have extraordinary natural ability—it is nevertheless above average—but she really does have *extraordinary* drive and determination, some of it coming from her family, but most of it from herself. She is one of the most determined students I have taught. Although her teachers and peers have great confidence in her, she often lacks confidence in herself. She enjoys and indeed does her best in independent work, particularly when she feels it relates to her own situation, but curiously enough she prefaces even excellent work with profuse apologies. Her desire to learn pushes her to participate in class (where her contributions are valuable), but at the same time her lack of confidence makes her somewhat tense when she does. What I have particularly enjoyed about teaching Sophie is that she has been developing more and more confidence in herself so that learning has become enjoyable for her. Now let me speak to your question about her 'clear, precise, subtle expression.' Sophie does not make many mistakes when she writes in French; her writing shows a sensitivity to nuances of style. What she lacks often when she writes is an ability to organize her ideas, particularly when she is forced by an examination to write quickly. In her most recent papers, she shows that she is developing the ability to synthesize and distinguish between the essential and the nonessential."

The Dean stopped reading. There was a silence. Finally, everyone heard Harry Chin take a deep breath. (Was it because he was a member of a minority group himself that he had covered his eyes with his hands during the reading?)

"I'm enormously impressed," he said, "with the successful effort of this school to help us know Sophie. Those reports are superb. Perhaps, however, they have grown to know Sophie *too* well because she is there around the clock, because she is so visible as a student officer, and probably because she is a minority student. But all to Sophie's benefit! My, how that girl must have grown. Here is a prime example of why boarding schools exist. Now I know what school to promote for my bright niece who is stuck in the New York City public system."

"Yes, those are impressive reports," said Nora Taylor, "partly for what they tell us about Sophie, and partly because they are so well written. If only the candidates knew they are at the mercy of a counselor's or teacher's ability to *write* in this admissions process!

"But what impresses us? What Sophie represents, or how

they present her? That's what puzzles me. If one searches carefully in those guarded and well-turned phrases, I think we hear that we are looking at a growing but nonetheless very insecure young lady, who hasn't yet seen her way clear to a consistent performance in the classroom or in student office. Wasn't the guidance counselor trying to tell us something we should know before we introduce Sophie to this sophisticated, rather cold, highly competitive environment? Much as I like Sophie, I can't help wondering if she wouldn't fare better at a college with more advanced support services and a slightly warmer atmosphere—and one perhaps even smaller in size than Oldebrick. Dean, could you read the counselor's remarks on Sophie's academic potential and her performance in the student government again? Those warnings need to be spotlighted, I think."

The Dean complied:

". . . Sophie has yet to make a realistic evaluation of her academic potential. She can be a good average student with consistent effort; she will never set the academic world on fire, no matter how hard she tries. She must come to terms with that reality before she can attain the equilibrium she requires for her best work. . . .

. . . She is now discovering the disappointing depths of student apathy; the need for tact, patience, and compromise in attempting to cut through procedural red tape, the burdensome obligations of her office, and the difficult expectations of a marshal as a moral exemplar. Once again, she has not grasped all the ramifications of a complex situation, and coming to terms with the difficulties of this position has again put Sophie under a strain this fall. . . ."

"I'm really confused by all this," young Adam McDermott hesitantly remarked. "On the one hand, Mr. Chin commends the school for all they've done for Sophie, and he is undoubtedly right—not to mention what Sophie surely did for this Waspy place in return. But here she is now, presenting her credentials for college admission, and we know her flaws so well that she is about to be crucified. What if she had stayed in her local high school back in California—even though it might be a zoo—had struggled to take the honors curriculum, had come up with the same SATs, had gotten A's and B's, and more important, raves from the school because they didn't know her subtle shortcomings and problems? I have the uncomfortable feeling that Sophie is about to pay a price for her 'advantaged' schooling, even though it undoubtedly benefited her in many ways."

"Well, I think I agree with Adam," said Butch Lassiter warmly. "But 'pay the price' or not, I'm won by Nora's honest question of how well we can accommodate this girl with our less-than-adequate advisory system and support services. She'll pay an even greater price if she enrolls at a college where she'll suffer. If we don't take Sophie, however, let's remember that she'll pay the price for *our* inadequacies rather than her own."

The comments on Sophie came in rapid fire.

"I'm suspicious of the label, or implied label, of 'disadvantaged' in this case," said Benson. "Yes, she is African American, but if I heard the report correctly, both parents went to college and hold responsible jobs, the father is very involved in guiding the daughter—probably *too* involved—she has gone to a superb school, and has tootled off to Japan. On the surface of things, she has had a hell of a lot more advantages than my daughter (whom I consider 'advantaged'). I find Sophie interesting, and a little sad. I'm glad we're reviewing her case. But my vote will not be bought just because she is black and we need more of them. It seems to me that our affirmative-action program should not be trying to reach out to the Sophies of the world but to those in far less grand circumstances. As a regular candidate for Oldebrick, I find Sophie beneath our standards. Color, in this case, strikes me as irrelevant."

"Being African American, Mr. Benson, is *never* irrelevant," Lois Ruffin retorted firmly.

"I somehow would have felt shortchanged if you had not made that comment, Ms. Ruffin," responded Truman Benson, attempting a smile which came as a smirk. "On the other hand, I'm looking forward to your guidance in this case. Your experience and commitment will help us here. What are your thoughts about Sophie?"

"Well, I'm of a mixed mind," Lois Ruffin responded with a

softened tone. "On one hand, I agree there is little evidence that Sophie is truly disadvantaged and should be given special consideration just because of her color. In fact, I question her fee waiver and wonder why the school approved it—there is nothing in the folder documenting her severe financial shortcomings. On the other hand, she is African American and, one, that has meant certain strains for her in an elitist school, and she has survived that trial with distinction, and, two, for some reason or reasons, we and a good many of our colleague colleges are down in African American applications this year, so we need her. Black for black's sake? A little of that. But more important, it seems to me, is the fact that she has fought a battle in a tough, stuck-up school; consequently, I find her emotional flip-flops no surprise at all. Also, it is going to take the needs of a few Sophies at this college to finally force us to get the supportive services that will help the kids of color survive here once recruited and enrolled. Sophie is an unusual affirmative-action case, because of her background, but we need her."

"Since we decided to hold voting until we've heard all seven folders, I'd suggest we move along," said the Dean. "Any more questions or comments regarding Sophie?"

"Not really regarding Sophie," said Mr. Chin, in the prayerful position again, "but would you comment on why a good secondary school as large as Sophie's does not rank its students? I find class rank a helpful barometer in this process, particularly when we don't know the degree of difficulty of attaining an A grade in one school compared to another school five miles down the road."

The Dean complied, glancing again at his watch. There was a general shuffling around the room. Adam McDermott and Kelly Darby started playing catch with a Danish over by the coffee urn until the Dean scowled. They quickly stopped and returned to their seats.

"Well, I think that is an important question, Mr. Chin. And I wish you all would listen, although I realize time is moving on. A good many schools, particularly the private ones, are reluctant to rank their kids, since grade-point averages can differ by only a hundredth of a point or so. Many schools feel—and I can see their point—that it is simply unjust to call one candidate "top fifth" and the next kid "second fifth" when only a B in ninth grade American History separates them. On the other hand, a good many validity studies at individual private colleges, many of them overseen by the College Entrance Examination Board, indicate that class rank is a very high predictor of in-college success, particularly in the freshman year.

"As you have suggested, we aren't certain of the quality of an A– GPA at Iowa City Central High unless we see where that average puts a kid in context with others. The top fifth at Iowa City Central High may *all* have A records—we don't know unless rank is recorded. The National Association of Secondary School Principals recommends a ranking system that many schools use. It gives added weight to Advanced Placement courses, Honors-level courses, et cetera. The NASSP formula strikes many of us at the college level as being fair and well formulated. I wish everyone would use it. I do understand, though, why tiny schools—those with thirty in the class, say—find it unfair to rank.

"Let's look at JOHN WENTE now." Everyone stirred to attention in his seat.

"A boy! I wondered if the class wasn't beginning to take on flagrant tones of feminism. Does this kid paddle?" queried Benson.

Benson's presence was no longer felt, it seemed, particularly by the other faculty members. Whenever he spoke, Dorsett, Lassiter, Chin, and Taylor did not stir or look up.

"Probably," said the Dean. "Wente is perhaps the classic case of a middling student who seems to have a lot going on the personal side. We can't fill the class with this type, but now and then we run across an applicant who is so compelling personally that we're willing to forgive a few academic holes.

"John attends a large public high school in a rather wealthy suburban area of New York. His school is regarded as superb: 80 percent head on to four-year colleges, so the curriculum is quite college-oriented. We've had a good draw from this school recently. Often, if a college attracts a few good kids one year and they talk positively when they return home for that first Christmas vacation, good kids the next year will follow.

"There are sixteen applicants from the school this year. Regrettably, John's class rank is toward the lower end of the group. But he draws such personal raves from all parties that we doubt if the school would question our inconsistency here. We're admitting a handful at the top of the class who are bright and a trifle drab; maybe John would help us strike a balance.

"On his application, John says he wants to major in Political Science, English, or Psychology. He says his most important extracurricular activity is being president of the Senior Class. He also is on the varsity tennis team, and varsity fencing team, and reports for the school newspaper. He is the chairman of the School Student Committee for a Safer Community—we'll hear a lot more about this later. His father is a lawyer; his mother does some freelance publicity work; he has one young brother. John urges us to read a few comments about his academic record before we dig into it. Here is his essay:

I feel I have qualities which make me the 'right' person to attend Oldebrick. One quality is that of progressive academic improvement. My transcript shows that I received an 83% in the ninth grade, 86% in tenth grade, and 89% in eleventh grade. My present average is in the nineties. This shows a pattern of growth and I feel that such a trend will continue during my college years. This quality of improvement will help me fit into college life and enable me to get the most out of my college education.

Another of my qualities is that of social maturity. I started in high school as an unknown freshman and became one of the best known students in the school. I achieved this because of both school and community activities. I have worked in my school's General Association since I was a freshman. Last year I was given the opportunity of giving a speech to the entire student body of 2,400. As Junior Class Social Affairs Committee Chairman, and as Senior Class President, I have addressed the 618 members of the Class on numerous occasions.

I am able to get along with people and have come to know many of my teachers on a personal basis.

Another quality essential to success is that of determination. I do not like to 'give up.' When I start something I finish with the best effort I can give. If I am involved in a report, essay or activity, I try to attain the best result possible out of the task. For example, I was able to obtain a traffic light to be placed in front of my school by overcoming the initial disapproval of village officials and trustees. I spearheaded the drive that resulted in the final approval of the light.

Another quality I possess is sensitivity to other people. I enjoy people and try to do what I can to help others. I like to do volunteer work. I have taught tennis to underprivileged children of my town and have tutored students in history. This is part of the give-and-take philosophy in my life as a member of the community. I like to get involved, and have either worked on or chaired a number of committees or organizations aiding my high school. These include committees dedicated to making the school a better place in which to study, committees planning activities for the student body, committees to provide better career education for those not planning to go on to college, and the student publications.

Finally, I believe I am an all-round person. In addition to my activities which I have described, I have been active in school athletics as a member of the varsity tennis and fencing teams. I was part of the team that captured the tennis sectionals and swept the State tournament.

I am sure that I will be able to contribute to, and benefit from, the Oldebrick College community. I believe that my transcript, extra-curricular activities, the personal interview, and the qualities described in this essay, indicate that I am the 'right' person for Oldebrick College."

Benson blew his nose. "Would that I had a vodka tonic tonight for every time that young man used the pronoun 'I.' He might be tough and aggressive when the rocks and the rapids threaten, but in calm waters he sounds like he'd be a pain in the tail."

"John's transcript brings few surprises, considering his warning to us. Look it over," the Dean said.

The group seemed more self-confident now in reading transcripts. Everyone quietly studied his copy of Wente's record, as the Dean talked on. *(See pages 48–49.)*

"Note that there has been steady growth from an early smattering of grades in the 70's to almost straight 90's now. John has taken a balanced courseload; notice, however, that, with the exception of senior European History, no courses are designated as Advanced Placement or Honors. His New York State Regents Exam scores are moderate indeed, and his SATs are paltry. His class rank is clearly affected by his slow start in high school—all those lowish grades in the freshman and sophomore years hurt his standing now. (This school, to my surprise, indicates they do not give added weight in rank to their more demanding courses.) Finally, notice that John had enough spunk and interest to attend the Phillips Exeter summer school, where all grades are listed as 'Satisfactory.' He drew no Honor grades there, but it does say something that he chose to go to enhance his own high school program."

For the second time, Harry Chin passed Rita Dorsett a note. This time she returned a faint smile, then adjusted her bun. One could sense pairings by point of view developing around the table, unstated but there.

"John's counselor writes:

John is an alert, articulate young man, consistently conscientious, anxious to do well, goal-oriented, and motivated to achieve. His personal warmth and sincerity, combined with an unusually mature outlook, have helped make him well respected by students and faculty alike. . . . John has been praised by his teachers for his genuine interest, his excellent attitude, his depth of understanding, his full acceptance of responsibility and his self-initiated participation in class discussions.

His American History teacher commented: 'John is an excellent student who contributes a lot to the class. He possesses real compassion for his fellow man and is willing to work for his ideals. He deserves the best education he can obtain.'

His Math II teacher describes him as 'highly motivated.' His Biology teacher wrote: 'John has shown a steady improvement from a B student to doing A work. Has excellent ability and is capable of working on his own with little guidance. He is a real pusher—works quite beyond his level, and thus, through sheer diligence, does very well.'

Playing the Game for Practice 47

John is well known at the school. He is President of the Senior Class, and has distinguished himself in athletics, particularly tennis. . . . During the past year he was the leader in the campaign to get a much needed traffic light in front of our school. For his leadership and dedication to this cause, he earned the praise and admiration of many community leaders.

John spent last summer at Exeter taking American Foreign Policy, among other courses. An already strong interest in history received further impetus at Exeter, with the subsequent result that he is currently enrolled in Advanced Placement European History.

Also, John has taught underprivileged children locally, has helped the tennis pro at a local club, and at present is employed weekends and after school working at a local pharmacy to make money for college.

John is a doer without ostentation. He is involved, industrious, and trustworthy. He seeks counsel when necessary, yet preserves his own integrity and independence. He is intellectually capable and emotionally ready to accept a challenging undergraduate program."

"You know," Nora Taylor said, "after hearing the candidate's essay first and then this recommendation, I get the uncomfortable feeling that John handed a list of his involvements to his counselor and the counselor just dutifully wrote them up. Frankly, I learned nothing new from that report except that he works in a pharmacy after school and on weekends. If a report that long ends up being so shallow regarding a kid who is seemingly quite visible, think what happens when the counselor writes about kids who are understated!"

Growing repetitious, as was Taylor's custom, she said: "As the evening progresses, grades and SATs are beginning to speak louder to me. A lot of these time-consuming reports from schools hide candidates more than they reveal them. I agree, however, that the school reports on Sophie were exceptional."

"Remember," said the Dean, "that John is in Advanced Placement History. I think it's interesting that he has given his instructor's form to that teacher for a recommendation, because AP History is probably his most demanding course. Here are the teacher's comments:

YEAR	CLASS RECORD — SUBJECTS (Include Subjects Failed or Repeated)	IDENTIFY LAB TV SEMINAR SUMMER	IDENTIFY HONORS ACCEL AD. PL. ETC.	1ST. SEM.	MARKS FINAL OR 2ND. SEM.	CRED OR UNIT	STATE EXAM. SCORES
9	English 1				89	1	
	Afro Asian History				90	1	
	French 1				74	1	
	Math 9				73	1	82
	Earth Science	Lab			80	1	74
	Phys. Education				PA	1/4	
10	English 2				93	1	
	Biology	Lab			84	1	93
	Math 10				75	1	80
	European Studies				92	1	
	French 2				85	1	
	Phys. Education				PA	1/4	
11	English 3LL				90	1/2	
	Language & Literature				88	1/2	
	Environmental Study				92	1/2	
	French 3				81	1	71
	American Studies				92	1	
	Speech/Drama				91	1/2	
	Anthropology				92	1/2	
	Math 11				83	1	
	Phys. Education				PA	1/4	
12	English Sen. Cr. Wr.			91			
	American Life & Prob.			91			
	Russian Studies			96			
	European Studies		AP	90			
	Drivers Education			95			
	Phys. Education					1/4	
	Physiology			88			

TEST RECORD	DATE	NAME OF TEST	RAW OR STD SCORE	PERCENTILE SCORE	NORM GROUP	DATE

NON-PUBLIC	PUBLIC	Enrollment in Grades	Percent Graduates Entering College
☒	☐	9–12	70 4 Yr. Col.	10 2 Yr. Col. and Other

Passing Mark	Honors Mark	LOWEST NUMERICAL EQUIVALENT
65	"90"	90 A	80 B	70 C	65 D

EXPLANATION OF HONORS COURSES

AP-Advanced Placement curriculum of CEEB
H-Honors group
("Regular" class groups do not carry any
suffix designation)

(See Summer School record below)

RANK IN CLASS BASED ON __6__ SEMESTERS

☒ EXACTLY 168 ☐ APPROX. _____ IN CLASS OF __529__

FINAL RANK _____

Check Appropriate Rank Information

☒ ALL SUBJECTS GIVEN CREDIT ☒ ALL STUDENTS
☐ MAJOR SUBJECTS ONLY ☐ COLL. PREP. STUDENTS ONLY

Explain Weighting of Marks in Determining Rank

*Rank determined on basis of all subjects
given credit <u>except</u> Physical Education,
Glee Club, Choir, Band, Orchestra.

~~OUTSTANDING ACTIVITIES HONORS AWARDS~~

PHILLIPS EXETER ACADEMY SUMMER SCHOOL

	GR	CR
Amer. For. Pol.-Age of Rev.	S	1/2
Psychology-Concepts & Methods	S	1/2
English 12-Literary Int.	S	1/2

NAME OF TEST	RAW OR STD. SCORE	PERCENTILE SCORE	NORM GROUP
Otis Lennon		105	
DAT VR&NA75ile			
CEEB SAT V460 M400			
CEEB SAT V590 M410			

John is a good student who works to the level of his ability, and then some. He is conscientious, well organized, and mature. When assigned research papers, he begins work at once and tries to obtain every source available.

John expresses himself clearly and precisely both in writing and in speech. Considering the fact that students today are rarely taught to write correctly, John's work is far above the average. Had he been taught traditional English by our school, he might produce even better papers!"

"Bravo!" exclaimed Truman Benson. "Who *is* this man? We should send him a medal."

"This man is a woman, Truman, by the name of Bernadette Jacobs. Write her! Surely some of these teachers wonder if we ever read their recommendations. Ms. Jacobs would be really glad to know we care. I'll give you her address at the school so you can write.

"But let me finish this folder. It's a fat one," the Dean said. "Which reminds me—there is a little quip that circulates among admissions people: 'The thicker the folder, the thicker the kid,' meaning we're suspicious, if the folder is chock full of outside recommendations, that the applicant has not felt secure in letting his record stand alone—that strings must be pulled to get in. We're coming to a pile of those recommendations now, but in John's case there is a difference: these letters seem to have been spontaneously sent. I don't have the feeling that John or his father went out hustling support. So often it is the father who feels such letters are necessary, and the result is embarrassing indeed: the solicited reference talking more about the civic spirit of the father and mother than about the quality of the candidate, who is sometimes not known at all by the senator, or the chairman of the board, or even by the business partner who happens to be an alumnus of Oldebrick. We in Admissions are human and reasonably intelligent: some of these letters create a bias against the candidate rather than for him. One no longer gets into college via 'the Old Boy system,' but somehow that word hasn't gotten out.

"Anyway, in John's case, we have a stack of letters singing his praise, often related to his great campaign of talking the town fathers into the traffic light in front of the high school. John must have spent months on that traffic light. Obviously he charmed the authorities. We have several letters from our own alumni regarding the campaign and John's effectiveness, as well as letters from the principal (that is unusual, I must say), from several members of the town council, from the area's state senator, and from the town's director of parks. Also, we have from John himself a sampling of newspaper clippings. And finally, let me read you a few comments from his interview here at Oldebrick:

> John is hardly an outstanding scholar, but he could probably handle our work if he lands courses of interest to him. He might bomb in science or math, but he seems vitally interested in politics and history, and perhaps will discover sociology and philosophy. He wants Law School, but unlike so many others we meet, he's leaving the options open. . . . Despite his disappointing record and test scores, I have the feeling this fellow has genuine intellectual curiosity. . . . In sum, John is probably a candidate we should seriously consider. He has certainly accomplished in the extracurricular zone at his school. Reading his folder prior to the interview, I expected more of a dynamo: not so. He is outgoing, but in a rather quiet way, solid, inquisitive, firm, and clearly one whom others would follow."

Ms. Darby of the admissions staff suddenly spoke again. "You know, I wrote that, and I'm disappointed now that I hear it. It's been four months since I interviewed John, but he is one of those candidates who lingers in your mind. I feel I really understated his personal strengths. And I think Oldebrick needs this fellow for diversity. True, he's not a superjock or a legacy or a minority student and his father is not worth a million dollars. And he is not brilliant. But he *is* one super guy, and I hope we have room for him. I feel I've done him a bit of an injustice by not using more superlatives in the interview report. He must have been my sixth or seventh interview on a full day."

"I'm perplexed," said Taylor, who'd been examining the docket carefully. "His SATs are absolutely pathetic and his Law

Boards will probably be similar. Four years from now the law schools will throw him out of the running before they even give his college grades and recommendations a fair reading. On the other hand, although I wouldn't want him as a college roommate, I'm becoming rather taken by his energy, his discipline, and his sense of purpose. In short, I guess he'd make a dandy lawyer. Curses on you, Dean, for introducing a good pre-law candidate with lousy scores. It upsets the vow I took upon entering here."

The committee members looked at each other. They seemed satisfied. One could sense a camaraderie developing. But then Benson . . .

"Somehow he isn't quite right for my canoe, and I really wonder if he's quite right for Oldebrick. Haven't we enough suburban, Polo-shirted, reasonably-bright-but-not-really, help-the-underprivileged-play-tennis types already lurking around the punch bowls here? This may be just the type Ms. Dorsett was rightly scorning before."

Rita Dorsett looked stricken. "Uh-oh. My speech served to hurt the wrong applicant. Truman, I really like this boy, Ralph Lauren shirt and suburbs or not. He sounds genuine." She smiled, then lifted her handkerchief to her cheek. "Somehow I have the feeling I'm not going to like this job."

Butch Lassiter was slowly circling the table now, pausing at his favorite window each round. Chin and Taylor seemed frozen to their seats, unlike the admissions staff, who were twisting and turning, already having read these cases and discussed them at length at staff meetings.

"Let's move on," urged the Dean. "It's late. Our fifth candidate of the evening is ANDREW JACOBSON. Like Patricia Murphy, he is introduced tonight to give you a sense of balance. Our admissions staff would also like to hear your reaction as faculty members to a conflict that pops up late in his folder. As you see from Andrew's transcript, we're looking at an exceptional student. His urban high school in Cleveland is probably not quite as strong as John Wente's school, but it is above average nonetheless. This school sends approximately 45 percent of its students on to four-year colleges, another 25 percent to two-year colleges. Andrew obviously has sought out every tough course he could find. Rarely do we see a more high-powered senior courseload. Note that he has gained extra weighting in his class rank for the Advanced Placement courses, which puts him in the top 3 percent. Also, note his College Board scores, which are sky-high. Andrew is a Commended student in the National Merit Program, the most prestigious honor program in the nation (which disappoints many of us, I might add, because National Merit gives much more weight to standardized test scores than to any other credential).

"Let's review Andrew's transcript." *(See pages 54–55.)*

There was obvious elation around the table as faculty members muttered about the high College Board scores under their breath. Nora Taylor, with a wry smile, held up two fingers to form a "V."

"Andrew's parents are both college-educated. They are now divorced. His mother is a school librarian. His father is a hospital administrator. The father will be paying college bills, and although he applied for financial aid, our analysis of the Financial Aid Form indicates this is a 'no-need' case. There are two younger children. Andy wants to major in Biology or Chemistry and wants to become a doctor. Last summer he worked as a hospital orderly, so he has done a lot more than most of our candidates to find out what the medical profession is all about.

"Regarding his extracurricular involvements, he says:

> I find my athletic involvement on the soccer and track squads to be the most meaningful of the previously mentioned activities I pursue. By their inherent nature as extra-curricular activities, they have broadened me as a person and allowed me to meet many new people. As sports they have developed me physically, but there is a further development involved. That development involves me as a person and my values. Perhaps the most important thing to be learned from athletics is that success is the result of hard work. Something athletics has instilled in me is the pursuit of excellence in whatever I do, whether it be on the track, the field, or my future profession. Lastly, my experience with athletics reflects what is hid-

CLASS RECORD
Include Subjects Failed or Repeated

YEAR	SUBJECTS	IDENTIFY LAB TV SEMINAR SUMMER	IDENTIFY HONORS ACCEL AD. PL. ETC.	MARKS 1ST. SEM.	FINAL OR 2ND. SEM.	CRED OR UNIT	STATE EXAM. SCORES
9	English I				B	5	
	Algebra I				A	5	
	World History				A	5	
	French 9				B	5	
	Physical Science				B	5	
	Electricity				A	2½	
	Phys. Ed./Health				B	1	
10	English II				B	5	
	Plane & Solid Geom.				A	5	
	U.S. History I				A	5	
	French 10				B	5	
	Algebra II & Trig.				A	5	
	A.P. Biology	Lab			A	5	
	Phys. Ed. II				A	1	
11	English III				A	5	
	AP Calculus				B	5	
	U.S. History AP				A	5	
	Chemistry	Lab			A	5	
	French IV				B	5	
	Phys. Ed./Dr. Ed				O	1	
	Dr. Ed. II (BTW)				S		
12	AP English			B			
	AP Calculus			A			
	AP Biology	Lab		A			
	PSSC Physics	Lab		A			
	Personal Typing (Sem)						
	Phys. Ed.			O			

TEST RECORD

NAME OF TEST		RAW OR STD SCORE	PERCENTILE SCORE	NORM GROUP	DATE
PSAT/NMSQT	V	62			
	M	72			
SAT	V	630			
	M	730			
SAT	V	620			
	M	750			

Passing Mark	Honors Mark	LOWEST NUMERICAL EQUIVALENT			
70	(if any)	A 93	B 85	C 74	D 70

EXPLANATION OF HONORS COURSES

RANK IN CLASS   BASED ON __6__ SEMESTERS

[X] EXACTLY   [ ] APPROX.   __15__ IN CLASS OF __550__

FINAL RANK _____

Check Appropriate Rank Information

[X] ALL SUBJECTS GIVEN CREDIT   [XX] ALL STUDENTS
[ ] MAJOR SUBJECTS ONLY   [ ] COLL. PREP. STUDENTS ONLY

Explain Weighting of Marks in Determining Rank

Only Advanced Placement courses
are weighted.

S - Satisfactory
O - Outstanding

OUTSTANDING ACTIVITIES. HONORS. AWARDS

COMMENDED STUDENT   MERIT PROG.
Soccer Team 9, 10, 11, 12
Winter Track 11, 12
Spring Track 10, 11, 12
Academy of Science 11, 12
Debate Team 10, 11, 12
Newspaper Photographer 11, 12

NAME OF TEST		RAW OR STD. SCORE	PERCENTILE SCORE	NORM GROUP
SAT	V	710		
	M	750		
Eng. Achievement		620		
Math II		750		
Physics		650		

den in each of us in some form. When I first went out for track last year, it was merely to stay in shape for the tennis team so that I could learn how to play tennis. Within a few months of hard work, I advanced from a novice to a member of a mile relay which won the state sectional championship."

"Sterile prose," Benson pointed out.

"Maybe his application essay will give him a little life," responded the Dean. "Here it is:

I'm weird.

That's a rather funny thing to say on an application to one of the finest institutions of learning in this country. Let me explain.

The dictionary defines 'weird' as odd or unusual. Yet when I indicated my career ambition, medicine, there did not seem to be anything unusual about that. After all, 'premeds' compose one of the largest categories of students in colleges today. Nearly all of these 'premeds' choose to major in either Chemistry or Biology. This is my first weirdness since I intend to major in Astronomy. Another weirdness is that along with being a good student, I am also an athlete who can make a substantial contribution to the Oldebrick track team.

On a more personal level, I don't smoke or drink or do drugs and am not afraid to assert my individual weirdness. I believe this is especially important in a college atmosphere where even on the smallest level, a person can be easily swallowed up and be vulnerable to many pressures.

Undoubtedly the most important factor in the selection of candidates for Oldebrick is that of scholarship. I believe that in this respect I qualify, as evidenced by my SAT scores and by my high grade average in high school, even with a schedule so rigorous that I was able to go through my entire high school program in three years."

"Yes, that's a little better," Benson said. "The wooden statue is still there, but at least we know now it doesn't smoke or drink."

The Dean continued. "Andrew sent us what appears to be a professionally prepared résumé (you can get this sort of thing for a price at counseling bureaus today) with headings of 'College Goals,' 'Career Goals,' 'Academic Awards,' et cetera. We don't learn anything new through this formal presentation except that he really seems to have distinguished himself in track: gold medals, silver medals, bronze medals at state and county meets. He was the anchor of a mile relay team that broke the school and county records. Despite these accolades, however, our track coach feels that Andy would not be outstanding at Oldebrick in track—he might be a contributor, but the times he has achieved so far would probably not put him in the forefront here."

"What?" Mr. Chin was astonished. "You actually check with our coaches on a candidate's athletic suitability for Oldebrick?"

The Dean stood and stretched. "Yes, we sometimes check with them—but the initiative often comes from them rather than from us. Actually, I wish other departments were as interested in our candidates! We rarely have Math or Physics or History or French calling over here to inquire about the quality or status of an applicant (unless the applicant is a relative). You know, when we really want to pursue a kid, faculty interest would be most helpful.

"With the coaches, we now have a fairly well-organized system. I meet with each coach individually in January and March, honing down each of their lists according to which students seem genuinely interested in Oldebrick, and which seem realistic admits academically. At times, the 'bargaining' gets a bit sticky and there are always some strained feelings. A few not so coincidental phone calls will come in from alumni pushing candidates I've told the coaches are 'maybe's' for admission. But let me repeat: If every department at this college took the interest in recruiting talent that the Athletic Department takes, we'd blow the doors off most of our competition, academically as well as athletically.

"I should add, by the way, that the coaches know that not all of their sports have equal clout in the Admissions Office. We'll push to structure winning teams in the most visible sports at Oldebrick—football, hockey, and basketball for men, and basketball, tennis, and volleyball for women. As you might guess, we never give enough 'special priority' to please all the coaching staff. But we are generous enough with some of these top athletes to twist my own conscience now and then. Sometimes it upsets me to see us taking mediocre students who can win games when we might be taking candidates who could win some graduate fellowships. Remember, though, that a good many of the highly rated athletes are not dummies. Some who are disciplined on the field are equally disciplined in the classroom, with outstanding and often surprising results. Andrew Jacobson, the fellow whose credentials are in front of you, is a fairly decent athlete who is second to very few in academics.

"So let's continue with Andy's folder. Here is his guidance counselor's report:

> Andy is great college material. He is extremely bright and an excellent athlete. He has a fine attitude toward learning and he has learned that much effort is necessary to achieve one's goals. He is more than willing to put forth this effort. In fact, he enjoys academic challenges. To illustrate, Andy is the only person to carry two enriched mathematics courses as a junior, and this year he is again taking Advanced Placement calculus in order to do independent work—a rarity in our system. He is quite science/math oriented, but he is also very verbal and he reads voraciously.
>
> Andy's teachers find him conscientious and one who has learned to use his time well. He has worked hard to develop a good background.

I'll skip around in this report. . . .

> Andrew is quite good in photography—has collected some excellent cameras and uses them for very good purposes. . . .

Jesus! . . .

> Andy has spent much time as a volunteer at our local hospital. He has worked in most of the departments and has had many opportunities to see the intricate and sophisticated happenings in a modern hospital.
>
> Another aspect of Andrew that is noteworthy is his keen interest

in athletics. He has been on our soccer team for three years and worked hard to become our 'most improved player.' He played goalie for our varsity team and has done much to promote our good record. Track is his major sport. He puts forth much effort in training and won the trophy as 'The Most Improved Runner' last year. He is a member of our mile relay team and also of our distance team. As a quarter-miler his best time was 50.9 seconds. His coaches feel he has great potential as an athlete, and with his excellent attitudes he should be an asset to your teams too.

Andy deserves an enthusiastic recommendation. He is the kind of student and person who does not come along very often and it is a great pleasure to recommend him to your college!"

"That report is embarrassing," said Mrs. Taylor a bit pompously. "Thank God for the Buckley Amendment, so families can now demand to see these reports. I'm marching with my senior daughter into the guidance office next week to see what kind of pap they threw at colleges about her."

"Maybe Andy was smarter than we think in having a professional résumé composed," Ms. Dorsett said, capping off the remark with her pressed smile.

"Well, remember that these counselors often have 300 to 400 seniors to report on. What can we reasonably expect of them? Here is what Andrew's Biology teacher has to say," said the Dean.

"Andrew is a highly motivated student. He is absolutely stimulated by a demanding academic environment. He never needs prodding. He made very good use of his time, particularly since there were interferences caused by his track and soccer involvements. He has a critical, analytical mind. He was able to convey his ideas verbly and defend his position with skill and clarity."

"That seems like scant praise for a student who appears on paper to be so exceptional," commented Mr. Chin.

"I'm not certain the Biology teacher is verbose. By the way, he did a dreadful job of trying to spell 'verbally.' Anyway, the assistant principal of Andy's school also writes a letter, which says, once again, what we've already heard.

"But now the curve ball. Andy came here for an interview last month. Sid Goldstein of our staff wrote the following:

> One of the myopic candidates: there is nothing in the world to him but becoming a doctor. Andrew's father is a hospital administrator, so perhaps this is part of the limited perspective. Doesn't have much to say for his high school, but did seek out the most demanding courses. Clearly has his sights set on the Ivies: wanted comparisons of our Biology Department to Penn's, Princeton's. Guess he has done a good job in soccer and track—perhaps more effort than actual accomplishment. Somehow this fellow seems to go through all the motions—but is any excitement generated?
>
> Andrew was quite ill at ease. In fact, he had very little to say. He was stiff. Was he just nervous, or did I do a bad job of getting him to open up, or is he just a set of impressive statistics? He seems egocentric and naive. What little he did say was in praise of his own accomplishments. I nearly upchucked when he went through the bit about being disappointed with his Math SAT of 750. Baloney.
>
> Yes, he's smart. But socially immature—perhaps that is an understatement. Frankly, I'm just not convinced that he would contribute anything to Oldebrick except one more admission ticket to medical school. Are we this hungry to improve our med school entry stats? Let Penn have him. But if he's as smart as he thinks he is, he won't go to Philadelphia for an interview.

"Sid, that's a strong statement," said the Dean. "Is there anything you want to add or subtract, one month later?"

"Not a thing," Sid Goldstein answered. "I think my report says it all."

"Well, I'd like to add a little," piped up Adam McDermott, the admissions fellow, growing at ease now with the group. "It seems to many of us in the student body—and I was just there—that Oldebrick spends too much time comparing itself to Amherst and Williams and Dartmouth, and nurturing its own inferiority complex because we're not quite in line with them, at least as popularly perceived. And usually the comparisons are made via statistics—our Board averages aren't quite as high, et cetera. So here comes a candidate who will help us *get* in line: He has all the right numbers. But dammit, we sacrifice a great

Playing the Game for Practice

deal that is important to Oldebrick if we go for this guy. He has no soul whatsoever. I don't want to stand up and sing the Alma Mater now, but I do want to say that Oldebrick has something going for it that we shouldn't lose sight of. We're casual but serious, bright but not insufferably brainy, into our studies but not morosely academic, and we care about one another and have a pretty good time. Do we crave med school entries *so* much that we will risk sacrificing a few of our subtle attributes—attributes, by the way, that may make us an even better place than Amherst or Williams or Dartmouth?"

Adam's face reddened as he tried to settle back in his chair. Kelly Darby and Sid Goldstein applauded to support their friend, but the faculty delegation ignored them.

"Adam, we know what you're saying and you said it very well," responded Rita Dorsett. "But you're using this young man as too heavy a symbol. In voting one Andrew Jacobson in or out, we're not charting the future of the college. Yes, he is something of a machine, but we have so few here with so much intellectual capability and accomplishment!"

"I wish the pre-med adviser were here," said Mr. Chin, "because I'm about to try to talk us out of this one, and the pre-med faculty should be given equal time.

"Frankly, I'm a bit tired of the get-the-good-grades-for-medschool syndrome. Those kids strike me as unoriginal, they try to elbow one another out of the way, they're strangely insensitive, and, well, I guess I end up agreeing with Adam McDermott and Sid Goldstein. Maybe Andrew Jacobson is a good match for Columbia or NYU, but for our residential college, where we all try to live together in the woods somewhat peacefully, I'm not certain. His numbers *are* impressive—and I'm surprising myself by speaking against him."

The Dean looked upset. After a pause he began. "I guess it is fair to say that I'm disappointed by the tone of this conversation, or at least the direction it seems to be taking. The consensus appears to be that 'you have to be nice to be necessary' at Oldebrick. Just because this kid isn't going to be everyone's choice for Social Chairman, you dump him and send him packing to the Ivies. Well, *why?* We spend so much time complaining that we don't draw a large number of students who profile out as impressively as those the Ivies get. And here is one. Not only is he distinguished academically, but he has also diligently worked at his athletics until he has become something of a champion in his own league. So what if he's stiff and naive and caught up with himself? It irks me to think that personality is more important to our committee than powerhouse academic potential and accomplishment."

The Dean began gently pounding his fist on the table, and continued. "And who is to say that the personality Jacobson conveys now won't be considerably improved four years from now? What kind of faith do we have in Oldebrick? I think this kid will meet some other high-powered types around here, will tone down a little, will turn to others more, and will, in time, mature. If we have a community here, Adam, then let it contribute to this kid's growth. He has a hell of a lot to give in brainpower. And that's what we're supposed to be all about."

It was the first time the Dean had let loose. No one seemed to feel comfortable in speaking next. And no one did.

"Let's look at our final two applicants of the evening, and then vote on all seven," the Dean said with a noticeable tremor in his voice.

"BETTE BASSIS is another candidate from the suburbs of a big city. She applied for Early Decision here and didn't make it, so we're looking at her once again. Bette attends a huge and well-known high school outside Dallas, and 'The Big D' should be underlined here, because our alumni in Dallas are very interested in her. Why have they singled out Bette Bassis? Frankly, I can't quite figure it out, but several recent calls and letters have convinced us of the seriousness of their interest. And I might add that the Dallas Alumni Club, as you may have heard, is one of our most influential and supportive alumni groups. Remember, it was they who gave the new arts building four or five years ago.

"Bette's father is a lawyer, her mother a housewife, and she has older brothers who are now out of college. Bette wants to major in Psychology (she spells the word p-s-y-c-o-l-o-g-y throughout her application) to prepare for guidance counseling at the high school level. She is very involved in equestrian activities—shows her horse throughout the country at A-rated AHSA shows. She works at a jewelry store to help defray expenses on the horse. Also, Bette is a cheerleader. Her application essay is, to a large degree, an attempt to justify her mediocre high school record. As a rhetorical strategy, she pretends that she has already been rejected by Oldebrick and is responding to our committee's decision:

Dear Admissions Committee:

Although my transcript did not please you and your staff, I feel as though you are overlooking the most important factor in evaluating these grades, this factor being improvement! Although the grades on the transcript were not as outstanding as a competitive college (like Oldebrick) might expect, the improvement from two slumping (4th and 5th) semesters to the past two semesters (6th and 7th) has been quite steady and shall continue into my final semester. However, grades alone are not the most important criteria in judging an applicant, contrary to many college's beliefs! The growing maturity that one shows through her grades is a much more important criteria to be judged. I believe that through outside experiences I have gained the maturity to sort out my emotional life from my school work and bear down to improve my grades. A person must be a more mature person to go to college in a changing atmosphere. Considering the change that Oldebrick must be undergoing due to the economic upheavals of the eighties and nineties, I feel that perhaps I will be better able to handle the situation than a 'straight A' student. Many of these students may not have ever had to learn to sort out the priorities of school work vs. outside influences and therefore would be unable to handle a changing situation. Hence, I feel that I am the right person to attend Oldebrick and reap the most profit from my education at Oldebrick in the period of change."

"Oh, pain!" blurted Benson. "Her letter to the committee has just confirmed that we all made the right decision in the first place. Why on God's green earth must we spend time on this one? She has Pi Beta Phi at U. Texas written all over her."

The Dean shook his head, conveying his own mixed thoughts. "Well, I really felt I had to give her a hearing in front of the full committee, considering the interest in her among alumni. And she undoubtedly could succeed here, if she put her mind to it. It *is* easier to survive here than to get in, is it not? This candidate is probably one who could graduate if admitted. Her transcript comes as no surprise after her warning She did not tell us, however, that her improvement in grades came via a fluffy courseload." (*See pages 65–66.*)

Taylor and Benson had abandoned the transcript after one quick glance, but the rest of the committee members were still poring over it.

"Note that she dropped Science and History after her junior year. Note also that this school rather carefully 'levels' courses. She has been mostly in '3' level courses, defined as 'above average.' The class rank is weighted according to level of courses. Bette is 296th in a class of 847, but remember that 85 percent go on to college from here. That means that her second-fifth ranking is no disgrace. But her College Board scores are all just above 500. The college counselor, who is an old friend of ours, says:

> Bette works very diligently and has managed to maintain a good average and rank in class over the past three years. She has been in our 'above average' academic classification in all subjects. The candidate has many cultural interests, with music and art being the most important to her. She has a talent in art, painting, and drawing.
>
> Bette spends a great deal of time improving her riding skills. She owns her own horse and has won many prizes competing in contests around the country. However, she does not make an occupation in this interest area and uses wise judgment in budgeting her time between this activity and others.
>
> We are of the opinion that Bette has more ability than her SATs indicate. She has a strong 27 composite on the ACT, which places her in the 92nd percentile for college-bound students. I suggested she repeat the SATs, and her second test scores may be reported to

SUBJECTS NOW IN PROGRESS								UNITS
SUBJECTS			Level	9	10	11	12	Extra	Earned
English	I, II, III		4	BB	BC	D			2½
	III, IV		3			B	C*		½
Lang.	French I				CrCr				1
	French II, III		3	CB	PC				2
	Spanish I		3				A*		
Math	Algebra I, II		3	BB			CC		2
	Plane Geometry		3		BC				1
	Trigonometry		3				B*		
	Lab. Periods	Yes							
Science	Biology	X	4	BB					1
	Chemistry	X	4		D				½
	Chemistry	X	3		B				½
Soc. Studies	Modern History		3		C				½
	US History		3			BB			1
	Sociology		3			B			½
Other Subjects	Consumer Econ		3				B*		
	Painting (10xwk)		3				B*		
	Drawing (10xwk)		3			A			½
	Drawing			PP					½
	Phys Ed			xx	xx		xx		½

DETERMINATION OF WEIGHTED AVERAGE

A weighted average is computed according to the ability level at which each major course is taken. Courses not designated by level are minor credit courses which are not used in computing rank.

The 2 level is regarded as the average high school level of competition. At this level A = 4, B = 3, C = 2, D = 1.

Grades in other levels are weighted by the following multipliers.

5 level (Advanced Placement)	1.8
4 level (Superior or Honors)	1.5
3 level (Above Average)	1.2
1 level (Below Average)	.8

you by now. This young woman has much to offer any college or community.

We did receive a new set of SATs on this candidate: 530 Verbal, 510 Math. Not much improvement."

"Well, your 'old friend' did the best he could, considering there is so little to work with," said Nora Taylor.

"Bette's senior English teacher reports as follows," continued the Dean:

> Bette is a perceptive and sensitive student of literature. Insightful understanding rather than precise intellectual analysis is her forte. Certain intellectual tasks that require precision make her shrink; she seems to have some diffidence about her ability to tackle such tasks. This makes her academic performance somewhat uneven.
>
> Bette's writing competence is well above average for a twelfth-grade student. She does not, however, participate regularly in classroom discussion. When she does, her contributions are valuable, but she seems reluctant to participate at times."

"Oh, how welcome honesty is in this exercise," said Ms. Dorsett. "That was a graceful but candid and fair report. I feel that I'm getting to know this girl. And I know plenty of Dallas alumnae." This time Rita Dorsett's smile and quick glance around the table found a nodding reception. The Dean was relaxed and smiling now.

"Let's hear what our alumna has to say. Bette was not interviewed on campus, so one of our former graduates interviewed Bette in Texas. Here is her report:

> This is a lovely girl. Also, I think she will attend Oldebrick if admitted. Seems to know what she's talking about in psychology, her intended major. I would guess that she is a responsible student. It is her outside activities, however, that seem rather outstanding. Being a cheerleader at her huge high school is a very big deal—several have gone on to cheer for the Cowboys. And Bette just loves horses; she's so enthusiastic about her horse that she works in a jewelry store to help her parents pay the transportation and entry fee costs for shows around the country. Bette speaks well; she seems socially

mature; she was most attractively dressed. In short, I think she's a perfect match for Oldebrick."

Harry Chin raised his hand. "Dean, could you comment on these alumni interviews? I realize that a good many colleges have a force of representatives around the country. But frankly, I find this lady's interview report a disappointment. I mean, it's so 'horsey.' Does she know what to look for in a candidate?"

Mr. Chin was earnest, as always, but pleased with his own little stab at humor. So were the others.

"Our alumni interviewers are hardworking people," the Dean said thoughtfully, "and they do seem more an asset than a liability. Candidates want the opinion of someone from their hometown before choosing a national college, so our alumni are obviously valuable to us. Their personal touch can persuade a candidate to choose Oldebrick over another college. So we try our best to keep them informed of what's going on here—fly them back to campus for conferences, have training sessions when we're in their home towns recruiting, et cetera. Too often, however, they have a tendency to represent the college as it *was* rather than as it *is*—I guess that's only natural. And they really are not as exposed to the academic credentials of a candidate as we are, so their comments dwell mostly on the personal."

The Dean paused, drumming his fingers on the table. It was obvious this topic perplexed him somewhat. "We do, of course, sometimes draw the wrong alumni volunteers to interview for us: the always-wanted-to-be-a-jock-but-never-quite-made-the-team types, who are embarrassing in their fervor to chase quarterbacks and goalies, and a few too many nonworking women who volunteer just to have something to do. On the whole, however, the alumni take their work seriously and are important to us. But as you will see, their reports tend to be quite uneven in quality.

"There is more in Bette's folder from alums. Excerpts from a couple of letters that arrived quite recently:

Playing the Game for Practice

I am writing regarding Bette Bassis, whose family I have known for many years.

Bette realizes her SAT scores and her grades/class rank are not the highest, but she feels capable of tackling the demanding education at Oldebrick. On the plus side for Bette is her diligence and perseverance in other areas. She has been working after school and on Saturdays at a jewelry store to help support her horse. She is a cheerleader, plays piano and organ and guitar. She has been an adequate student and now really wants to concentrate on her studies and self-development. She is interested in Psychology, especially relating to teenage problems and also how this relates to animals.

I feel Bette has a lot of spunk and is capable of accomplishing whatever she really wants to do. To demonstrate: Bette says that if she doesn't make Oldebrick on this round, she'll apply later as a transfer. Take her now!—she is a personable young lady of good character and discipline.

"Another alumna throws us a bit more grit:

I understand Bette Bassis is applying to Oldebrick and will attend if admitted. Thank God! We Alumnae/i in Dallas have been befuddled by some of your recent choices in our area—clearly, grades and a liberal point of view seem to mean more to you than character and personal promise. We're a bit fed up. Now we throw you a challenge: Bette Bassis. She is bright, purposeful, an accomplished equestrian, and she is *clean*. We trust she will hear positively from you. If not, the College will not hear positively from some of the alumnae/i here."

"That self-serving biddy probably hasn't given us a penny," quipped Benson.

"*Wrong*, Truman," replied the Dean. "During the recent capital campaign she gave an endowed scholarship for the disadvantaged, with priority to Latinos from the Southwest. She is also a Trustee for the Dallas Art Museum, has donated heavily to our gallery, and has been most helpful in advising our curator. You certainly missed the target on this one."

Everyone glanced at Benson, hoping to catch him wincing in humility. They were not rewarded.

"And finally, we have just received a letter from Bette Bassis herself:

> While I fully appreciate and realize the tremendous burdens placed upon you in selecting from the great number of applicants those fortunate enough to be admitted, I hope you can take time to ponder my earnest desire to attend Oldebrick. If I understand college admissions correctly, you will undoubtedly admit some with records better than mine, and they may end up on your campus only because they're not admitted at, say, Rice. Why not generously stretch a bit and admit one who so desperately wants Oldebrick as a first-choice college? Well, I just thought I'd like to make a final plea. . . . Thanks."

Rita Dorsett leaned forward. "Oh, poor dear. . . . And doesn't she have a point regarding those who *want* to be here and tried for Early Decision versus those who come reluctantly, and would rather be in Hanover or Chapel Hill or Palo Alto?"

"That's a tough question," the Dean responded. "We obviously favor Early Decision candidates because they are declaring Oldebrick first choice and we'll get 100 percent of those we admit. Last year, remember, we admitted about half of all our candidates, but we admitted a higher percentage of our E.D. candidates: 'One in hand is worth two in the bush' in this business. Williams and Bowdoin and Amherst and a few others often take a quarter of the class Early Decision because they know their losses will be heavy to the Ivies come April.

"Once here, however, our Early Decision admittees can become some of our most disappointed freshmen. They found what they thought was the perfect college early in their senior year of high school, and they continued to fantasize it into Utopia during the succeeding months. Once they are here, any flaw they find disappoints them greatly. On the other hand, some kids here who were dying to go to Duke or Princeton come to Oldebrick with a bit of a chip on their shoulder. But then, almost inevitably, they love the place by the end of the first year and become some of our strongest supporters."

"Let's move on," urged Benson. "Desire or not, wealthy

alumni support or not, I can only hope we'll uncover better candidates than Ms. Bassis. I'm all for prompting smiles from the rich, but not at the expense of selling my soul."

Ms. Darby of the admissions staff spoke up. "Someone else can recruit in Dallas next year if we don't take this one. At a tea in my honor several of those ladies gave me a piece of their mind about how Oldebrick was going down the drain with the 'hippie types' we have been admitting. Turn down Miss Clean here, and I think we should just skip Dallas for a while until the ladies simmer down."

Adam McDermott winked at Kelly Darby and whispered audibly that he'd travel to Dallas on the next round.

"The *final* candidate of the evening is a total contrast to any other candidate we've considered thus far," said the Dean, a touch of excitement in his voice. "This is a kid from Alabama who discovered us late and applied late (we excuse a few who seem to have legitimate reasons for not getting their materials in on time). Just how THADDEUS RUFTUS stumbled upon Oldebrick from down in the boonies of Alabama, I'm not certain, but we're glad he did. He lives on a farm, has several younger brothers and sisters, and attends what appears to be a slow-w-w high school. No one in Thad's family has attended college. A nearly full scholarship, by the way, will be needed. His application is sketchy and the reports from his school are even sketchier.

"I must admit I'd like to take a chance on this fellow because he's so different for us. But in actuality, we know little about him, so I want you to hear his story before I get carried away.

"Thad says he wants to major in Math or Astronomy. His Math SAT of 620 and his Math II Achievement of 700 indicate he might know what he's talking about. His other scores, by the way, are SAT Verbal 580, English Achievement 470, and Physics Achievement 650. You have his transcript in front of you. (*See page 73.*)

"Frankly, we know little about the quality of Thad's school. They sent no profile, but they did indicate on the school report that 28 percent go on to college—that's well below the national average. Note that Thad took the basic courses. He ranks 24th in a class of 138; they weigh all grades evenly, so his two C's in Typing didn't help the rank. Considering the fact that this fellow is so bright, one does wonder why he didn't get straight A's, particularly if the school is below average. We'll never know, but I'm guessing there are two reasons: one, on school days he works from 5:00 to 7:30 A.M., and again from 3:00 to 6:00 P.M., on the family farm, and that is bound to make a dent in his school performance; and two, the great majority of his schoolmates are not going to college, nor did anyone in his family—in other words, there is not much company for discussing educational goals.

"Thad is a National Merit Semi-Finalist, and he has been named to 'Who's Who Among High School Students,' a national honor society in which we put little stock due to its questionable means of selection and recruitment of secondary school students. Beyond that, there is little to report from Thad's application except the fact that he spends three to four hours per week as a newspaper reporter and always participates in the county science fairs with great success."

The Dean's enthusiasm had perked up the committee. Butch Lassiter returned to his chair once again. "Here is Thad's essay, written in longhand, and a bit of a mess:

An area of moderate interest to me is whether or not genetic engineering is safe. I see the question as two-fold: will we use it for good or will we use it to destroy each other. It can do good by possibly providing a means to increase food crop yieldage. It can be used to evil by giving the military leaders a means to kill off the enemy with terrible diseases or destroy the local ecology.

The solution that will be accepted won't be acceptable to everyone because some people are naturally cautious and others are trail blazers who won't or can't see the evil potential of something of this nature. The solution that I feel will be accepted is 'proceed with caution.'

Genetic engineering can be a panacea for society's ills or a weapon more terrible than anything physics can produce. The choice is in

3. STUDENT'S ACADEMIC HISTORY

MINIMUM PASSING MARK		OTHER PASSING MARKS USED (AND NUMERICAL EQUIVALENT)		
GRADE & YRS.	COURSES TAKEN (AND SPECIAL LEVEL WHERE APPROPRIATE)	MARKS		CREDITS
I	English I	C	B	1
	Algebra I	B–	B	1
	Science	A	A	1
	Civics	A–	A	1
	Typing I	C	C	1
	P.E.	S	S	1/2
II	English II	B	B	1
	Biology	B	A	1
	Geometry	B	B	1
	Spanish I	A	B	1
	P.E.	A	S	1/2
III	English III	B	B	1
	U.S. History	A	A	1
	Chemistry	B	A	1
	Algebra II	B	A	1
	Spanish III	A	A	1
IV	English IV	B		
	Spanish III	B		
	Trig.	A		
	Physics	B		
	Calculus H	A		
	Athletics			

the hands of the layman, of the politicians, but most of all, in the hands of the scientists."

"What an obscure topic for John-Boy Walton to try to write about," said Benson. "I'd enjoy a hayseed at Oldebrick as much as the next don, but I can only hope someone else will get him for the opening course in English. Actually, I really do think we need this type of kid here. How many deep southern accents have you heard in your classrooms lately?"

"Well, Truman, Thad's writing is the only area adequately discussed in his folder by school authorities, and you're not alone in your reaction. His History teacher writes:

> Thad is 'outstanding' in intellectual ability and academic achievement, 'excellent' in disciplined work habits and potential for growth, 'good' in original thought and taking initiative, but 'below average' in written expression of ideas. Thad always makes it his business to know the subject matter, but is inconsistent and disorganized in his presentation and evaluation. He has a real thirst for learning (and is the *only* student in our school who spends spare time quietly reading in the library, alone) but has a way to go in written expression. His deportment in class, by the way, is (most of the time) alright.

"Thad's counselor really doesn't help the boy at all. It appears he just didn't take the time:

> Thad is a fine boy, who will go far if given the opportunity. He is well liked by student and faculty. He has a 3.3 average out of a possible 4.0. I am certain you will enjoy him.

"And that's all we know about Thaddeus Ruftus. Intriguing in the context of our usual suburban applicant. What do you think?"

"I'm with you, Dean," said Harry Chin promptly and deliberately. "He will probably end up in our department. Not only does he have ability, but he has the potential for growth that we so enjoy working with. I think we should admit him, high cost and rough diamond or not."

"I'm *certain* we should admit him," Lois Ruffin said quietly.

Playing the Game for Practice

"This white kid is just like most of the students of color we'd like to attract. He is from a different, somewhat disadvantaged situation, and Oldebrick could open nice new doors for him. And he'd teach us all a whole lot."

"Whom would you room him with?" queried Nora Taylor. "Yes, I find him interesting, and a change of pace for us, and I think he'd achieve. But how comfortable will he feel here? Whom will he share campus life with? Frankly, I think he'll be miserable at Oldebrick, at least for a while. We should take him *only* if we put a flag on his folder indicating that the Dean of Freshmen should follow him carefully and take special care in assigning a roommate."

"Ms. Taylor, he only looks different," Mr. Chin said, leaning forward. "So many of our freshmen, including those who arrive with the 'right' demeanor, are scared and uncertain and lacking confidence. This boy, it seems to me, already has developed a sense of independence that will be obvious very, very soon. Also, our department is small and we'll watch him."

"This thoughtful conversation pleases me," said Rita Dorsett a bit ponderously. "But it raises questions: For example, what is this young man like as a person? We really don't know. He didn't let us know much, and his school didn't help except to say he might need assistance in English. Here is a case where I wish we had an interview report. We need to know more about Thaddeus. Would he be able to adjust to Oldebrick? We should be searching for an answer to that question, for his sake as well as for our own. We're investing, if I heard the report accurately, a full scholarship in this young man. Is this money properly spent? I personally feel it may be, but I'm not convinced we've done our homework quite thoroughly enough yet."

"Well, you're probably right," said the Dean. "We have very few, if any, alumni in Thaddeus's area of Alabama, I'm afraid. But let me call the Alumni Office in the morning and see if we can get Thaddeus interviewed down there, pronto. If we can, I'll ask the alum to phone in the report quickly and we'll talk about Thad again before the week is out. I must admit, my own enthusiasm for 'differences' became a bit unbridled. Yes, Rita, you're right. Let's have this kid interviewed. It's better than a quick vote, impetuously giving away a place in the class and a bundle of financial aid for four years here, plus running the danger of making the boy miserable. I'll report back to you in a few days."

With positive nods all around, the meeting moved on.

"Okay, it is past 10:00 P.M. and we must vote. But is there any relevant general topic we have not stumbled upon yet and ought to discuss to make tonight's (and tomorrow's) decisions more informed?"

"Yes, the SATs," said Taylor. "My own daughter was sick to her stomach the night before the test, just worrying about getting into college. Probably my own dinner-table talk over the years hasn't helped her any; I'm obviously high on tests. But what really are the facts? Do those with the highest scores tend to do the best work here? Are we right to turn down kids who score under 500 on either Verbal or Math? You know how I've always been talking up tests. But frankly, I'm running a little scared now, with so many human dimensions sticking out of these damned folders."

"The topic is huge, Nora, and I know you don't expect to cover all the bases at this late hour. But let me try to respond briefly," said the Dean, a little impatiently.

"Here at Oldebrick we've found that almost all the students who do exceptionally well by traditional standards—Phi Beta Kappa, graduate magna cum laude, et cetera—entered Oldebrick with high Board scores. Among that group there are few surprises when one checks back to both SATs and the secondary school grades. However, there are plenty of surprises when one checks the SATs of those who get into academic trouble here. Too often, that group *also* entered Oldebrick with well above average Board scores. Obviously, something didn't click in terms of attitude and discipline: the kid's fault? Oldebrick's fault? Who knows? But plenty of youngsters who enter with very strong SATs bomb out. In short, we've had enough experience to know that numbers alone do not tell all. And that is why I believe in rather thoroughly scanning the 'characterizations' submitted by teachers and counselors. Their adjectives can give us important clues regarding the applicant's determination, genuine academic interest, and self-discipline.

"Some years ago, Bowdoin College shocked admissions circles by announcing that it would no longer require candidates to submit College Board results. The move was noteworthy because Bowdoin has long been considered very selective. Although some of Bowdoin's competitors felt this was a 'grandstand play,' the Bowdoin statement was rather convincing. Essentially, it said that the SATs had become overemphasized and that a highly selective college could go about its business of choosing a new class without standardized test scores. Bowdoin also questioned whether minority kids and those who 'freeze' were not significantly disadvantaged by required SATs. The announcement also cited what the college considered an 'evidence gap' regarding the SATs.

"As a postscript, let me read you this little poem a student sent to Bowdoin in support of its announcement:

Do the numbers of the SAT reveal what one is like?
Can one who times a sprinter know how far the man can hike?
Can one who weighs a person know how much that man can eat?
Can one who counts the seeds predict the total crop of wheat?

"I love it!" exclaimed Ms. Dorsett. "That poem says it all for me, Nora. I'll be disappointed if you categorically vote 'yes' for high scores, 'no' for low scores. Let's use the Board scores as just a piece of the pie. To do otherwise would be simply unfair, law school admissions frenzy or not."

"Let's vote, for Chrissake!" yelled Benson. The others jumped, but everyone agreed the time had come.

The Dean began. "Remember that you should be voting for approximately half the candidates who are presented, so try to pace yourself accordingly. Raise your hand if you are in favor of a candidate, and I will record that individual's total number of votes. At the end of the week I'll admit those with the highest vote totals, approximately 125.

"As I explained to you at the beginning of the evening the

seven candidates we read tonight are fairly representative of our applicant pool. In his or her own way, each suggests different problems of admission policy. But remember, I included a couple of outstanding candidates in this group tonight just to add balance and give you some perspective. Those you see the rest of the week will be more marginal and truly 'muddy-middle.' Obviously, there are no clear answers."

The Dean had a full audience. There was not a sound in the room but his voice.

"Because these seven candidates constitute a microcosm of our applicants, let's do more than just see which three or four you feel should be admitted. After we determine the three with the most votes, let's further eliminate two of the candidates (just for fun, not for good) to simulate the kind of class Oldebrick *might* have if our applicant pool grew larger and we were able to move closer to the Ivies and Caltech and Georgetown in selectivity."

READER STOP!

It is decision-making time, so to play your own hand in the college admissions game, vote now on the candidates.

Oldebrick is in a position to admit three of the six candidates just presented. (The seventh and last candidate's folder was considered incomplete, you will remember, and discussion of his application was postponed pending further investigation. It is only fair to tell you right now, however, that the alumnus interviewer who drove miles to see Thaddeus was extremely impressed by him. Not only did he seem an extraordinarily eager student, but also a hardworking fellow who was able to put in five hours per day on the family farm. After the interview report had been called in, the committee unanimously voted to admit the Alabamian. Thaddeus will come to Oldebrick on full scholarship.)

VOTE! And have your arguments ready so that you can participate in the committee discussions that follow.

Playing the Game for Practice

"I'll try to do a very brief recap of each candidate before I ask you to raise your hands," said the Dean. "While I recap, you can review the transcript in your folder.

"First was Trudi Jameson, from the good day school in the Midwest. Trudi has two sisters who went here. Her Boards are a little lower than our medians; she ranked twentieth in a class of sixty-seven, with a moderately difficult courseload. This year she is taking things she obviously enjoys. You will remember that Trudi has traveled a great deal, is strong in the theater, and wrote the 'I am I' essay. She seems to have a lot of bounce and self-confidence, and she had a positive interview here. There is no indication of how seriously interested in Oldebrick she is—but she obviously was interested enough to come out and see us, all the way from Wisconsin. Besides being a decent student who wears a big smile, Trudi raises two important questions: how loyal should we be to a family that has already sent two students to us, and how far are we willing to go to increase enrollment from an underrepresented area like the Midwest? Well, enough. How many favor Trudi?"

"I don't like this!" exclaimed Rita Dorsett. "Five whole days of playing God. Really, each young person tonight, with the possible exception of one, seems to me to be a positive addition to Oldebrick. And I'm to raise my hand for *three?*"

Mr. Chin clapped his hands softly, delighted. "No, no! This is interesting. Each one of us has complained at one time or another that Oldebrick is not quite as selective as Swarthmore or Brown. And now we balk at rejecting even some who appear truly mediocre by all traditional yardsticks. Come on, Rita, get tough," he urged with his first broad smile of the evening.

"Up with the hands," said the Dean. A few hands went up halfway, then came down. Everyone seemed to be waiting for others to vote. After a few false starts, most hands remained raised. Seven of the eleven favored Trudi.

"Seven. Next is Patty Murphy, who is working in New York for a semester, attended a decent but not terribly demanding day school, had a near-perfect record, a straight courseload, powerhouse SATs with Achievements not quite as strong, a real interest in art, and is somewhat bent toward medicine, largely because of her little brother's problems."

"Stop, stop, stop," said Benson. "Anyone who doesn't vote for this near-perfect creature should not report for future meetings."

"Vote for your own canoe, Truman," retorted Rita Dorsett firmly. "But I must say I am moderately surprised that any young lady could win your ringing endorsement."

"Hands, please," interrupted the Dean. All eleven shot up.

"Unanimous. Next is Sophie Wilson, the African American who has had her ups and downs academically, socially, and emotionally. The product of what appears to be a middle-class family; strong paternal influence; president of the student body of a powerful prep school; wrote her essay on the exchange trip to Japan; the girl whose school wrote so completely and sensitively about her moods, her uncertainties. And let's remember Lois Ruffin's reminder that our black pool is down somewhat this year."

"Yes, I think we need this girl. She can survive here if we keep an eye on her," Lois Ruffin said calmly but with precision.

"I still question the match of this girl and Oldebrick," said Benson quietly.

"Votes?" probed the Dean. After a good many quick glances at one another, five hands went up.

"*Jesus!*" exploded Ms. Ruffin. "Does the college's commitment mean *anything* to this group?"

"Yes, it does," said Truman Benson explicitly. "And I trust we'll be looking at other students of color who are perhaps more stable and accomplished than this one. And perhaps more deserving—in several senses of the word."

The air was a little heavy, and the Dean moved on, "John Wente, the boy with the traffic light, is next. Remember: large suburban high school, Exeter summer school, president of the senior class, academic record that consistently improved, tons of letters from the town fathers praising him, dreary SATs, pre-law, strong interview impression here."

Without much hesitation, every hand shot up. And everyone seemed surprised to see everyone else in favor. There were a few smiles. Wente, despite iffy statistics, had convinced even Nora Taylor. And Taylor smiled.

"Unanimous. Now we move to Andrew Jacobson. Bright, bright, bright: A record and sky-high SATs, super courseload in an above-average high school; strongly bent toward pre-med; disciplined athletic involvement in soccer and track; probably interested in the Ivies; and the one whom Sid Goldstein panned the hell out of in the interview. Who's for Andrew?"

Again, hesitation. Finally, six hands went up and stayed up. Three admissions staff members were voting against, and so did Mr. Chin and Butch Lassiter.

"You're kidding," said the Dean sternly, and he paused a short while. "*Six?* Well, it is inappropriate for me to question votes of this committee, but I do fail to see the everlasting flaw in this young man. Yes, he is intense. One might say he's obnoxious in his youthful, myopic goal orientation. But he's bright if not brilliant, and he's disciplined, accomplished, and even balanced, as demonstrated by his earnestness in athletics. With all the painful paranoia that Oldebrick carries because the Ivies and a few similar colleges seem to stay slightly ahead of us, how can we shut the door on this supertalented fellow? Again I ask: Do you have to be nice to be necessary at Oldebrick? I'm surprised by this vote, and frankly, disappointed. But so be it." The Dean looked down, tense.

Again a hesitation around the table.

"You make me feel more than a little guilty, Dean," said Mr. Chin, barely audible. "You undoubtedly suffer more than we in comments people make about the quality of the students here. But, you see, I agree with Adam McDermott in what he said about Oldebrick and its unique 'flavor' of community. If I wanted to be part of a college which prided itself in having student-technicians who grind it out for four years, I would not remain here. Yes, I want bright students in my classroom. But I want young people with a little compassion even more. I will not vote for Andrew Jacobson, knowing that he wants Penn or Princeton anyway and would probably be happier at one of those places."

The Dean was visibly perturbed—his upper lip always stiffened when he was tense, and it was nearly frozen now. He flipped through the pages of Jacobson's folder rather mournfully, as though he were saying goodbye to a friend. Then he continued.

"Our next candidate is Bette Bassis of Dallas, the young lady who is dying for Oldebrick, applied Early Decision and didn't make it, took Level 3 courses with adequate results, is an equestrian and a cheerleader, and the gal who brings strong backing from one of our most powerful alumni organizations."

"She's as drab as an overcast day in Newark," offered Benson. "Let's vote."

"All right, how many favor Bette Bassis?" This time, there was no indecision. Only two hands went up.

"Bette is already out. And because she musters so little enthusiasm among us, and because I know the phones will be ringing like crazy if we put her on the waiting list, my impulse is to reject her. Any objections?" There were none.

"If my rough tally is correct, you have just voted in Patricia Murphy, John Wente, and Trudi Jameson. Trudi has one more vote than our friend Jacobson. Also, if my tally is correct, the eleven of us cast forty-two votes. If each of us had voted for half the candidates, there would have been a total of thirty-three votes for the six candidates.

"So now I must give you a terse little warning. If you want Oldebrick to be more selective, hold back on your 'heart' votes. And please remember to look at the forest rather than just the trees: In forming our microcosm class, so far you have eliminated our minority representation, you have said to hell with the wishes of monied alumni, and you have axed one of the two best scholars of the group—because you felt he wasn't a nice enough fellow for our warm community. I don't mean to rap knuckles here, but do be aware of the consequences of your votes tonight in terms of the structuring of the class."

"Golly, are you going to keep badgering us all week over Andrew Jacobson?" asked Butch Lassiter. "I'm one of those who voted too many times because I thought most of these kids were pretty good material. I don't feel any more strongly *for* Trudi Jameson than I feel *against* Andy Jacobson. In view of that, I'm withdrawing my vote in favor of Trudi so that she and Andrew will be tied. We can squeak in one more freshman, can't we? We may lose Andrew to the Ivies anyway."

"And we may lose Trudi to someone, too," said the Dean. "I just don't feel it is fair to second-guess where these kids might end up going to college. They applied to Oldebrick in good faith, so let's vote on them in good faith. We know we're going to lose half of our admittees to other good colleges—that's a given. Let's not try to guess at this point which kids we might lose.

"Because the week will be even more turbulent if I start allowing vote swapping, withdrawing, et cetera, I think we'd best say firmly right now that once a hand is up, the vote sticks. And there will be no second-thought additions to votes. Let's go with our hunches at this late stage, or we'll never finish. We all know this is not an exact science . . . thank God.

"However, so that I can sleep tonight, and because I didn't lay down the law regarding vote changes until just now, and because I think you made a real mistake on Jacobson, I'm going to let Butch's change of mind on Trudi stand. That means that Trudi and Andrew both get into the class. And we'll just have to get tougher as we move along."

There was an exchange of uneasy glances around the table, as if people were wondering if the Dean was not being a bit high-handed. But his decision stood, and no one commented.

"In a more cosmic sense, let's consider what we've done in terms of overall selectivity. Tonight we admitted four out of six (with one pending), or 75 percent, of our applicants. Most colleges in America would be thrilled to admit all seven. It is estimated that a strong majority of private and public colleges will open next September with empty beds.

"Some so-called 'selective' private colleges in America today would be in a position to turn down only one or perhaps two of the candidates we reviewed this evening. Here are the names of some fine institutions that have admitted two-thirds to three-quarters of their candidates during the past few years: Washington University (St. Louis), Denison, Bennington, University of Colorado, Mount Holyoke, RPI, Marquette, Rollins, USC, Smith, Vanderbilt, Syracuse—and even Oldebrick a few years ago, when we went through some sparse times due to image problems. Now we and a few other colleges are in the position of admitting approximately half our candidates: Tufts, Bucknell, Carleton, Macalester, Connecticut College, Rhode Island School of Design, Northwestern, Wellesley, and Vassar.

"If we were admitting only one-third of our applicant pool, consider the pain of selection. That would have meant, in tonight's exercise, that both Trudi and Andy would have slipped down to the waiting list. We'd have ended up taking only Patricia Murphy and John Wente—one near-perfect student, one dynamic person. A very small number of colleges in America are in the position of admitting approximately one-third of the applicant pool. Among them: Wake Forest, Bates, Pomona, MIT, Georgetown, Columbia, Davidson, Chapel Hill (UNC), Middlebury, William and Mary, and Bowdoin.

"Some of our faculty, as you know, want us to have top Ivy selectivity. I'd rather be the director of admissions than the director of rejections, so I don't aspire to admitting one kid out of four or five applicants. But Amherst, Brown, Caltech, Dartmouth, Duke, Harvard/Radcliffe, Princeton, Rice, Stanford, University of Virginia, Williams, and Yale do just that. If we were to get into that fortunate (or unfortunate?) position, we'd have to make a choice between Patty and John. Just for fun, let's see what you as a committee would do. Everyone can vote only once. How many would go for Patricia Murphy?"

With surprisingly little hesitation, nine hands were stretched high. Only Butch Lassiter and Truman Benson abstained.

Truman nodded approvingly at Butch, grabbed the last Danish, and left.

They were all in their seats at nine the next morning.

2.

The Candidate Looks at the College

Now that you have audited what happens at the end of the line, it is time to make enlightened choices at the beginning. Your first project is to settle on a list of colleges and universities that seem a good match for you. Remember: There are probably several "right" choices, not just one.

If you remain skeptical of popular mythology regarding the college search, you will be off to a good start. Let's look at a few of the most common misconceptions.

Myth I, NAME: "THE MORE PRESTIGIOUS THE COLLEGE, THE BETTER THE COLLEGE"

On climbing down from the chapel pulpit of an old-boy-gone-coed prep school in Boston (having made a Sunday evening chapel talk which I was instructed should be "uplifting but not religious"), I was ushered to the rear of the Gothic structure by an impressive senior girl. Since it was mid-April, I asked how she had fared in college admissions returns.

"Gloriously," she exuded. "I'm so lucky: University of Virginia, Pomona, Vermont, Duke, and Yale all admitted me. It is nearly embarrassing."

"Good grief," exuded I. "How could one possibly decide by

the May first deadline which of those prestigious colleges to attend?"

"It couldn't be easier," she stated firmly. "Yale is Yale, and I must go."

Miss Cup Runneth Over went on to say that her intended college was located in a city which she defined as "the pits," probably had classes larger than those at Pomona, and was said by some to be a bit less warm in accommodating women than men. But Yale is Yale, and she must go.

The higher a college's position in the popular pecking order, the more likely it is that an admitted student will ultimately pick it, regardless of compelling reasons to go elsewhere.

Colleges pay thousands of dollars to enrollment management specialists for "recruitment and marketing plans" and even more to public relations firms to invent dramatic new viewbooks to be sent to candidates and parents who request information. The publications are informative, selectively honest, comprehensive though concise, and very appealing to the eye. The viewbook is intended to be an "incentive piece" to prompt students to read the full catalogue and visit the campus for a tour and interview. But no matter how appetizing the new Ivyish college's viewbook and catalogue, no matter how tantalizing that picturebook campus and role-model student tour guide, the college knows that if Johnny Marks is admitted to one of the institutions reputed to be slightly *more* prestigious, off he'll go—urban blight and large classes or not.

At this point, parents must enter our discussion, with emphasis on mothers. Mothers are very important to the college selection process. They are often quiet, but they are always there. We in the admissions office are aware of their background presence, and grateful for it, and surely the candidates are, too. It is often the mother who has read or takes the time to read the college viewbooks so she can tell the family over dinner how College H differs from College Y. It is usually the mother who calls the admissions office to arrange for the tour and interview and asks for the names of the cleanest and least expensive motels in the area. It is often the mother who asks the student tour guide the gritty questions about drugs and sex on campus and the percentage of pre-meds admitted to medical school last year.

And there is Dad. Fathers seem to dwell a little heavily on price, or what the associates at the office and the boss's wife say about St. Tom's U. versus St. Jim's. We in admissions can't help wondering at times which has priority with the dads: a good match between offspring and college or finding the institutional banner (accompanied by financial aid incentives) that will fly highest during the business lunch.

Unfortunately, both mothers and fathers impose old college images on new college candidates. (Imagine the adjustment in the home of the young *man* aspiring to Vassar whose sister wanted Dartmouth!) Parents are important to the college search, but they sometimes cannot resist stepping over the boundary of discreet influence. Going to college is Today with consequences for Tomorrow. Helpful as parents can be, Yesterday looms all too heavily in their minds when colleges are discussed. Parents, more than any other party, are guilty of perpetuating the prestige-equals-quality myth.

Guidance counselors and principals must share the guilt, however. Placement in "name" colleges becomes the badge of success for all too many schools, for the schools must answer to their public or private boards. How tempting it is to push a very talented Joe or Jane into a public or private Ivy, whether or not he/she will be happy there, in order to bolster next year's Where-They-Went-to-College profile and cool political heat.

The candidates themselves, of course, should not escape blame. Funny thing: High school juniors and seniors scrutinize colleges wonderfully well when deciding where to apply. One would think that the same careful scrutiny would be applied after letters of acceptance arrive. But no. When the options are finally at hand, and financial considerations have been put in perspective, the fame of the name rules supreme. You just don't turn down Harvard to attend Cornell; you don't turn down Berkeley to attend Oregon; you don't go to Mount Holyoke if invited to Brown; you can't turn Williams down to attend Bucknell, or snub Smith to attend Pine Manor. Some immovable force keeps the pecking order intact, much as we in admissions try to alter it. Our failure to succeed is demonstrated most poignantly every late April when the thanks-but-I'm-going-elsewhere letters from admittees arrive. A sample or two from my own files:

> As indicated on the enclosed card, I shall not be attending Bowdoin in the fall. Instead, I will be at Harvard. I feel, however, that after all you and the College have done for me, more than a simple card is required. Your every assistance while I visited your college, your invitation to a second weekend on campus, the letter from a professor—all were overwhelming. Nowhere else, at any time, did I receive such attention. Unfortunately, despite all you have done for me and despite all the obvious attributes of Bowdoin, I cannot turn down Harvard. I have made this decision not because Harvard is necessarily better or greater than Bowdoin, but rather because my life-long dream has been to attend it. Until the letters arrived, reason within argued that a small, personal college would perhaps be better for me than a large one. But when those fateful envelopes were opened, emotion took control and I found myself unable to reject my desire of so long. Sadly, I say goodbye.

From a Vassar fan held prisoner by her brother at Princeton:

> I am writing this letter to you from my brother's dormitory room at Princeton. My decision to attend Princeton has been downright anguishing. It was only this weekend that I felt I could actually enjoy the college experience at this Eastern Establishment. For the first time I have found it electric and stimulating! These adjectives I always knew applied to Vassar. The Vassar people I met—be they students, faculty, or administrators—were all amiable, the kind with whom I'd like to be associated. Yet Princeton, perhaps only because of its fame, has always held a "trump card." Sorry.

In all fairness, many young people—and certainly their parents—justify falling toward the big-name school by arguing that graduate school placement and the first permanent job search will be made easier by having attended a prestige college. And that was once true. But it is no longer *as* true. . . . Graduate and professional school admissions offices have democratized now—in philosophy and in practice—just as the college admissions offices have: they all want a socio-economic-ethnic mix, and not a full class who came from "just the right places." Look at the Rhodes Scholarship list of winners these days: Harvard, Yale, Princeton, and their brothers used to have a lock on this top honor, it seemed. Well, no longer—the annual Rhodes list is now peppered with state university graduates and small-college liberal arts graduates, as well as the usual top-line private Ivies. And so it is on the freshman-class roster at law and medical schools now—and at IBM, General Motors, and Procter & Gamble! The rule of thumb for all these school/employers is: Was this candidate superenergized, and did this candidate make the most of her opportunities at the institution she last attended?—and, of course, Was the achievement there noteworthy in the context of that competition?

The general prestige of an institution may indeed denote quality, although images are often woefully dated and distorted (consider winning football teams: what does *that* have to do with whether the pre-law program is superb or mediocre?). Remember: some of the average of the old schools may not be quite as good as the best of the newer schools, particularly as one compares specific majors and programs. The "name recognition" and prestige of an institution, although difficult to discount, should not point to the college for you.

Myth II, LOCATION: "TO RETIRE TO THE OCEAN OR THE WOODS WITH MY BOOKS—OR, IF NOT, TO BOSTON—WOULD BE UTOPIA"

The location of a college is an important consideration indeed. But sitting in the middle of Perfect City or surf-sand-and-sun or mountains-and-glacial-lakes hardly gets at the core of what college is all about. It is easy to be miserable in the most ideal college locale if one doesn't probe beneath surfaces *and* question one's own adaptability well ahead of time.

Colleges and universities—*all* of them—are eager to sell their produce today, and "packaging" becomes key. Promotion of activities available in the area of the campus has become important to the colleges' marketing campaigns.

I well remember arriving at Bowdoin in Maine in the late sixties to head admissions. Here was a college of glorious tradition, founded in 1794, which had graduated Hawthorne and Longfellow and America's first undergraduate black (John B. Russwurm, in 1826). But for some reason, despite consistency of academic quality over the years, Bowdoin had slipped from national visibility and applications were declining. Part of the problem, it appeared, was the trend at that time of teenagers wanting a city college. To "save the world" one couldn't desert the city—only there did the ghettos call, only there were the visible podiums to demonstrate actively against America's wayward foreign policy. (Indeed, the extracurricular involvements of urban college students in that era helped change a nation.)

But trends and times change, too. Suddenly in the seventies, the ecology movement came roaring in. "Our moment!" said Bowdoin and Williams and Middlebury and Dartmouth, for in the eyes of the young, helping save the environment became a compelling option to bettering the human condition within urban boundaries.

We at Bowdoin lost no time providing collegiate music for the new bandwagon. The sensitive, seemingly troubled and certainly studious young man on the cover of the viewbook was dismissed in favor of pictorial displays that would impress Audubon: quaint fishing villages with (endangered) sparkling waters, magnificent sunsets, (endangered) verdant forests, and shots of backpacking extravaganzas. And it worked. Applications to the Bowdoins of the nation (we were clearly not alone in our newfound campaign and glory) soared; meanwhile, there was a momentary decline in applications to urban universities, which were suddenly labeled "unsafe and troubled." (Granted, educational innovations at Bowdoin and other rural colleges in the early seventies helped to boost their stock, but locale seemed to deserve top honors for the turn-around.)

The Candidate Looks at the College

Bowdoin was honest in accompanying the descriptions of its academic offerings with pictures of the wonders of coastal Maine; the pine trees and the rocky shoreline and the incomparable sunsets were all there. But just as Uncle Sam instructed the nicotine salesmen to put a warning on the label, so might someone have gotten to us at the colleges. Kids should be warned that an idyllic natural location is not a "natural" for all.

Who wouldn't want to go to Bowdoin after seeing the campus on a sunlit, foliage-drenched Saturday afternoon in mid-October? Who wouldn't be captured by the seals bobbing two miles away at the shore? Nature-starved high schoolers from Manhattan and Boston and Los Angeles fell for it in droves. And after settling in, many were utterly happy there. But others found that four years without a subway, without "culture" beyond the campus, without the anonymity and freedom that tall buildings and crowded streets provide, was a strikingly different experience from the weekend visit.

True, one could argue that Manhattan kids need Maine and that Maine kids need Manhattan during those broadening college years. But academic adjustment and accomplishment through hard work may prove enough of a challenge without also risking a completely foreign locale. To each his own, of course, but teenagers must seriously examine their ability to adapt to dramatically different surroundings before being won over by the lush brochures put out by both country *and* city colleges. (Are the distractions of glorious Boston and its quarter of a million college kids going to provide the most conducive college-years atmosphere for *every*one?)

As a postscript, I can't resist commenting that Miss Cup Runneth Over's description of New Haven as "the pits" seems a trifle unfair. True, New Haven, Poughkeepsie, Oakland, Providence, and Durham are not the garden spots of America. But they, and many other "unattractive" moderate-size cities, are big enough and interesting enough to offer quality relief from the campus. They are diverse enough to provide an arena for volunteer work that is both meaningful and, because the towns are small, visible; and they are all within proximity of unpaved areas of woods and grass and water and fresh air. The facade of ugly/urban cannot be overlooked, but some college locales tout versatility beyond looks—and some of the prettiest are limited indeed. Know thyself: Will the campus area distract from, or encourage, serious college pursuits?

Myth III, SIZE: "THE SMALLER THE COLLEGE, THE MORE PERSONAL THE EDUCATION"

Granted, everyone knows everyone in a tiny school, but is this stimulating, or is this boring? The communal comforts of the small college are clearly what some institutions push in justifying a hefty price tag.

Becoming a friend of both fellow student and professor can truly promote a warm learning environment. But surely there is a case to be made for the educational value of a diverse student body, which assures that a student will be exposed to cultural and lifestyle differences. At some point the notion "I like Reserve because everyone knows my name here" becomes a bit vapid: Reserve may be shortchanging this student in offering such limited exposure. Little places that do not structure diversity (by choice, or because they have too few applications) can be stifling in their rigidity and lack of differences. And larger places can be surprisingly personal as one moves from small group to small group: at least there is choice.

The diversity of the student body is only one aspect of the question of large university versus small college. A more important issue is the faculty's accessibility to the individual student.

A favorite question of college candidates today is "What is your college's faculty/student ratio?" We admissions officers are always ready with a pat and persuasive answer, but often we fudge. Most colleges include the following in their ratio figures: faculty members on sabbatical leaves; administrators who are technically part of the faculty but who teach little (if at all); and "nonacademic" faculty members such as full-time coaches or music librarians. A more penetrating question would be "How many students in your college's average class?"

At many private and public institutions today, including some of the famous ones, the faculty has been "frozen" because of financial constraints. This means the size of the faculty, by administrative decree, must remain constant or be cut back by "natural attrition" until the financial crunch eases. Obviously, political conflicts rage on a campus when this situation develops. Meanwhile, a faculty freeze is often accompanied by a "natural growth" in the student body (luring more tuition-paying students results in looser purse strings), so individual classes grow larger.

At some small liberal arts colleges where the add-and-subtract method of accommodating the faculty freeze is too painful to be exploited, some departments remain underenrolled (foreign languages, for example, today), while others bulge with students (Communications and Biology are two examples now). Often an institution just cannot keep up with fads among students, as academic vogues rise and fall without fair warning. Students aspiring to the business world were subject to peer harassment in the late sixties; then, the Economics and Business Administration classrooms were flooded for a couple of decades, but now are subsiding once again.

Any college, large or small, can become "personal" if a student hits it off well with a particular faculty member. Oddly enough, given all the talk by college candidates of not wanting to be "just a number," students often don't take the initiative. (If they only would, there would be great rewards.)

To determine the "personalness" of a college, careful prodding must be done. Neither the gross size of the institution nor the faculty/student ratio necessarily provide accurate insight into the faculty/student ratio within a given department during a given term.

Should one really care how large the class will be if John Kenneth Galbraith is willing to teach undergraduates at Harvard? At many institutions there is "a course you *must* take before you leave here," popular because of a particular professor rather than because of the subject matter. That class is usually big. And when basic terms and concepts are being transmitted in Sociology I or Biology I, does it matter whether the professor is close enough to touch?

If one is paying an exorbitant price, however, one would seem to earn the right to assured attention. To get at the core of the matter, ask an admissions office how many freshman advisees a professor has at his college; ask if the person who lectures and conducts discussion in most courses is the same person who grades the papers (and do many of them speak English?); ask how often typical professors eat with the students, or whether there is a separate faculty lunchroom (so interaction midday becomes a moot point); ask whether full professors teach freshman courses; ask whether the famous names at a famous institution teach undergraduates at all!

Big versus small college? There is no pat answer to this important question. What one gains at a large school because of the diversity of courses offered and people assembled, one may lose in feeling a member of an impersonal, fragmented community. But "personal" has many faces, and counting noses will not alone suffice.

Myth IV, MAJOR: "ANY PROMINENT COLLEGE WILL BE GOOD IN MY FIELD"

Wrong, wrong, wrong. Rumored general strengths of institutions can be deceptive, and the candidate must investigate below labels in the viewbook. Often, even at a liberal arts college, a specialized faculty within an academic department gains strength and fame and "settles in," unwilling or unable to shift departmental emphases with shifting times, needs, and demands. A "good" Art Department may specialize in Art History, be mediocre in Studio Art, and may not acknowledge photography worthy of credit at all. A "good" Music Department may not be uniformly excellent in theory and performance, and some of the best music departments may not accredit jazz or electronic music. Does an institution's Math Department bend toward the theoretical or the practical? Does the Psychology Department bend toward the Experimental or the Clinical? *Which* languages does Middlebury teach well?

However, before you become too immersed in researching the subtle shades of a major at specific colleges, a reminder is in order. Most of the selective, private colleges of the nation— and some of the smaller Public Ivys too—hold fast to the traditional liberal arts program ("which trains you for nothing but prepares you for everything," Bill Wilson, a former dean of admissions at Amherst, said frequently) and immerse a student in general education for about two years. Even many of the large state universities, although requiring a student to pick a major or "school" up front, require general education courses for much of the opening two years.

Mount Holyoke College states the liberal arts, or general education, philosophy in an admissions publication:

> Mount Holyoke is committed to the liberal arts and the principles of philosophy such an education symbolizes. The liberal arts college maintains that the search for knowledge and with knowledge, compassionate understanding, is a central and not a peripheral human activity. It specifically provides the tools of mental inquiry and tries to reveal their variety, their inner logic, and their relatedness. It seeks to develop individuals committed to humane values, capable of rejecting oversimplifications of ideology or method, and liberated from narrow definitions of themselves and others and of human problems in general. It is an education that is evaluative, not merely factual and descriptive.
>
> These are utopian ideals, and rightly so, but the world of a college that seeks to live by them is nevertheless a real and rigorous world —a world where a life of a particular sort is intensely lived: a life of the mind above all, and of individual and joint endeavor.

Liberal arts colleges realize that students often—and quite honestly—change their minds about their academic concentration after sampling the great smorgasbord of courses in the freshman and sophomore years. Usually secondary school students have had in-depth exposure only to basic disciplines: English, History, Physical Science, Mathematics, Foreign Language. A freshman-year introductory course in Anthropology or Biopsychology or Asian Studies or Computer Math can whet appetites and open new, exciting vistas. At most colleges, it is not unusual for as many as half of all freshmen to change their minds regarding a major after exposure to new disciplines during the first two college years. (This can be a problem at some larger schools, where if students are admitted to specialization early, mobility is prohibited, or sometimes disallowed.)

Some small liberal arts institutions are so supportive of investigation and change regarding the college major that they view applicants who appear determined to specialize in a particular area with some suspicion. A common example on the current scene is the student who is hell-bent on being premedical. Almost all selective colleges today lament their unrealistically high percentage of "pre-meds." Many of these students have not even tasted an advanced course in biology or calculus in secondary school before making their plans.

Since a change in one's academic major is a real possibility for many students, one might feel that a large institution would be "safest" because of its wide spectrum of courses and majors. There is some merit to this argument, but the smaller institutions have a comeback.

Realizing their relative deficiency in the number of courses and majors offered, small colleges tap each other's resources so that an individual student can gain from two, or perhaps several, colleges' offerings during the undergraduate journey. Colleges in the same city allow and encourage cross registrations with each other. Twelve colleges in the Northeast* are involved in a formal exchange program through which a junior from one college can attend any of the other eleven colleges for a semester or a full year and return to his home college for the senior year.

Both large and small colleges offer broad opportunities for independent study for the student whose needs cannot be met

---

* Amherst, Bowdoin, Connecticut, Dartmouth, Mount Holyoke, Smith, Trinity, Vassar, Wellesley, Wesleyan, Wheaton, and Williams.

through standard curricular offerings. And many colleges are generous in allowing students to "create" years for credit abroad or at other American universities that have specialized programs.

One must remember that enrolling at a college or university today, in contrast to a generation ago, does not necessarily mean four years of staying put. Not only is moving around possible, but many good institutions encourage it. And if one settles on a major that the original college is ill equipped to offer, a transfer is a possibility. As most colleges have grown more accommodating to mobility, they have simultaneously adjusted to the possibility of students' permanently leaving midstream. Transfer students from other institutions then fill the holes. As a result, there can be heavy transfer traffic these days.

All good colleges, large and small, are limited in what they can offer well, and are often uneven in across-the-spectrum curricular quality. The candidate must analyze the depth and breadth of a specific institution's offerings, realizing all the while that a broad exposure may well lead to change in his or her major field, if not in the college also.

Myth V, SOCIAL TYPE: "SINGLE-SEX COLLEGES ARE DEAD"

For men, it is so: The all-male academic bastion has nearly fallen. Harvard and Yale and Williams and Dartmouth and all their macho cousins, including West Point, are now admitting women. When conservative Washington and Lee opened its gates to freshman women, an era of gender-specific exclusive education in America passed. (A few noteworthy all-male private college remnants can still be found: Hampden-Sydney of Virginia, and Morehouse of Georgia, for example. Wabash College of Indiana continues to be for-men-only, but this is probably because a major endower attached strings to a fortune. A couple of public all-male institutions persist, continuously in court to keep the women out.) Today, men must count on going to college with women.

But for women, there are many single-sex options. And they are worth considering. Throughout America there are healthy private women's colleges: California has Mills and Scripps; the deep South has Sweetbriar, Randolph-Macon, Hollins; the Northeast has Chatham and Simmons, plus the prominent and still-selective Seven Sister remnants—Smith, Mount Holyoke, and Wellesley. (Other Sisters in the Northeast are now so cozy with men's institutions that they don't qualify for the all-women's college list: Barnard, the across-the-street half sister of Columbia; Bryn Mawr, the morosely academic live-in mate of Haverford; and Radcliffe, once the fabled mistress of Harvard, now deceased wife. Vassar now has roughly equivalent numbers of men and women, much to the consternation of its old sorority.)

Until women are given an equal place in the American social and economic fabric, educating them separately is warranted, say the proponents of all-women's colleges. Jill Conway, former president of Smith College, argues the position convincingly:

> There are three major pedagogical reasons why women benefit from undergraduate study in an all-female student body. First, women students in such an environment are free to choose their area of academic specialization without reference to sex stereotyping. Thus, women's colleges have historically produced a disproportionate number of women who have gone on to achieve the doctorate in mathematics and science, and today they graduate many more majors in economics and political science than their coeducational equivalents.
>
> Secondly, undergraduates have always been thought to learn more when exposed to a civilized and humane environment that gives them insight into themselves through access to the experience of their peers. Similarly, it is clear that women in a single-sex student body build a network of friendships with other talented women that is a source of support throughout their lives and a powerful force for the creation of female identity. For natural and self-evident reasons, the bonding of the young in coeducational settings tends to be pairing across sex lines. In fact, there is some evidence that friendships among women are inhibited in coeducational environments.
>
> Finally, women in a single-sex—and thus self-governing—student

body take on managerial and leadership roles in greater numbers and on different terms than is possible in society at large. In the running of an all-female student world, women see themselves as part of the solution of problems rather than as part of the enduring problem of female subordination.

The chief weakness of feminist thought has been to see liberation for women as freedom to adopt male styles of action and traditionally male occupations without penalty. However, this tends to downgrade or ignore the importance of nurturing the young and to oversimplify the complex social arrangements we need in order to come to terms with human generativity.

The difference between the coeducational college and the all-female institution is that, at the women's college, she does this in a world in which she is in charge instead of one where she may feel the need to win acceptance.

There are outspoken critics of this view. One is Philip Jordan, president of Kenyon College (and former dean of Connecticut College, once all female, now coeducational):

Women's colleges nourished confidence and ambition in their students by freeing them from crosscurrents created by male peers and by providing examples to follow in the mature women who taught and oversaw them. But now that *male* bastions have fallen, the case for separating women is weak.

Why should women need a collegiate interlude of separatism before re-entering a society where, in graduate school or on the job, women work and compete with men? . . . Able young women today need no special treatment, just treatment and opportunity equal to that given to men.

Women's colleges were founded in response to the restrictive social attitudes of the last century. They flourished and did their job well. Now it is time for the next step: to take full advantage, for the good of both men and women, of the new freedoms that women are winning. This can best be done by educating men and women together, not apart.

The coed-versus-women's-college debate has subtleties deserving more than a passing glance. For example, "coed" often means male domination (reflective of the nation as a whole) with women present: big crowds and campus social events too often center around men's athletic contests, men's fraternity parties, etc. (Oddly, however, women frequently do not complain about this problem at the "coed" institutions most guilty of remaining macho.)

Selective women's colleges do seem to have a higher transfer-out rate than comparable coed institutions. Surely this relates somewhat to such factors as locating specialized academic programs or wanting to move closer to home. But some say that this phenomenon simply confirms the male domination of society as a whole: College women meet men and transfer to their institutions. Regardless, the single-sex college is *affirming* for women, remains a strong and popular option today, and should be seriously considered.

Myth VI, COST: "THE IVY-TYPE COLLEGES ARE NOW FOR THE RICH AND THE POOR: THE MIDDLE CLASS HAS BEEN SQUEEZED OUT"

History confirms old notions regarding the rich. The traditional elitist public and private colleges of the nation catered for years to the blue bloods. Much as the public and private Ivies and Seven Sisters and all their cousins brag about their institutions' open doors, there is little evidence to suggest that the doors have been unlocked for long. We thought the blue-jeaned scruffy hippies of the late sixties all looked alike? Take a look sometime at a University of Virginia or Smith or Yale yearbook of the forties or fifties. For every headband and unwashed lock hiding a saddened face of the early seventies was a striped tie or circle pin and blond hair cascading over endless blue eyes four and five decades ago.

For a long time those who attended the elitist colleges were, quite simply, mostly whites who could pay. But concurrent with zooming prices came a surge of conscience regarding equal access for all ethnicities and socio-economic groups to the best and/or most established of American colleges and universities. Largely thanks to student insistence on fairness during the turbulent sixties and seventies, literally all prestigious institutions now support ambitious affirmative-action programs, with priority accorded disadvantaged students of color.

So visible have the programs for the disadvantaged become that the second part of our "myth" is confirmed: "Olde Ivy *does* pay the (talented) poor to share the library and the football stadium with the (talented) rich." Both of these contingents are well represented in Williamsburg, Palo Alto, Ann Arbor, Hanover, and other Ivyish hometowns. But it is not fair to infer that the huge group falling financially *between* the richest and the poorest have not been provided for.

Is the middle class being squeezed out of Olde Ivy? No, no, no. Middle-income families frequently qualify for financial aid, making access to highly selective private and public institutions quite possible. Selective colleges today are eager to construct a freshman "classful of differences." Doing so obviously requires committing significant financial aid to those who cannot make it on their own—not just those at the lower end of the scale but also families with mid-level or surprisingly high incomes who, because of educating several children at once or living with legitimate costly commitments such as family health problems or elderly parents, genuinely need assistance.

Although there is a rush in America toward the "no-need" or "merit" scholarship (*aggressively* at institutions nervous about filling their beds), nearly all the most prestigious colleges use the majority of their considerable resources in financial aid to assist those who have *proved* financial need, at whatever level. While there may be some favoritism shown in the *admission* of an athlete, a student of color, or a legacy (see Chapter 3), there is negligible favoritism in *aiding* these special-interest groups at Ivyish institutions. Again, financial assistance at the most selective colleges is offered largely (but not exclusively) on the basis of proved financial *need*.

But alas, the financial aid story has grown ever more complicated recently: surely no one aspect of the college admission process has undergone more radical change and scrutiny during the past decade. Today's rising costs make financing a college education an increasingly critical concern for students and their families, regardless of income level. With the estimated cost of a freshman year at any one of the private Ivyish colleges approaching $25,000, more middle-income—and some high-income—families are understandably seeking accurate information about financial assistance. (A colleague who works at a prestigious prep school in a Los Angeles suburb where one assumes that family income would be adequate to cover the costs of even the priciest colleges reports the number of families attending financial aid workshops has more than quadrupled during the last five years.)

The Basics

Families must first understand that there are two basic types of financial aid for college:

1. *Need-based aid.* Money is allocated solely on the formulated "ability to pay" of the student's family. But because institutions use a variety of formulas to *determine* "ability to pay," the amount of financial aid offered from one school to the next will vary.
2. *Merit awards* (or non–need-based aid). This term refers to scholarships and awards given for significant talent and achievement—academic, athletic, leadership, artistic, and so on. Financial need may be incorporated to some degree in determining the amount of these awards (e.g., National Merit Scholarships), but in most cases an analysis of need is not part of the process in awarding "merits."

More on Need-Based Financial Aid

Understanding concepts of financial aid for college is complex in and of itself, but it is further complicated by the fact that the criteria, rules, and regulations regarding *federal* and *state* assistance programs change annually and sometimes dramatically. We will attempt a general overview of the need-based financial aid arena, however, greatly assisted by specific examples and guidance from one selective private institution (see Appendix II regarding the California Institute of Technology's financial aid program and instructions). *But remember*: It is of utmost importance that you check directly with the financial aid offices of the institutions to which you are applying to make certain you have timely, accurate, and complete information about the steps you should follow to be considered for financial aid at specific colleges.

In recent years, federal guidelines on financial aid have been dramatically liberalized: for example, mandatory student contributions have been pared, and home equity has been removed from the basic formula of a family's assets. These changes have allowed thousands more students to apply for assistance. But unfortunately, because of the sluggish economy and government budget deficits, far less money than expected has become available for this increasing pool of applicants. This scenario has resulted in both federal and state programs shifting aid dollars from *grant* programs to *loan* programs. Thus, students are facing an increasing debt load upon graduation as the amount of "free money" continues to shrink.

A college's need-based financial aid package awarded an admitted student will usually include three types of support:

1. *Grant*. This is "free" or "gift" money, and does not have to be repaid.
2. *Loans*. Both student loans and parent loans are available. Money lent to *students* usually carries a lower interest rate; payback generally begins soon after graduation. For some student loans the amount of payback is reduced if the student performs certain services (e.g., teaching in a rural or inner-city area via newly instituted national programs). The particulars of *parent* loans vary greatly, although for most the payback begins shortly after the student begins college.

3. *Work-study*. The student is employed, often on campus, for a stipulated number of hours per week. The money earned is applied against college costs.

Every student who applies for financial aid must fill out the Free Application for Federal Student Aid (FAFSA); as the name implies, there is no charge to complete and file this form. Students may obtain this application from their school counselor in December of the senior year. There are four agencies that process the FAFSA: the American College Testing Program (ACT), the College Scholarship Service (CSS), the Pennsylvania Higher Education Assistance Agency (PHEAA), and the U.S. Department of Education. Families should check with colleges to see which processor an institution prefers; a college may indeed use a particular processor's supplemental form (for which there may be a fee), to determine a candidate's eligibility for *institutional* aid (given in addition to federal aid). Some schools may also have, in addition to the FAFSA and the processor's supplemental form, even more institutional forms for the family to complete. (Beginning to get the picture that this is a paperwork nightmare?) So always check with the colleges to be certain you have completed all of the documents each institution requires. A crucial detail you *must* honor is each college's deadline for receiving needs analysis application forms. (If you are applying for supplemental loans, you will have to fill out separate applications; generally you obtain the supplemental loan applications directly from a bank or lender.)

Once you have submitted your financial aid application to a college, you will also have to submit verification of the information presented on the application. This is usually accomplished by submitting your and/or your parents' tax returns for the previous year. The college may also request additional documents (bank statements, mortgage information, business records, records of child-support payments, etc.). Final award offers are not made until these verification documents have been submitted, so be certain that your family tax forms are completed early (don't wait until April 15!).

More on Merit-Based and "Restricted" Financial Aid

Several years ago a young woman in the South made headlines because she had been offered over $300,000 in total financial aid from her college choices. Some of it was need-based, and being an underrepresented student of color probably boosted her cause. But much of the money that fell to her came in the form of special restricted scholarships because, as the famous ad said, "She earned it!" How? By doing her homework. She became knowledgeable about the many types of college-based special awards available (see Appendix II for a related bibliography), checking eligibility requirements carefully (by, among other things, researching her family history, as awards are often tied to country of origin, wars in which a relative may have fought, companies for which a parent worked or works, religious affiliation, etc.), and applying in a timely fashion. She did the work herself, coming up with more information than a computer-generated list would probably have produced for her specific profile.

Indeed, there are applications to fill out, essays to write, recommendations to obtain, interviews to attend, and projects to complete. And one must pay attention to deadlines—they're critical. But done right, this research can generate tremendous cash dividends in the merit and restricted scholarship categories.

It is true that many merit awards honor cumulative outstanding records in the classroom, on the ball field, or in the concert hall. But there are less obvious awards to be claimed: who would have guessed that a huge scholarship endowment at Yale, restricted to farm-oriented young men from Henry County, Indiana, went begging for years because no one in Henry County knew of it! (Because the scholarship went unclaimed for decades, the heirs of the donor expanded its geographical area to include the county of nearby Indianapolis, and the money goes begging no more.)

And Finally, on Financial Aid

There is no segment of the college admission ordeal that creates more anxiety than applying for financial aid. Concepts may at first seem confusing, but there are many people out there to help you. Your first important resource will be your college counselor. Also, financial aid officers at most colleges and universities tend to be friendly and helpful and are willing to answer questions when you call, or at least steer you in the right direction to get answers. Many financial aid professionals hold workshops for the general public in January and February. You do not have to apply to a college in order to attend the workshop they are hosting—and the seminars are usually free. Check the calendar in your high school's college counseling center or the local newspaper for information on these workshops, which are open to both parents and students.

The financial aid process cannot be conquered overnight. It takes prolonged preparation and grit to get through all the forms and to complete them in such a way that your unique situation is presented honestly but in the best light. Junior year in high school is not too soon to start gathering general information.

One way to learn more about financial assistance programs and related matters is to ask individual colleges and universities, by telephone or during a campus visit, these questions:

- At your college, does the student reduce his or her chances for admission by applying for financial aid?
- What percentage of your students normally receive financial aid based on financial *need*? And what percentage of your institution's grant money goes to *need*-based grants?
- What percentage of your students normally receive scholarships based on *merit*—academic, athletic, whatever?

And what percentage of your institution's grant money goes to *merit*-based grants?
- How much does your college usually increase costs (room, board, tuition, and fees) from year to year?
- If an accepted student must submit a room deposit, when is the deposit due—and is it refundable? (The deposit should be refundable in full up to May 1, if the college or university is a member of the National Association of College Admissions Counselors.)
- If my family demonstrates financial need on the FAFSA forms, what percentage of the established need will typically be met/awarded? When can I expect to receive an official financial aid notification letter?
- If a student receives additional scholarships from outside organizations, what impact will this have on financial aid he/she might receive through the college's financial aid office?
- What commitment can the college or university make to keep the composition and amount of a student's financial aid award consistent from year to year?

No matter when you read this section, changes in financial aid programs and procedures will probably *just* have happened. Regardless, we thought it would be useful to publish one selective (private) college's exemplary financial aid program and instructions, related to the 1993/94 academic year. (Please refer to Appendix II. But remember, you must check with your colleges of choice for updated programs and procedures, specific to those institutions.) We are grateful to David Levy, Director of Financial Aid at the California Institute of Technology, Pasadena, California, for sharing his instructions to candidates. Caltech, it must be noted, awards most of its financial aid on the basis of financial need, as do most other highly selective colleges, both private and public.

IN SUMMARY

Now that you are armed to debunk all college admissions–related myths circulating among your nervous classmates or your mother's telephone grapevine or your father's commuter train, it is time to take some steps on your own:

1. See your school's college counselor *early* (fall of the junior year, at the latest) to talk candidly about where your secondary school record puts you vis-à-vis the "selective level" of college to be considered. You may feel the school counselor is out of touch (rarely true) or has little time for you (often true—counselor loads continue to rise, and in some schools counselors have been eliminated altogether). But a friendly overture by you will demonstrate your interest, and you will almost always receive sympathetic advice. You may be disheartened by straight talk from the counselor, but remember: he/she has passed through hundreds of college acceptance and rejection notices in recent years and has as good a handle as anyone on which college requires what level of accomplishment, particularly with respect to applicants from your own high school.

In recent years, many families have begun utilizing the services of independent college counselors to supplement the assistance they receive at school. These private counselors charge a fee for a variety of services, from assistance in college selection to test preparation. Many are highly qualified, having worked as school college counselors or college admission officers prior to going into private practice. But it is important to find out the qualifications of the individual and the services provided before spending money for something you may already be receiving for free at school. The National Association of College Admission Counselors has developed strict guidelines for independent counselors, and membership in NACAC or the Independent Educational Counselors' Association is one good measure of a person's qualifications (Appendix IV). But remember: *No one* (outside of you yourself, perhaps) can guarantee you admission to a particular school!

2. Utilize *all* the resources available to you. Although some of the printed materials found in the guidance office or college center may be outdated, many schools now have a college video library, which can serve as a very helpful first introduction to a college. Also, there are various computer programs you can use to define your criteria for selecting a college, resulting in a list of colleges that fit these criteria. Check out your school's college center to find out what resources are available to you. Doing college research is your job, not something you can or should expect someone else to do for you.

3. Write directly to colleges that interest you for informative materials. Colleges are hungry for your inquiry, and will respond with volumes of literature, sometimes far more than you are prepared to read! A simple postcard requesting a viewbook and application will suffice. (The complete college catalogue, which includes a very detailed description of admission criteria, graduation requirements, and course descriptions is rarely available "just for the asking," as it costs so much to produce. The catalogues can usually be found in your school college center. For top college choices, you can purchase a copy of the catalogue by writing the college bookstore, or buy one if you visit the campus.)

4. *Study* the materials you are sent. The pictures can be entertaining (and are designed to create a mood—you'll often see New England campuses in the colorful fall rather than the bleak winter), but hard prose is what you must absorb. Pay particular attention to profiles of the freshman class. Most selective private institutions make these available today (but, alas, too few of the more selective publics) and they are helpful indeed in charting one's chances for admission. For example, you can test yourself on nearly every scale of the exhaustive freshman-class profile published annually by Williams College. Are you a "long shot," or are you rather a sure bet for Williams next year? An astute reading of the following tables brings you closer to the answer.

5. Talk with people from your hometown about the institutions that seriously interest you. Current undergraduates returning for Thanksgiving, Christmas, spring break, or summer

WILLIAMS COLLEGE

CLASS OF 1996

	Men	Women	Total
Completed Applications	2,406	2,185	4,591
Number admitted	573	590	*1,163
Percent admitted	24	27	*25
Entering Freshmen	262	262	**524

*Includes 11 accepts after Early Decision deferral, 14 from waitlist, and 16 who postponed from Class of '95.
**An additional 11 admitted students postponed enrollment until Fall 1993.

EARLY DECISION STATISTICS

	Men	Women	Total
Early Decision applications	248	228	476
Number admitted	92	92	184
Percent admitted			39%
Total class entering via Early Decision			34%

SUMMARY OF RECENT ADMISSION STATISTICS

Class	Final applications	Early Decision applications	Total admissions	Early Decision admissions	Number of freshmen
1987	3,962	322	1,126	139	515
1988	4,364	331	1,225	128	511
1989	4,685	341	1,226	123	516
1990	4,660	352	1,143	129	506
1991	5,099	416	1,200	136	511
1992	4,963	413	1,207	147	544
1993	4,329	393	1,225	138	519
1994	4,345	389	1,205	151	508
1995	4,190	370	1,213	160	518
1996	4,591	476	1,163	184	524

ACCEPTANCE RATES BY HIGH SCHOOL TYPE

	Total number applied	Percent of pool	Number accepted	Percent accepted	Number entering	Percent of entering class
Public	2,650	58	680	26	290	55
Independent	1,684	37	425	25	211	40
Parochial	257	5	58	23	23	5
	4,591		**1,163**		**524**	

RESIDENCE OF CANDIDATES FOR ADMISSION

	Number applied	Number accepted	Percent accepted	Number entering	Percent entering	Percent in class
New England	1,031	182	18	103	57	20
Middle States	1,590	464	29	196	42	37
Midwest	506	135	27	66	49	13
South	324	111	34	47	42	9
West	664	162	24	76	47	14
Southwest	135	41	30	12	29	2
U.S. Territories, other countries	341	68	20	24	35	5
	4,591	**1,163**	**25**	**524**	**45**	**100**

FINANCIAL AID DATA

Percent of those in Class of '96 aided who had demonstrated need	100%
Percent of the class receiving scholarship aid	36%
Tuition, room and board, 1992–93	$23,250
Average financial aid package (job, loan, scholarship)	$15,000
Range of financial aid awards to individuals	$1,000–$24,000
Range of family income of students assisted	$0–$125,000
Scholarships & grants awarded to the Class of 1996	$2,250,000

COMPLETION STATISTICS

Freshman retention	97%
Students in the Class of '92 who graduated within four years	87%
Students in the Class of '92 who graduated within five years	95%

RANK IN CLASS BY PERCENTILE

	Total number applied	Percent of pool	Number accepted	Percent accepted	Number entering	Percent of entering class
98-100	807	18	331	41	121	23
95-97	649	14	172	26	82	16
90-94	506	11	99	20	43	8
80-89	430	10	54	13	34	6
70-79	194	4	30	15	19	4
60-69	40	1	4	10	3	.7
0-59	63	1	3	5	1	.3
Unranked	1,877	41	470	25	221	42
	4,591		1,163		524	

RANGE OF COLLEGE BOARD SCORES

SAT Verbal

	Total number applied	Percent of pool	Number accepted	Percent accepted	Number entering	Percent of entering class
750-800	120	2	102	85	38	8
700-749	625	14	368	59	128	24
650-699	1,081	24	286	26	136	26
600-649	1,006	22	163	16	80	15
550-599	761	17	121	16	70	13
500-549	502	11	83	17	48	9
450-499	245	5	23	9	16	3
400-449	91	2	4	4	3	.7
200-399	66	1	2	3	1	.3
Not available	94	2	11	12	4	1
	4,591		1,163		524	100

SAT Math

	Total number applied	Percent of pool	Number accepted	Percent accepted	Number entering	Percent of entering class
750-800	580	13	287	49	91	17
700-749	1,199	26	381	32	169	32
650-699	1,123	24.5	241	21	124	24
600-649	799	17	137	17	77	15
550-599	435	10	56	13	32	6
500-549	203	4	33	16	19	3.5
450-499	94	2	10	11	6	1
400-499	40	1	4	10	0	0
200-399	24	.5	3	13	2	.5
Not available	94	2	11	12	4	1
	4,591		1,163		524	100

ACT (American College Testing Program) SCORES

For the 696 applicants taking the ACT, the average composite score was 29. Of those accepted (173), the average was 31, and the average for those entering (72) was 30. Of accepted candidates taking the ACT, 75% had composite scores of 29 or better.

CLASS OF 1996: DOCUMENTED DISTINCTIONS

Distinction	Percent
National Merit or Achievement Scholar	9%
Head of student government	10%
Distinction in music	14%
Distinction in studio arts, theatre, dance or creative writing	14%
Research or honors in the sciences	18%
Distinction in athletic endeavor	24%
Head of service organization	16%
Debate captain, editor-in-chief of yearbook, newspaper, or literary magazine	16%

AMERICAN STUDENTS OF COLOR

Recent Freshman Classes:

Class of	Total Size	African-American	Asian-American	Latino	Other Am. Minority	Percent of Class
1996	524	36	44	36	8	23.7%
1995	518	43	57	41	12	29.0%
1994	508	47	52	22	3	24.4%
1993	519	34	47	27	8	22.3%
1992	544	56	45	28	3	24.2%
1991	511	32	37	22	0	18.0%

Ten Years Ago:

Class of	Total Size	African-American	Asian-American	Latino	Other Am. Minority	Percent of Class
1986	497	29	18	6	NA	10.6%
1985	508	23	11	14	NA	9.5%
1984	501	37	14	9	NA	11.9%
1983	489	40	11	18	NA	14.1%

Total Student Body:

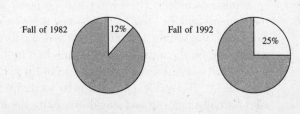

Fall of 1982: 12%   Fall of 1992: 25%

☐ Students of Color
▓ White or Caucasian

vacations will provide the most accurate and up-to-date insights. If you don't happen to know people attending these schools, check these possible sources: your school's guidance office or the guidance offices of neighboring high schools to see if recent graduates are attending colleges high on your list; the admissions offices of the colleges themselves, which may be able to put you in contact with current students from your hometown. Also, chats with local alumnae/i can be helpful, if one is good at selective listening. Too often the alums romanticize "good old days at Oldebrick U" and tell you about the college they attended rather than the college that exists today. A few alumni in each major city, however, are well trained by their institution solely for the purpose of talking to you. Write or call the admissions office to learn how to contact a local representative.

6. Visit the colleges that interest you the most. Seeing the campus firsthand will tell you a lot about a school, more than the rumor mill or the college's own "sales" literature. But even before you finalize your list of top choices, you can visit schools in your own backyard to help you get a sense of what you want and need in a college. Visit a huge rah-rah campus, a midsize urban university and a small liberal arts college to see what would be most comfortable for you, academically and socially. Attend the admissions office's general information session and, if possible, arrange for an interview (if for no reason other than to "practice" and to see what it's like).

College visits will accomplish different objectives depending on *when* you visit. If you visit during the summer following your junior year, you'll certainly get to see the community in which the college is located, attend an information session, and have a much better chance of booking an interview appointment with an admissions officer. However, what you *won't* see is most of the students and the "real" faculty—and these two populations, along with the setting, are often what give a college its distinct personality. So the meaty visit can come best in the fall of your senior year, when you return to the two or three campuses that top your list. If possible, go on a Friday to attend a few classes, take your sleeping bag and stay overnight in the dorm (the admissions office will help to arrange this), and check out what happens on campus outside the classroom on the weekend. *Always* sit down in the student union and ask several undergrads, independent of one another, "What's wrong with this place?" The answers will provide a healthy balance to all the pap in the slick admissions literature you receive, not to mention the unbridled enthusiasm of alums.

Students are now applying to more colleges, and often in geographically diverse areas, so it may not be possible to visit all campuses prior to admission. Some families wait until *after* students are admitted, and then visit their top two or three choices for several days before a final decision is made. The crucial issue is not so much when you visit, but that you *do* visit before you commit to four expensive, critical years.

7. If you are visiting a campus that accommodates individual interviews at the admissions office, schedule one. In the summer an interview appointment will be easier to procure, and you will receive a royal welcome because the crowds for the next class haven't arrived yet. In the fall or winter you may miss an admissions officer altogether because they are on the road visiting high schools; if you can book an appointment, the interview may be a bit rushed because the crowds have descended. If you are planning to visit, call at least three weeks in advance to book a student tour, an information session, and, with luck, an interview (hours are usually 9 to 5 weekdays; some schools are open 9 to noon Saturdays). The interview is important for two reasons: (1) your unanswered questions about the college can be cleared up at this time (although the tour guide or the students you meet in the student union may be more able to help you find answers); and (2) you can present your case for admission in conversation, which (regrettably) is often considerably more effective than the case for admission you will present in writing. (On the whole, students talk better than they write today, so most enhance their chances for admission via the interview.)

8. Apply to a "long shot" or two, a few "maybes," and at least one "safety." Which colleges fit the preceding definitions must

be decided by the counselor, candidate, and parents together, not by any one of these parties alone. Often college admissions officers will help you with these personal definitions if you can muster the courage to ask.

9. Spend time, effort, and imagination on the application. Remember, you're nearing the point of entry into your adult life. Why limit your options by postponing a serious application effort in favor of one more cheerleading or soccer practice, or one more hour of volunteer work at the hospital? After seventeen years of thoughtful involvement and accomplishment, you have something to record and present. The colleges are eager to review it. The highly selective colleges today have a wealth of B+ averages and 560 Verbal scores, but too few genuinely interesting candidates. Show the college how truly exceptional you are!

3.

The College Looks at the Candidate

STRUCTURING THE CLASSFUL OF DIFFERENCES

Despite outrageous price tags, the certain tension and exhaustion that will accompany the quest of "getting in," and even the knowledge that superb undergraduate education is available at far more accessible places, hordes of candidates and parents continue to court the most prestigious institutions. The highly improbable odds of an out-of-state student being tapped for Berkeley (13 percent), or any student from any state being tapped for their neighbor, Stanford (22 percent), seem not to deter.

So the tired old question of "Who *does* get in?" is important to discuss.

There is an underlying principle to be understood: the philosophy and practices in place at the top of the selectivity scale are basically in place throughout the order of selective colleges, with all hurdles being incrementally lowered the further one descends the ladder. So what are the most selective universities and colleges looking for (with implications for their less choosy cousins)? Is it what you know or whom you know? Is there some special talent one must possess to win the trip to Amherst or Ann Arbor?

The lavish catalogues and tweedy admissions officers are frustratingly evasive. Of course, the higher the College Board or ACT scores and the higher the grade-point average, the better the chances for admission. But what of the nebulous "personal evaluation"? More to the point, how is it that Ann Alexander, in the top 10 percent of her class with 600 SATs, president of the student council and chairman of the Community Drug Abuse Program, is passed over in favor of that popular but not particularly academic boy from the same school whose height, weight, and speed seem to be his most impressive statistics?

Highly selective colleges do not judge all applicants by means of a uniform standard, with the possible exception of a few "*Public* Ivys" who evaluate *in*-state candidates by a well-publicized formula. Consciously or (in some cases) subconsciously, the schools admit five (or more) freshman divisions, often using a separate norm for each category, and then lump the composite together as a "class" (usually deemed "best ever"). This means that applicants compete against one another *within* categories predominantly, not against all other candidates judged by a single admissions standard. The top scholar, the extraordinarily talented violinist, the Vanderbilt alumnus' son, the nifty all-round kid, and the African American are not going to nudge one another out of the running. Instead, they're competing against others of similar interests and similar talent or identity for that particular group's fair share of the class.

There are at least five categories that must emerge intact as each highly selective college structures and completes its freshman class.

1. *The Intellects*. The faculty of every college and university complains about the intellectual shortcomings of the student body. All professors want scholars who are developing prodigies at entry and will chase ideas with discipline and creativity thereafter. And admissions officers do listen to the faculty. As a result, superior intellectual ability and achievement are likely to be admitted, even if the applicant isn't lovable, the future "human contribution" is questionable, and the alumni couldn't care less if this one

gets in. If a student has opted to take every tough course the high school offers, has emerged with a near-perfect record, and has exceptional intellectual power as demonstrated by standardized aptitude *and* achievement tests (proving that the good grades are no accident), that student is *almost* always given the nod. But there aren't enough "perfect" students around to fill even the most selective colleges' classes. And even if there were, a few would be passed by to make way for other types of candidates the elite college wants, needs, and always gets.

2. *The Special Talent Category.* Every Bowdoin freshman class has a super hockey goalie. Hockey is the rallying sport at Bowdoin, where a winning team makes the long winter a tad more bearable. A good goalie does not compete against the 3,143 candidates for the 426 freshman slots. He competes against the two or three other hockey goalies applying, in the hope that he'll be judged the most likely of this little subgroup to keep the puck out of the nets and, somehow, survive the academic rigors of Bowdoin. Each year Texas will get its offensive and defensive lines in order, Penn will end up with a roster of minor sports celebrities, Princeton will get its distance freestyler, and Miami of Ohio its fullback. Now and then an expert oboist or vocalist or sculptor will squeak through the "special talent" door, but on the whole it is athlete against athlete. Forget the high class rank and the high SATs. Academic survival is what counts here, and the official rationale is in support of those winning teams that put the college name in headlines, boost morale on campus, and most important (reportedly), lure the alumni to dig a bit deeper into their supportive pockets.

3. *The Family Category.* Tax money helps to fill the coffers of the public university system, although even the publics are now aggressively recruiting monies from the private sector, and certainly from their alums. The private colleges have always counted on the generosity of their alumni to help pay the bills. Many alums are happy to do so in grat-

itude for good college years. Nonetheless, universities and colleges constantly float inducements: gala reunions, winning teams, and perhaps most important, the "edge" a son or daughter is promised in the admissions process. Most selective institutions are generous in admitting alumni sons and daughters—at some private colleges the percentage of legacies admitted is twice as high as for all candidates. The same applies to more removed relatives (grandsons, nieces, sisters, etc.) if the alumnus/a has given generously of his or her time or money to Alma Mater.

At some institutions the "family" extends beyond alumni. Harvard, for example, is good to hometown candidates from Greater Boston. On the whole, however, the Family Category relates to the alumni; and the stronger the alumni tie, the stronger the favoritism in admissions. Legacies compete against legacies to claim a segment of the class. Each class at Yale ends up including 10–15% legacies. "It's a tricky area," said Yale's alumni chairman of the Committee on Undergraduate Admissions in the alumni magazine. "How much is too much? Certainly we're cognizant that it's easy to backfire into a club mentality, a cozy relationship that involves dual standards. On the other hand, I don't think we should feel self-conscious when talking about the need for a higher percentage of alumni children. We recognize in very cold, practical terms that Yale has no automatic claim on the future. It exists partly on the strength of the emotional support that it gets from a loyal and enthusiastic community of people." The "Public Ivys," it must be said, are beginning to echo this language more audibly.

4. *The Social Conscience Category*. Because the elitist institutions of the nation were dominated for so long by white children of the Protestant establishment, most of these colleges have tried during the past two decades to make good on their overdue debt to society for years of exclusivity. Great progress has been made in accommodating students of color, particularly African Americans. Many of

the selective colleges had their social consciences stirred by student demands in the late sixties and resolved to make the percentage of underrepresented minorities in each entering class comparable to the percentage of an ethnic group in the nation's (or the home state's) population. Some institutions—the University of Virginia, Stanford, and UCLA, for example—have come close to realizing this goal, thanks to ample resources and energetic recruitment. "The motivation quotient" is the vital criterion in judging applicants in this category, and often a student—because of inadequate secondary schooling and a lack of incentive from family and society—will be judged more on potential than on accomplishment. The size and quality of the minority-applicant pool dictates how flexible the admissions standard will become. In fact, lawsuits are not uncommon when any one ethnic group feels it still is not getting its "fair share" of the class. (Asian Americans, whose superb academic credentials usually argue in favor of representation well beyond the "percentage of population" formula, are understandably outspoken on this issue today.) But one thing is certain: a respectable representation of students of color is an essential component of the prestige college's class today, alongside an increasingly complex "rainbow" of gay and lesbian students, older students, and "different learners," as well as the customary broad socioeconomic mix.

5. *The Well-Rounded Kid Category.* This is the toughest category from which to emerge a winner. Most well-meaning and generally accomplished candidates fall into this huge group. They don't wear special labels or make special claims on a segment of the class. They usually don't have organized lobbyists hovering around the admissions office via phone or engraved letterhead. They're just the good kids who are quite decent but not outstanding as students, who help in a significant way to run the school, and/or the community, and who have the intelligence, energy, and inclination to help the community and the nation keep

moving along at a good pace and in the right direction.

The prestige college is swamped with "nice," accomplished, well-rounded kids, and the admissions office is remorseful that more cannot be accommodated. Although most of the faculty are less than enthusiastic about this "type," the alumni like them, particularly if they're good family friends or relatives. Meanwhile, the admissions officers meet dozens and dozens of them on the road and in office interviews, knowing full well that only a small percentage can be taken.

If an applicant falls by default into Category 5, he must somehow make himself noticed to win a place—by the essay, by the interview, or by any means possible (and responsible). For one thing, it is certain that she or he will be competing with hundreds of others in this division. Furthermore, this category has the least clout in claiming representation in the freshman class. Now and then, accidental factors such as a candidate's wealth or his geographic location (most selective colleges want broad geographic representation) can give a candidate a boost.

Remember: Many of the applicants who fall into Categories 1, 2, 3, and 4 are *also* well-intentioned, upright, and affable, so it isn't that the "good kids" are being overlooked altogether! Although only a small *percentage* of applicants from huge Category 5 is admitted, the number is large—usually the *majority* of a prestigious college's freshman class.

Admissions categories vary in importance according to the institution. Female-oriented colleges are less preoccupied with athletes than male-oriented colleges. Oberlin, Berkeley and the University of California at Santa Cruz, Swarthmore, Reed, and the University of Chicago seem to reserve more of the class for Category 1, the high-powered intellects, than other prestigious institutions do, large or small.

A few institutions will readily admit that the category method (perhaps less rigidly adhered to than I have suggested here) is indeed the way a class is born. Many institutions are reluctant to make that confession publicly, and some colleges may not themselves realize that their long and tortuous candidate-against-candidate review eventually results in a class that might have emerged more easily through systematic category-oriented eliminations. A university or college simply can't apply a uniform standard of "academic and personal excellence" and end up accidentally with an adequate showing of students of color and legacies, with a basketball team, and with geographic distribution.

As one president of Yale said, "The admissions office is the umbilical cord of the university." If the undergraduate college has many purposes (an arena for training the mind, a national instrument for social access and change, etc.), the admissions office must make certain all the human potential is there. Diversity—by design—is essential to each incoming and outgoing class.°

JUGGLING THE SPECIFIC FACTORS

No matter how closely specific universities and colleges follow the "Categories" method of selection to achieve class diversity (usually the more selective the college, the more closely the method is followed), most colleges agree on what components are basic to a fair evaluation of the candidate. These are appraisal of the degree of difficulty of the student's high school courseload, school grades and class rank (incorporating a guesstimate of the quality of the secondary school), standardized test scores (the College Boards or a substitute battery of tests such as the ACTs†), the application essay, the interview, the depth of extracurricular involvement and achievement, the student's employment record, and recommendations from school author-

° This section of the book, a description of the categorization process in undergraduate admissions, appeared in similar form in *Harper's Magazine*. Readers might be interested in responses from admissions professionals regarding Mr. Moll's "category" theory. See Appendix III.
† American College Testing Program, headquartered in Iowa.

ities and teachers. Individual colleges differ somewhat in the weight accorded these factors in the selection process, and how to best evaluate motivation, staying power, and creativity.

But almost all selective colleges—public and private—make two general evaluations of the candidate: (1) an academic evaluation and (2) a personal evaluation. Of course, college A may give more weight to one of these areas than college B, but the two evaluations are almost always made. Let's probe these zones somewhat more carefully, knowing (as every admissions officer can attest) that the boundary between them is difficult to draw.

THE ACADEMIC EVALUATION

Courseload: How Demanding?

A's in Glee Club and Hygiene aren't as interesting to selective colleges as B's in Advanced Placement History and Calculus. Before a college records the grade-point average (GPA) of a given applicant, an analysis is always made of the degree of difficulty of the courseload. Obviously, this is not an exact science, but colleges usually can spot the student who has ducked the tougher courses to avoid getting lower grades. Colleges today, as in the past, are most comfortable with the "basic disciplines." Admissions officers are impressed by applicants who have done well in the most difficult courses offered within the "core curriculum" of a given secondary school.

Most selective colleges, both private and public, have a liberal arts bent and will expose new students to a wide range of curricular offerings before asking the student to choose a major discipline (often by the beginning of the third year but sometimes earlier). They feel, consequently, that the job of the elementary and the secondary schools is to prepare young people in "the basics," leaving peripheral disciplines and frills for later. This concept obviously created tension in the early seventies, as elementary and secondary schools introduced "experiential" education and attempted to evoke greater student interest by allowing free choice in curriculum. The result—still lingering in some school systems—was often a much heavier concentration in the humanities, social sciences, and the arts, with a minimum of exposure to the sciences, math, foreign languages, and tedious English grammar. But as linguistic skills among teenagers declined, national College Board averages fell, and college faculties complained that they were having to teach remedial grammar when they were hired to teach Shakespeare. "Back to basics!" became the cry in most high schools.

To be certain, the "back-to-basics" movement in the secondary schools draws nods of approval at the colleges. And the admissions offices follow suit. A sampling of the high school course of studies recommended in college catalogues:

Duke: Each application is evaluated in terms of the student's program of study in secondary school, academic performance, the overall quality of the application and essay, standardized testing, recommendations, and the candidate's personal qualities. At the minimum, candidates for admission should present four years of English, at least three of mathematics, natural science, a foreign language, and two years of social studies. Students are encouraged to enroll in advanced-level work in as many of these areas as possible since this provides the best preparation for Duke.

M.I.T. expects that its applicants will have taken the broadest, most rigorous program available to them in high school. Ideal preparation for study would include English (four years), history/social studies (two or more years), mathematics through trigonometry or beyond (four years), laboratory sciences (biology, chemistry, and physics), and a foreign language. Interested students whose high school program does not match this in every detail are also urged to apply, since the selection of an entering class with broad interests will be guided as well by the quality of the applicant's work, by special strengths, and by apparent promise on grounds of intellect, character, and particular goals.

Wellesley does not require a fixed plan of secondary school courses as preparation for its program of studies. However, entering students normally have completed four years of strong college preparatory studies in secondary school. Adequate preparation includes training in clear and coherent writing and in interpreting literature, history, training in the principles of mathematics (typically four years), competence in at least one foreign language, ancient or modern (usually achieved through three or four years of study), and experience in two laboratory sciences.

Students planning to concentrate in mathematics, in premedical studies, or in the natural sciences are urged to elect additional courses in mathematics and science in secondary school. Students planning to concentrate in language or literature are urged to study a modern foreign language and Latin or Greek before they enter college.

There are often exceptions to the preparation suggested here, and the Board will consider an applicant whose educational background varies from this general description.

The best rule of thumb is for the candidate to take a balanced program of the most demanding courses his or her secondary school offers. No college will quarrel with that; to the contrary, applicants are given bonus points for their willingness to pursue the toughest possible curriculum despite the risk of getting slightly lower grades.

Regrettably, schools do not always adequately explain "levels" of various courses on candidates' transcripts. This is difficult to do, of course, since two teachers in the same department can be decidedly different in "degree of difficulty." But it seems only fair to the motivated candidate for the school to designate Advanced Placement (AP) courses and honors-level courses on the transcript. Most schools do, but not all. Would that all schools were as specific in defining course levels as New Trier High School, in Illinois. Each course on the transcript is accompanied by a level designation:

5 = Advanced Placement
4 = superior or honors
3 = above-average
2 = average
1 = below-average

There are too few New Triers, so the candidate must check with his school guidance office to make certain that advanced courses are pointed out to colleges on the transcript. If the designations are not made clear by the school, the candidate himself must get the message to the college: this is probably best accomplished in the application essay. Some bright, well-motivated students today are hurt by the absence of course-level descriptions on the school report.

A realtor-uncle of mine told me that there were three things to remember in buying a house: "Location, location, location." As selective colleges approach the academic evaluation of a candidate for admission, there are three overriding considerations: "Courseload, courseload, courseload." A bit of an overstatement perhaps, but the high school student who has opted for the roughest possible courseload demonstrates (often quite unconsciously) the motivation that selective colleges equate with the drive to learn and to succeed. Given the luxury to choose among candidates, a college will nod to the "B" record in the honors courses much more readily than to the "A" record in fluff. And the colleges can almost always tell the difference.

Grades: Is an "A" an "A" at School B?

"The past is the best prologue to the future." Every admissions officer believes that, so every candidate must stand on his or her record. Presupposing that the courseload is balanced and demanding, a college applicant's high school grades become the second most important factor in the admissions folder.

A consistently strong record is, of course, the best. But the most recent grades in the most demanding courses interest the admissions office the most. Grades in the basic disciplines of the junior year and first semester of senior year carry greatest weight.

Colleges will be humanly forgiving if made aware of interim handicaps and distractions that hurt the GPA—health problems, family problems, school problems, financial problems, love-life problems. But any candidate can come up with excuses for not performing along the way, and admissions officers grow weary of hearing "I'd have done better if . . ." If Rice has five candidates for every place in the class, why shouldn't they go for the one who has consistently performed and has overcome whatever obstacles were placed in the way?

Admissions officers are aware of the impact of environment on performance. Candidates for any selective college or university come, of course, from a variety of environments. Ironically, it is probably slightly to a candidate's disadvantage to come from an advantaged background. If a youngster is the offspring of well-educated parentage, has been carefully guided to make the most of top-level courses at a college-oriented high school or private school, has been exposed to world-and-local-affairs discussions around the dinner table for seventeen years, and has been constantly reminded of the advantages that come to those who reach higher levels of education, *shouldn't* she or he be expected to have produced somewhat more in the classroom than a working-class candidate who works after school to help make family ends meet, attends a mediocre high school where the minority aspire to higher education, and is habitually subjected to "time to get a job, get married, and settle down" talk?

Selective colleges look at a candidate in terms of where she has been, where she hopes to go, and at what pace and with what resolve she seems to be traveling. And we know that some bright kids find academic incentive late. We are sympathetic—to a point. But direction and discipline must be evident by the time of freshman entry. Again: the more recent the achievement, the more important it becomes.

After the student comes up with the grades, the college must interpret them. This is no mean trick. There is no consistent pattern of grading in America's school system today. If the colleges were to vote, the A-to-F system would probably win out, or the traditional 0-to-100. Colleges find these systems easiest to cope with, partly because they are most familiar with them. But today, one transcript might record a 1-to-7 system, the next a pass/fail system, and the next a high honors/honors/pass/low pass/fail system. Some admissions offices try to convert all grading schemes into one system in order to uniformly compare one candidate with another. But most colleges just try to cope with what the high school sends—if the grading code is hazy, more weight is usually assigned to that uniform quantifier, the standardized test scores.

But are all A's the same? No, and admissions officers know that. Some teachers are easier graders than other teachers within the same school, but that can hardly be deciphered by a university analyzing the transcript. Colleges know, however, that secondary schools differ markedly in competitive level, and consequently in grading patterns. The effort that produced an A at laid-back Central High might only have produced, with similar effort, a C+ at super-competitive Phillips Exeter Academy (N.H.) or Lowell High School in San Francisco. As a result, many colleges actually track how graduates from a given high school perform at college compared with graduates from other high schools, and bring that information to bear on new applicants. Some colleges make freshman or sophomore *predictions* of grade-point averages on applicants, based on the data of previous enrollees who graduated from that high school. Also, secondary schools' "profiles," which are often sent by schools with a candidate's transcript, help the admissions office interpret the school's level of quality and competitive tone: where their recent graduates attended college, the number of AP courses offered, and the average SAT or ACT scores say a great deal in interpreting what a given B+ is all about. (See the Highland Park [Ill.] H.S. profile, p. 130.)

Class Rank: Cold, Crass, and Valuable

One way to know how difficult it is to get an A at West High is to see a student's grade-point average (GPA) put in context with the averages of other students from the same school. High school class rank is, in a way, a crass and cold appraisal of a student's accomplishments, but it is an important ingredient in

HIGHLAND PARK HIGH SCHOOL

433 Vine Avenue • Highland Park, Illinois 60035
(708) 926-9226 • Fax # (708) 926-9348
James H. Warren   Jane A. Gard
Superintendent   Principal

School Code #142-275

Class of 1993

SCHOOL AND COMMUNITY: Highland Park and Deerfield are two four-year high schools in District 113. With an area of 24.8 square miles, the district is located 25 miles north of Chicago and extends from Lake Michigan four miles to the west. Though largely a suburban residential area, some light industry is included. The district serves students from Bannockburn, Deerfield, Fort Sheridan, Highwood, Highland Park and Riverwoods. Highland Park is a four-year comprehensive high school which anticipates an enrollment of approximately 1507 for 1992-93 with 378 graduating seniors. It is accredited by the State of Illinois and the North Central Association.

FACULTY 154 members; 10% have a BA; 87% have an MA or beyond; 3% have a Ph.D.

PROGRAM OF STUDIES The high school offers a comprehensive educational program. Please note the following explanations.

Levels Ability groupings occur selectively throughout the curriculum.

Level 1 indicates Advanced Placement or Accelerated courses.
Level 2 indicates College Preparatory classes.
Level 3 indicates classes where the curriculum has been modified.

Advanced Placement These college level courses are offered in English, European History, United States History Economics, Psychology, Calculus AB, Calculus BC, Biology, Chemistry, Physics, French, Spanish, Computer Studies, Art History, and Studio Art.

Accelerated Courses Honors classes are available in Mathematics, Physics, Chemistry, Biology, English 3, American Literature and Composition, Accounting, and Languages beyond the first year.

College Preparatory Courses Most courses in the curriculum are designated Level 2. With the exceptions indicated above, accelerated courses are not available in the Social Studies and English Departments. If students take Algebra 1-2 or Geometry 1-2, Level 3, and complete the courses in summer school or during the junior year they have covered the same material taught in Level 2 courses.

GRADUATION REQUIREMENTS

The high school requires 20.5 units (41 credits) including:

English	3 units (6 credits)	Fine Arts	.5 unit (1 credit)
Mathematics	2 units (4 credits)	Applied Arts	.5 unit (1 credit)
Science	1 unit (2 credits)	Phys. Education	3.5 units (7 credits)
U.S. History	1 unit (2 credits)	Traffic Safety	0 units (0 credits)
Social Studies	1 units (2 credits)	Consumer Education	(a course or profcy.)
Health	.5 unit (1 credit)	Electives	7.5 units (15 credits)

POST HIGH SCHOOL EDUCATION: CLASS OF 1992

4 year college	2 year college	Work	Other	TOTAL
82%	12%	5%	1%	100%

ACADEMIC EVALUATION

GRADING SYSTEM

The school uses a letter system with the following equivalents:

A = 100-93	C = 76-73	E = 59 & below is failing
A- = 92-90	C- = 72-70	X = doctor's excuse
B+ = 89-87	D+ = 69-67	H = pass in a pass/fail course
B = 86-83	D = 66-63	G = withdrawal
B- = 83-80	D- = 62-60	
C+ = 79-77	E = 59-0	

I = incomplete; the grade must be earned during the first three weeks of the next semester

AU = Audit

GRADE WEIGHTING POLICIES AND PROCEDURES

Highland Park High School allows students to report to colleges either a weighted or an unweighted rank-in-class. The transcript will show both a specific rank and percentile identified as either weighted or unweighted.

Unweighted This rank includes all courses taken, except Physical Education and those taken pass-fail, without regard to level. The rank is based on a conventional four point scale using plus and minus grades.

Weighted The weighted rank is computed using the following values for all courses except Physical Education and those taken pass-fail.

Grade	Percentage	Level I	Level II	Level III
A	100-93	6.00	5.00	4.00
A-	92-90	5.67	4.67	3.67
B+	89-87	5.33	4.33	3.33
B	86-83	5.00	4.00	3.00
B-	82-80	4.67	3.67	2.67
C+	79-77	4.33	3.33	2.33

C	76-73	4.00	3.00	2.00
C-	72-70	3.67	2.67	1.67
D+	69-67	3.33	2.33	1.33
D	66-63	3.00	2.00	1.00
D-	62-60	2.67	1.67	0.67
E	59-0	0.00	0.00	0.00

TESTING PROFILE FOR 1992-93

ACT	COMPOSITE MEAN SCORE		SAT	VERBAL MEAN SCORES	MATH
	23.5			480	540
322	seniors tested		289	seniors tested	

ADVANCED PLACEMENT 240 students took 427 exams in 17 areas.
23% of the grades were 5's, 33% were 4's and 30% were 3's.

COUNSELING STAFF Each counselor is assigned students at four grade levels. Students remain with the same counselor throughout their tenure in the high school.

CHAIRMAN - Vernon L. Hein, Ph.D.

COLLEGE CONSULTANT - James A. Alexander

COUNSELORS

Mr. David Bene'
Ms. Patricia Cannon

Mr. Duane Frahm
Ms. Gloria Haddy
Mrs. Sandra Hoeg

Mrs. Regina Manley
Mr. Sheldon Schaffel

the college admissions process. Colleges not only like to receive rank in order to make a specific GPA more intelligible, but they also want it because validity studies have indicated again and again that class rank is one of the most valuable predictors of college success. The few quantifiers that seem to work are in demand, and class rank is one of them.

The smaller the secondary school, of course, the more unfair class ranking may be. A dean of admissions at UNC Chapel Hill once said that he would forever wear the scar of having ranked in the lower half of his high school class—he graduated second in a class of two from a one-room school. In large schools, shades of percentages can keep a student from ranking in the upper half or upper third or upper fifth of his class. But performance is performance, and the colleges like to know rank in order to place a given GPA in context.

Several alternative methods to assess class rank precisely have been developed in recent years by "grouping" students in less arbitrary categories. Some private schools utilize a helpful grade distribution chart in each of a student's courses (for example, English III) to demonstrate the comparative strength of a particular student to his or her entire class (see Loomis Chaffee School [Connecticut] chart, p. 136).

A study in the Spring 1993 issue of *The Journal of College Admission* (by Joan Isaacs Mohr and Norma Talley) found that a majority of high schools do provide some type of rank in class, and a majority of colleges do utilize the information. The study also found that most college admissions directors prefer that high schools *weight* grades in computing GPA—that is, give added points for AP and/or honors courses. Highland Park High School in Illinois (see profile, p. 130) computes both a weighted and unweighted GPA to rank their students. They explain that they do this because of the wide representation of students in their population, from bilingual and severely learning-disabled to the highest number of National Merit semifinalists in the state in the 1992–93 school year. An individual student may choose which GPA he or she wants sent to colleges.

One of the inherent qualities of the American system of education is variety. But when trying to judge applicants' past performance and future potential, the selective public and private colleges feel most comfortable with traditional quantifiers—precise grades, rank or grade comparison statistics, and test scores—fleshed out with personal and insightful comments from teachers and counselors. Neither type of information can stand alone.

Those Detestable Tests

One day I walked into a St. Grottlesex–type school for my college's scheduled "information session" with juniors and seniors. My delight in being told by the guidance counselor that there was great interest in my institution was softened considerably by the way he introduced his candidates. I was handed a list that went something like this:

Jane Ackerman	V	540	M	510
Joann Knowlton	V	610	M	630
Abe Feldman	V	580	M	600
Liz Smith	V	620	M	560

In a "personal" school touting individualized education, kids were being introduced as SAT scores! An extreme instance perhaps, but this was not the first nor the last time I had the experience. No wonder candidates feel their scores are tattooed on their foreheads and it is their fate to wander through life muttering at every turn, "I am a 510."

And colleges are just as bad, if not worse, in overemphasizing standardized test scores. At Ivy-type gatherings there is far too much informal talk (after one finishes the "How many did *they* take from the waiting list to fill the class?" gossip) of what this and that institution's SAT averages are this year compared with last, implying a conclusive qualitative comparison of the two classes. And although in recent years colleges and universities have moved to reporting scores for the middle 50 percent of

The Loomis Chaffee School
Windsor, Connecticut 06095
(203) 688-4934

Student Name:
Address: 37 Highwood Drive, Manchester, CT 06040

Junior-Year Grade Distribution

Course	Teacher	Student Grade	A+	A	A-	B+	B	B-	C+	C	C-	D+	D	D-	F	#in Class	Median Grade
0030 ENGLISH 3	SZK	A-			4	3	3	11	5		1					27	B-
0340 GERMAN 4	ILM	A		5	2	2										9	A
0432 US HIST. ADV	RKA	A		1	2	3	3	1	2							12	B+
0547 PRECALCULUS/CALC.	SWR	B+		1	2	4		5	2	1						15	B-
0637 PHYSICS 1 ADV	1260	A-	1	2	4	4	2	2	1	1						16	B+

Senior Year Courses

0075	FWS	ENGLISH SEMINAR ADV
0350	FWS	GERMAN 5AP
0477	W	HISTORY INDEP. STUDY
0550	FWS	CALCULUS BC
0744	S	PR MYTH, DREAM, RITUAL
0829	FWS	ART SEMINAR AP

the freshman class (e.g., for the Oberlin class of '96 the midrange SAT Verbal is 560 to 650, the Math 580 to 680), still college faculties focus far too much on these College Board signposts, erroneously defining an entire new freshman class by one factor.

Ironically, it is the College Entrance Examination Board itself that keeps *warning* schools and colleges and kids and counselors and parents against such extremes of emphasis. The Board reminds us all that the test scores are intended as a *supplement* to other important data, and "if properly used," can become an important interpretive tool, benefiting both applicant and institution. Of course they're right. But the problem is that no other single means of appraisal is so uniform—high school grade patterns differ from school to school, and class ranks are computed by different means, if at all. So, by default, College Board (or ACT) scores become a universal language for defining the quality of a candidate or the quality of a college's freshman class. Until other methods of candidate evaluation become more consistent, we'll probably all continue to be guilty of overemphasizing test scores.

During the past several years the College Board has conducted a major overhaul of its admission testing program. The revised version of the examinations first appeared in the 1993–94 school year. The SAT is now called SAT I, and is taken by approximately *one million* students per year. The new test, still three hours long, no longer includes antonym questions. The test now is composed of analogy, sentence completion, and reading comprehension questions. The reading comprehension section has been expanded, and focuses more on critical thinking skills. The math sections cover the same content areas as the old SAT, but students will now find open-ended questions —that is, they must derive an answer as opposed to selecting from five choices. (And students are now able to use calculators during the exam.)

Students who are seeking entry at the more selective colleges are also required to take three one-hour SAT II tests (formerly called Achievement Tests). Most colleges will require the Writing Test (similar to the former English Composition with essay), Math (Level I or II), and one other offered by CEEB. Schools and colleges recommend that candidates take the Preliminary SAT (PSAT) in the fall of the junior year of high school; this test also serves as the initial qualifier for the prestigious National Merit Scholarship. Between spring of the junior year and winter of the senior year the candidate should take the SAT I at least once, often as many as three times. He/she may take 1, 2, or 3 SAT II tests at one or more of the sittings. (A student's college counselor will have information on the dates of these administrations.)

One word of caution. Sometimes students—with parental encouragement—in their eagerness to create a competitive edge, begin to take these exams too early. But readiness, maturation, and exposure to curriculum do play a significant role in a student's performance. One cannot expect to earn a rousing math score if one hasn't yet taken Geometry!

(In recent years, as the nation has become more knowledgeable about learning needs and students who are differently abled, special administrations of the College Board Examinations have been devised to meet the needs of these students. Tests are available in large print, on tape, with readers, and on an extended-time or individualized-administration basis. Students must qualify for a special test administration; you may obtain specific information from your college counselor or from the Educational Testing Service, [609] 921-9000.)

Considering the importance of the College Board tests, there should be clear agreement on what they are and how they should be utilized. But definitions remain vague.

A recent president of the College Board wrote:

> It might be useful to consider what the SAT is and what it does. First, let me suggest what the SAT is *not*. It was not designed as a measure of a *school's* performance and should not be used for that purpose. To single out the schools as being responsible for the current decline in scores, for example, is unwarranted, unfair, and scientifically unfounded.

Secondly, the SAT is not a measure of some innate and unchanging quality that somehow mystically categorizes people. It does not gauge the worth of a human being, or his or her capacity to function well or creatively in society.

What, then, *is* the SAT? *It is a measure of developed verbal and mathematic reasoning and ability.* It measures those abilities that are most commonly needed for academic performance in colleges and universities. Therefore, how students perform on the SAT is a useful and well-validated indicator of how they might do in one college or another. It is intended to supplement the school record and other information about the student in assessing competence to do college work.

It is a uniform measure of the same mental tasks, expressed on a common scale for all students. Thus, it operates as a "leveling agent," or if you will, a democratizing agent, cutting across differences in local customs and conditions, and affording admissions officers help in the assessment of the *academic* potential of students in relation to the differing academic demands of institutions.

Interpretation is as much a problem as definition. Often candidates and parents ask what the median SAT score of a given college's freshman class is, and mistake the median figure for the bottom line of that class. When Colgate says that its SAT Verbal median of accepted candidates is 600, it means one-half the admittees are below that score. But so frequently the reaction is, "Oh, if I don't have around a 620, I don't have a prayer of getting into Colgate!"

To prevent this common misconception, some colleges now avoid releasing means and medians of SAT and Achievement scores. Following are examples of SAT range at three institutions. They are plotted somewhat differently, but all are helpful as a counseling tool for the student who wants to predict his or her chances at a particular institution. (*See pages 140–45.*)

Granted, almost everyone (though not Nora Taylor from Oldebrick!) laments overemphasis of SATs in college admissions talk. But just how important are these tests? Private colleges rarely place as much importance on test scores as on the degree of difficulty of the high school courseload and the grades and class rank attained. On the other hand, the more selective pub-

Kenyon College

The following tables are not meant to describe the Class of 1996 as much as they are intended to suggest the relationship of test scores and class rank to admission decisions. Every decision made by the Kenyon admissions staff will take personal qualities, strength of program, and other factors into account as well. The first figure in each column is the number of applicants; the second is the number of admittees (i.e., applicants/admittees).

ACT COMPOSITE

	30-36	27-29	24-26	20-23	Below 20	Total	% Accepted
Top decile	120/116	105/103	55/43	25/20	5/4	310/286	92
2nd decile	26/26	46/42	61/50	30/19	3/0	166/137	83
2nd quintile	16/14	40/27	47/30	21/8	7/2	131/81	62
3rd quintile	3/1	14/4	16/8	15/4	4/0	52/17	33
Below 3rd	0/0	3/0	2/0	10/2	3/0	18/3	14
Unranked	17/17	48/39	54/29	41/16	7/1	167/102	61
Total	182/174	256/216	235/160	142/69	29/7	844/626	74
% Accepted	96	84	68	48	24	74	

SAT VERBAL APTITUDE

	700-800	650-690	600-640	550-590	500-540	450-490	Below 450	Total	%Accepted
Top decile	53/50	79/73	101/98	104/100	69/62	33/27	32/18	471/428	90
2nd decile	8/8	18/16	49/43	75/66	61/49	44/26	22/10	277/218	79
2nd quintile	10/7	16/14	43/31	66/50	54/38	53/25	21/6	263/171	65
3rd quintile	2/0	10/4	13/4	21/10	28/13	21/8	22/6	117/45	38
Below 3rd	0/0	1/0	8/2	5/1	8/1	5/0	7/1	34/5	15
Unranked	32/26	77/63	151/112	189/129	216/124	132/49	70/16	867/519	60
Total	105/91	201/170	365/290	460/356	436/287	288/135	174/57	2029/1386	68
% Accepted	87	85	79	77	66	47	32	68	

SAT MATH APTITUDE

	700-800	650-690	600-640	550-590	500-540	450-490	Below 450	Total	%Accepted
Top decile	105/99	109/101	97/91	92/87	41/35	11/7	9/6	464/426	90
2nd decile	24/21	53/45	59/50	60/50	41/27	20/16	15/6	277/218	79
2nd quintile	23/19	38/32	59/45	59/41	40/19	27/12	15/3	263/171	65
3rd quintile	11/5	13/8	22/11	25/14	21/3	18/4	7/0	117/45	38
Below 3rd	1/1	5/0	7/0	8/1	4/1	8/2	4/0	34/5	15
Unranked	76/62	124/99	165/121	203/127	176/88	78/17	47/5	867/519	60
Total	240/207	342/285	409/323	447/320	323/173	162/58	97/20	2029/1386	68
% Accepted	86	83	79	72	54	36	20	68	

FRESHMAN PROFILE:
The University of California (Berkeley and Davis Campuses)

The Freshman Profile summarizes by UC campus the qualifications of applicants and admitted freshmen for the fall 1992. The Profile is most useful as a guide to the selection process, rather than to predict your chances for admission to the University. Separate figures are included for non-engineering and engineering programs.

Grade point average (GPA) intervals are listed vertically and Scholastic Aptitude Test (SAT) composite score (mathematics plus verbal) intervals are listed horizontally. Each block in the chart represents a pool of applicants with GPA and SAT scores within the specific intervals indicated.

GPA ▼	ALL PROGRAMS EXCEPT ENGINEERING SAT COMPOSITE					
	490-790	800-990	1000-1190	1200-1390	1400-1600	OVERALL
BERKELEY						
2.82-2.99			131/21 16%	39/0 0%	3/0 0%	173/21 12%
3.00-3.29	179/11 6%	500/79 16%	729/127 17%	304/50 16%	26/7 27%	1738/274 16%
3.30-3.59	173/24 14%	608/165 27%	1133/247 22%	569/136 24%	44/21 48%	2527/593 23%
3.60-3.89	116/15 13%	573/160 28%	1489/408 27%	1081/449 42%	125/111 89%	3384/1143 34%
3.90-3.99	11/3 27%	97/23 24%	332/104 31%	325/219 67%	47/45 96%	812/394 49%
4.00	39/12 31%	345/115 33%	1908/769 40%	3363/2770 82%	997/980 98%	6652/4646 70%
OVERALL	518/65 13%	2123/542 26%	5722/1676 29%	5681/3624 64%	1242/1164 94%	17063/7326 43%
DAVIS						
2.82-2.99			180/39 22%	36/14 39%	1/1 100%	217/54 25%
3.00-3.29	259/76 29%	745/244 33%	876/272 31%	245/159 65%	11/11 100%	2136/762 36%
3.30-3.59	231/138 60%	838/307 37%	1312/589 45%	467/397 85%	17/17 100%	2865/1448 51%
3.60-3.89	140/80 57%	730/348 48%	1485/1102 74%	631/614 97%	45/43 96%	3031/2187 72%
3.90-3.99	20/13 65%	94/61 65%	265/246 93%	177/177 100%	11/11 100%	567/508 90%
4.00	45/26 58%	347/267 77%	1399/1330 95%	1453/1440 99%	243/240 99%	3487/3303 95%
OVERALL	695/333 48%	2754/1227 45%	5517/3578 65%	3009/2801 93%	328/323 98%	13903/8631 62%

In each block, the first figure is the total number of applicants and the second figure is the number of applicants regularly admitted. The figure in bold type on the second line is the percentage of students who were regularly admitted.

GPA is defined as a student's GPA in the "a–f" requirements as calculated by a UC admissions evaluator or, if the evaluated GPA was not available, the student's GPA as self-reported on the application for admission.

The campus overall total includes freshman applicants whose GPA and/or SAT composite score were out of range or unavailable. Data as of September 1992.

GPA ▼	ENGINEERING PROGRAMS SAT COMPOSITE					
	490-790	800-990	1000-1190	1200-1390	1400-1600	OVERALL
BERKELEY						
2.82-2.99			17/2 **12%**	5/0 **0%**	0/0 **0%**	22/2 **9%**
3.00-3.29	25/0 **0%**	42/0 **0%**	78/2 **3%**	42/7 **17%**	0/0 **0%**	187/9 **5%**
3.30-3.59	13/0 **0%**	75/0 **0%**	153/10 **7%**	110/14 **13%**	12/2 **17%**	363/26 **7%**
3.60-3.89	19/0 **0%**	94/5 **5%**	231/22 **10%**	232/75 **32%**	41/20 **49%**	617/122 **20%**
3.90-3.99	2/0 **0%**	22/0 **0%**	68/11 **16%**	81/30 **37%**	10/8 **80%**	183/49 **27%**
4.00	8/0 **0%**	60/4 **7%**	393/87 **22%**	870/523 **60%**	387/353 **91%**	1718/967 **56%**
OVERALL	67/0 **0%**	293/9 **3%**	940/134 **14%**	1340/649 **48%**	450/383 **85%**	3409/1204 **35%**
DAVIS						
2.82-2.99			14/4 **29%**	5/3 **60%**	0/0 **0%**	19/7 **37%**
3.00-3.29	10/0 **0%**	55/4 **7%**	110/30 **27%**	40/28 **70%**	1/1 **100%**	216/63 **29%**
3.30-3.59	10/1 **10%**	77/17 **22%**	199/91 **46%**	95/85 **89%**	6/6 **100%**	387/200 **52%**
3.60-3.89	5/0 **0%**	86/45 **52%**	235/163 **69%**	171/168 **98%**	15/14 **93%**	512/390 **76%**
3.90-3.99	1/0 **0%**	13/6 **46%**	65/57 **88%**	48/48 **100%**	6/6 **100%**	133/117 **88%**
4.00	4/1 **25%**	53/43 **81%**	310/292 **94%**	424/422 **100%**	79/77 **97%**	870/835 **96%**
OVERALL	30/2 **7%**	284/115 **40%**	933/637 **68%**	783/754 **96%**	107/104 **97%**	2279/1636 **72%**

LEGEND: applicants/regular admits
percent regularly admitted

Entering Freshmen with Class Rank *(Public and Private Schools)*

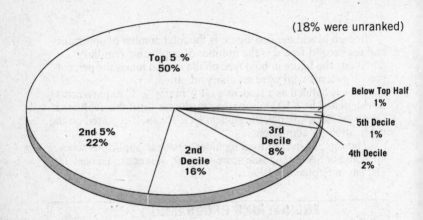

(18% were unranked)

- Top 5 %: 50%
- 2nd 5%: 22%
- 2nd Decile: 16%
- 3rd Decile: 8%
- 4th Decile: 2%
- 5th Decile: 1%
- Below Top Half: 1%

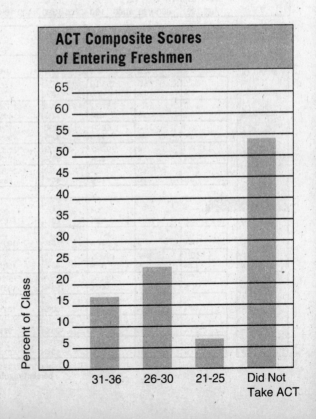

SAT Scores of Entering Freshmen

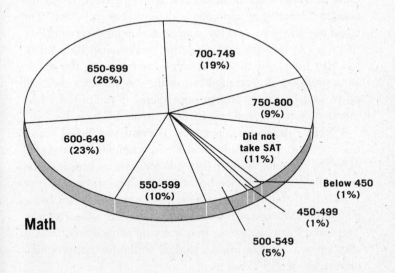

Math

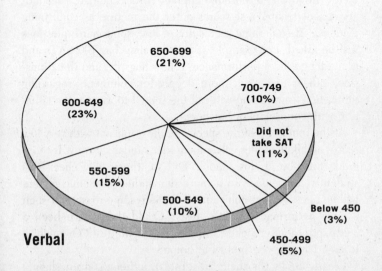

Verbal

lic institutions, such as UC Berkeley and Michigan, *must* depend on "numbers," including test scores or GPA. Given the tens of thousands of applications they receive each year, they could not possibly spend the time on evaluating each candidate that is spent by a Barnard, Carleton, or Pomona. (Remember, too, that frequently the way students are treated in the admissions process is a good predictor of the way in which they will be treated by the institution once there. If you're judged by numbers, you may well end up being treated like one!)

A former dean of admissions at Harvard says Board scores become a priority consideration for his committee if they fall *over* 750 or *under* 550; if they fall somewhere between, the scores fade in importance because that range is "normal" for Harvard. Of course, some colleges have a reputation for being a bit more conscious of Board scores than others—Georgetown, Tufts, and Penn are names frequently mentioned—but no institution will admit or reject a student on the basis of very high or very low scores alone.

As indicated earlier, an A record is harder to achieve in some high schools than in others, so test scores provide a leveling factor. Following a thorough appraisal of a candidate's secondary school record, test scores enter the picture as confirming evidence. If something seems out of line, some hard questions will be asked. For example, if a young man has 700 SATs and a middling school performance, yellow flags fly, and the admissions officer digs a bit more deeply for comments regarding motivation—maybe he will call the school to discuss the situation with counselors or teachers.

At the other end of the spectrum, the applicant with very low scores and high grades will come under similar scrutiny. Is there grade inflation at this school? Did we thoroughly check this student's courseload? In a more demanding academic milieu, will he have any "stretch" left? Was there some reason for such a poor performance on the tests? Could there have been a learning disability? sickness on the day of the test? Or might a foreign language be spoken at home?

Clearly SATs (or their substitutes), although given slightly different weights from one college to the next, are an important part of the candidate's résumé because colleges seem satisfied with the tests' predictive powers. Even at maverick Bowdoin, one of the handful of highly selective colleges where submission of standardized test scores is optional, a memo from a Chemistry professor to the chairman of the Faculty Admissions Committee said:

> I would like to make clear a few points which might be open to misinterpretation. In no way do I favor a return to the strong emphasis on SATs which may have characterized admissions policy at highly selective colleges in the past. But I do feel that the score is a useful number and that it should be required of all applicants. My classes, and the College as a whole, are better places as a result of the presence of some students with low scores, but let us not kid ourselves any longer by saying these same students have been accepted because of potential to do science. We need students who can merely survive in science while they make a real contribution to college life in another area, but we also need students who will be *distinguished* in science. Those accepted because science is a strong suit should have significant potential as indicated by their SATs and Achievements and a well-defined interest in science which is more than skin deep (more than "I would like to be a doctor"). There will certainly be special cases where the SAT is not a meaningful measure of potential to do science, but I think they will be rare indeed.

Although the SATs seem most often to be the topic of popular discussion, many colleges look at the SAT II tests, the one-hour tests of knowledge in specific areas, with as great or even greater interest. A letter to Vassar from the Research Division of CEEB said:

> A memorandum regarding aspects of the Vassar validity study is enclosed. Finding that the CEEB Achievement [now titled SAT IIs] average tends to be a better predictor of Vassar grade average than the SATs has been a fairly consistent result of validity studies conducted at similar colleges the past ten years or so.

Students and parents always have a raft of questions regarding standardized testing—and no wonder, since the test scores are correctly rumored to be important in the admissions program but are an "agent removed," some external force that one cannot easily address or have control over. Actually, several organizations have an answer to every question, just for the asking. Write:

> College Entrance Examination Board
> 45 Columbus Avenue
> New York, N.Y. 10023-6917
> (212)713-8000
>
> or
>
> American College Testing Program
> Box 168
> Iowa City, Iowa 52240
> (319)337-1332
>
> or
>
> Fair Test
> 342 Broadway
> Cambridge, Ma. 02139
> (617)864-4810

Let's quickly discuss what you always wanted to know about standardized tests but perhaps had no one to ask. Following are some of the questions raised most frequently:

1. *How and when do I learn my scores?* Within five weeks after a test date, a student will be sent his scores with more-than-adequate comparative percentile rankings, explanations, and so forth. Within five weeks of each test date, the colleges that the student has designated will receive the test scores.
2. *Are the tests getting harder?* Through a complicated equating process, a given score today indicates the same level of mathematical or verbal ability as it did years ago.
3. *Are the tests really predictive of how I'll do in college?* In most validity studies of the SAT, the high school rec-

ord is a better predictor than either the Verbal or Math score *alone*. However, the validity of the combination of scores *and* the high school record is higher than that of high school record alone. Studies of the ACT show similar results. (But then, again, one study showed height was a valid predictor; remember, colleges don't rely on any one factor!)

4. *How can what I know become such a precise number?* Test scores should be viewed as approximate rather than exact, using a range of about 60 points. For example, if a student's "true" score is 500, chances are two out of three that the score he or she will actually make on the SAT will be between 470 and 530.

5. *Do I have a good chance of improving my score if I repeat the test?* For those students whose scores change when they repeat the test, 65 percent have score increases, while 35 percent have score decreases. The average score increase is only 15 points.

6. *If I take the SAT I several times, which score will a college use?* Most selective colleges will use your highest "split," your highest verbal and highest math score earned, even if they occurred on different test dates; some will use your highest total from a single test date; a few will use your latest score and a few will average your scores. Because there is no uniform answer to this question, it is wise to ask the policy of each institution to which you are applying.

7. *If I can't answer a test question, should I guess?* The answer to this question depends in part on which test you take—the ACT or the SAT I and II. On the ACT your score is based solely on the number of correct responses. Thus there is no penalty for guessing, so answer *every* question. On SAT I and II, however, your score is determined by the number of correct answers minus a fraction of the number of incorrect answers. As questions are arranged in ascending order of difficulty, it is possible

for astute test takers to maximize their score by knowing when to guess and when not to guess.

8. *What about SAT prep courses?* The controversy surrounding these programs and the validity of *their* claims has escalated as the number of coaching programs has proliferated (which, of course, has happened in response to colleges "hyping" the scores of their incoming class), and as claims and counterclaims between the College Board and prep course proponents have been picked up by the media. The abilities and knowledge measured by these tests have developed over a student's entire academic life. No one can expect to compensate for years of intellectual laziness by cramming for five to ten weeks. But look at the situation in terms of a college course. If one did none of the reading and none of the course work, then studying for three days straight just before the final would be of very little benefit. On the other hand, if one worked diligently throughout the course, it would be foolish not to review and study for the final exam. Also, it can be beneficial to become familiar with the format of the exams. Do be wary of programs that tout phenomenal score jumps in a relatively short period of time. As with most things, the quick fix doesn't work.

9. *What if I'm nervous or really tired the day of the test?* Anxiety and/or fatigue may influence performance, but there is much you can do to control these factors. *Don't* set yourself up by staying out until 2:00 A.M. the night before the test! *Do* have everything you need to take with you—your #2 pencils, picture ID, test admission ticket—set out ahead of time so you're not frantically rifling through drawers searching for them twenty minutes before the test is scheduled to begin!

10. *Are the tests biased in terms of culture, gender, or socioeconomic level?* There is ongoing discussion and concern about the ways in which the test sponsors can assure that the tests are as unbiased as possible. Organizations such

as Fair Test monitor exams continually and conduct their own studies to examine these very issues. Again, no instrument alone is the best measure of anyone's accomplishment or potential. As discussed in the section on the Social Conscience category (see page 120), strong motivation and maturity of purpose become primary factors in evaluating underrepresented and/or disadvantaged students.

THE PERSONAL EVALUATION

The College Essay: A Procrastinator's Dream

Surely there is no assignment known to man that is postponed longer than the application essay. Suddenly the college candidate is no longer reporting grades, birthplace, or lists of brothers and sisters and activities and addresses and dates. Instead she or he is asked to fill an ominously large space with "what is important to me."

Regrettably, most do it poorly.

Most probably do it poorly simply because they postpone the task for so long, and suddenly have to dash off the essay the Sunday evening before the application deadline. For some reason, applicants don't seem to take this assignment as seriously as a term paper. And that is too bad.

The application essay is the candidate's chance to take the admissions situation into his own hands and emphasize to the college "what *is* important about me." Enough of the colleges' terse little questions, with just enough space provided for terse little responses. Here is the free-for-all section of the application, which students could use joyfully, imaginatively, provocatively, and politically if only they would seize the initiative in their oft-stated plea "I want to be treated like more than just a number in the admissions process."

Too often, when the essay finally gets written, it has a distinct ring of "what I think they want to hear" rather than "what I want to say." Too often the essay simply puts into prose what already has been stated in the application: a list of activities in sentence form. And that is drab, very drab.

A seventeen-year-old doesn't have to be first cellist of the County Youth Symphony or all-state halfback to have something interesting to talk about. Every kid who has passed through the teenage years has something worthwhile to say. And we admissions officers listen. In fact, a near-reject can be pulled from the "out" drawer if the essay is sterling—it happens often.

The Harvard dean of admissions reports that the essay gets a moderate weighting in his college's admissions process, unless it is particularly good or particularly bad, in which case it becomes important. The dean also says that his committee often does not receive enough information about a candidate and that the essay therefore takes on added importance. The Harvard dean urges candidates to tell their story, whatever it happens to be, with care, and to develop strong points thoughtfully and persuasively. He cautions, however, that fake interests and involvements are usually caught by admissions committees: "Things that are fake clank," he says.

What do colleges hope to learn through the application essay? First, whether or not the applicant can put a sentence together. There is a linguistic skills scare today, so the colleges are extremely interested in students' ability to write: the essay, the English grades, the comments of the English teacher, the SAT Verbal and the English SAT II test scores all contribute to a college's appraisal of the student's ability to communicate. The essay provides a piece of the puzzle, even though admissions officers realize that some application essays have been rather carefully screened by a parent, a sister, an English teacher, or a college adviser. (Because of this screening, a handful of institutions require that the candidate submit a graded paper from a high school course in addition to the application essay. Not only does the college receive a rather typical sample of the applicant's in-school writing, but also a grade, plus a teacher's criticisms.)

As important as it is to learn how well a student writes, the admissions office also wants to learn what a student has to say about himself or herself when given a free hand. Colleges fully realize that most application questions are perfunctory information-gathering necessities. In a way, then, only the essay allows an admissions officer to have a personal conversation with an applicant—if the applicant will allow that to happen. Too few do.

There are no specific rules on writing the application essay. But there are a few general guidelines to be seriously considered. Despite the fact that the essay is not an admissions committee's conclusive insight into a student's ability to write, the applicant should be certain that the essay is not bogged down with dreadful spelling and illegible handwriting (and yes—it's okay to print out the essay on a computer). The length of the essay should concur with what has been requested; during the late-winter "reading period," admissions officers have thousands of pieces of paper to peruse and simply can't—and won't—read beyond a reasonable length. The essay should say something that the rest of the application doesn't say, or at least should elaborate on something another segment of the application barely suggests: a talent, an interest, thoughts on a world or local problem, a personal accomplishment.

The subtleties of a candidate can be captured nicely in the essay. One of the best essays I remember was by a young man who wrote "On Always Placing Last in Cross-Country." With articulate humor, he convinced the admissions committee, through tales of arduous running, that he could survive the toughest required academic course and could be counted on to "travel the extra mile."

Perhaps it is best at this point to display a few real-life examples. First, an extreme example of—of what? not caring? not spending the time? not thinking? not drying out? not being serious about the application? Tragically, this essay was submitted to a highly selective college along with a very decent set of grades, adequate test scores, and glowing school recommendations:

well if you want to know me better, I guess I should write about my favorite subject, myself. Now your probably thinking I'm conceded or a little zany but not conceded. I'm always looking for new people and places to discover, thats why I love working at McDonalds. I try to do everything in my power to make the customers smile, especially when they're grouches. I have 1001 different facial expressions and more actions to go along with them. I love nature and any type of athletic competition fascinates me, especially hockey. Playing a nice and hard game of tennis is my idea of fun. Cooking is one of my favorite hobbies, besides what else do you do on rainy days. I have two brothers who I try all my new recipes on. Last time I looked they were still alive. I'm a very logical person, at least that's what all the horoscopes and handwriting analysis say, and I plan what I should do every week on Sunday and about Wednesday something turns up and all my plans are wrecked. That's life! I would love to go to _____ College because I love your location, the college campus, the interest taken in the classes, and it seems the people there are more concerned with learning than getting messed up with something else. I always try to live for the future because you should "think only of the past as its remembrances give you pleasure" (Jane Austen). That, by the way, is my favorite saying. Ha! Ha! I didn't exceed 500 words!!!!!!!!!

So much for the down side. Now let's look at a few essays that have struck admissions officers in selective colleges as successful in conveying individuality, maturity, and sensitivity.

A.

How It Feels to Be Two of Me

No, I am not a twin, and this is not an essay about vision problems or schizophrenia. I say that there are two of me in the sense that I am like the Greek god, Janus: two-faced, not meaning deceptive, but that there are two sides to me. I seem to be composed, in every sense, of two different, opposing elements.

The first and most obvious binary combination in me relates to my physical being—my race. Born in California to immigrant Chinese parents, my ethnicity is always referred to as that dreaded hyphen, Chinese-American. But growing up this way has been a positive experience. I have the benefits of both worlds. I have been raised as a person eternally presented with options: choices between two different philosophies, two different ways of learning, two different ways of looking at the world. Granted, since my parents generally advocate the traditional Chinese positions of obedience, respect towards elders, humility, hard work, and no social life until the coveted age of twenty-two, while I on the other hand have been bombarded since birth by the American principles of rebelling, questioning authority, proudly extolling the virtues of the Constitution, and dating whomever, whenever, there are a few clashes between parents and child in our household. Last year they really made my life miserable. However, this year each side is learning to give a little, and I like to think that I have achieved a reasonable and favorable balance between the two spheres that influence my life.

The next bipartite feature of me is not as obvious as the first. Contrary to popular belief, there are two sides of my personality. Which side people see depends on how well they know me. The first impression that I make on acquaintances is usually that I am very quiet, studious, serious, reserved, and shy, even. I think I act that way when I first meet people in order not to shock them with my true self. You see, if you were to recite those adjectives to closer friends of mine, they would, in all probability, not have the faintest idea of whom you were describing. If you mentioned my name in relation to any of those words, they would definitely all collapse in fits of laughter. The flip side of the grave studybug is the me that my friends and family know: the loud, crazy, sarcastic and wry procrastinator with an offbeat sense of humor, always ready to roll off to the movies and armed to the teeth with silly anecdotes and corny jokes offered to anyone who cares to grin.

Lastly, of course, is the binal nature of my academics. As anyone browsing through my transcript would notice, I seem to do best in the humanities. I do enjoy my English and history courses, and especially enjoyed the seminar class I took last spring. However, I also have a secret passion to be a math whiz or to consider the world of medicine. I know I'll have to do serious work if I decide to follow those paths, but I do have something going for me—my genes! My father tends to shy away from social functions, and was a very quiet, studious young man with an artistic sensitivity who desired to be a writer and poet. On the other hand, my mother is a very fun-loving, outgoing type of person, and she was bright enough in math that she was the only woman in the entire electrical engineering department at her university in Taiwan. It is only fitting that the two halves of my personality and interests so closely parallel those of the two people who came together to make physical me.

And how does it feel to be two of me? Well, I think it feels pretty great. And so do I.

—Jade Jeng

B.

I am 5'9" with a stocky build. My main facial feature is a set of red mutton chops and a matching crop of hair. My hair style is not the only anachronism attributed to me: I prefer folk music to rock, and an acoustic guitar to an electric. I identify myself as a realistic optimist. I still live under the fable that man is basically good, and over a period of time each will reach his potential.

No one could ever say that I am afraid of work or that I actively search it out. I am a poor chess player, looking forward to little improvement, and tennis is a fun game for others.

My family experience has taught me how to deal with people. I am the second oldest of four children, the other three being females. Harriet, who is attending Yale, has visions of a Supreme Court appointment; Frances has a collection of almost all the clothes in the world; and Aurenna wants to be a fullback.

There is an urge in me to express myself in music and art: I have written poetry and have composed songs. I am a member of a few school choirs and perform occasionally with my guitar. My guitar gets the applause. Besides music and writing, I backpack, hike, camp, and canoe for recreation. I am also into photography and leathercraft. I keep mending my shoes. Another pastime I have is reading. I have an extensive collection of books ranging from Shakespeare to Doonesbury. If anything, they are a constructive vice.

I am going to college to learn. There are many things both academic and social that I am curious about. Through my studies I hope to find something I could base a profession on. But it is simply College that attracts me, where many find knowledge that before was not theirs.

—Wade Komisar

C.

I believe there should be a nominal or no-cost neutering program for dogs and cats to curb the proliferation of strays. I don't believe in a mandatory retirement age. Some program of consulting work should be worked out for those who wish to remain in their fields but who wish to cut down the work hours. I think it should probably be a lot more difficult to get married than it is. Perhaps at the time of applying for a license a period of time should have to elapse during which classes or counseling would be required. I believe in a liberal arts education and that these institutions should be distinct from vocational schools. Vocational schools should have their images upgraded. They are necessary and no less noble than colleges, just different. We don't have enough skilled artisans—just amateurs. People wander into professions like carpentry, plumbing, etc. Efficient apprenticeship programs could be worked out.

Why can't mental health agencies advise the public to seek a twice yearly checkup, very much the way dental societies do?

I believe in a close-knit family. I believe we lost out when the extended family was sacrificed in the cause of a mobile society. I find the world divides itself in two camps on the question of how supportive a family should be. There are those who say that too much support fosters weakness and dependency. Then there are those who say that there is no such thing as too much loving and caring. Put me down for number 2.

Let's hear it for cloudy days. Days that allow us to stay indoors to read, go through old letters, and experiment with nail polish without guilt.

I'm against: generation gaps, working for grades, smoking in public, perfume in restaurants, too many rules, too few rules, boots for strolling, designers' monograms on clothes, haircuts that have names, food additives, exercise that requires counting, cabs that are hard to climb into, mindless TV for children, mindless TV for adults, and department store prices.

I'm for: zip codes, daily garbage pickup, brevity, the N.Y. Times, Chinese food, the diversity of New York, boots for riding horses, cats, comfortable shoes, James Herriot, anything Irish, shorter school days, more career exposure in school, fresh bread, and modified vegetarianism.

—Jessica Miller

D.

Life has a dual nature and I have experienced both sides. There have been times of bliss as well as times of grief and I have found that each can have value if only understood. I have grown up in Harlem where many times the understanding has been harsh, but the merit still remains. Perhaps ostracism at the hands of my peers (caused by my light skin-color and West Indian background) was a terribly rugged road through childhood, but just how valuable are the lessons of self-communication and individuality? Is it not essential to learn that one can not always be what others may want him to be, or more importantly, that he doesn't have to? Despite the numerous attempts, I have never been separated from my sense of self, never the victim of egotistical homicide; each attempt induces palingenesis.

Intermediate School 201 was always known as the school without windows, simply because it was one of the first buildings designed not to have any. It was in this architectural "wonder" that I experienced my first encounter with the universe of sound and emotion that I feel lies dormant in every mind—the art of poetry. Although encouragement came from many sources, my own beginnings were largely due to the impression left upon me by poetess Sonia Sanchez and the few but still treasured words she wrote for me quite some time ago: "To Brother Carlos, keep on being Black and together; Black love, Sister Sonia Sanchez." Many years later, as I look back on that experience and my entire junior high school career, I realize that I.S. 201 had many more windows than we thought.

Although I had been exposed to a great many ideas while still going to school in Harlem, I was nonetheless ill-prepared for the kaleidoscope of diverse peoples and experiences I have encountered in my more recent years. Ours is not a universe of one; many stars are shining and in Stuyvesant High School the glow can be ofttimes overpowering. But I have found that if I view each person as an individual, many lights will be broken down into colors of realism and sincerity that my eyes can accept. As president of the Black Students' League, or as a former member of Stuyvesant's Acting Class, my experiences have also been many and varied, but each is the same in one aspect: whether an experience is "good" or "bad" it is still unique and every moment should be savored. "The pedigree of honey does not concern the bee; a clover anytime, to him, is aristocracy."° I accept each moment, each event and every individual as rare, for in actuality they are.

There is much that I would like to do in life, and my only restrictions, I believe, are whatever limitations I place on myself or allow to be placed on me. My major goal is to contribute as much as I know I will make use of, via programs such as the Archbishop's

---

° Emily Dickinson.

Leadership Project, a highly selective group which for the past ten years has sought to develop the leadership potential of young Black men. However, my most important aspiration is to move ever closer to erasing the phrase "I wish I had" from my vocabulary.

—Carlos Griffith

E.

I took a short break from my typical program today, appeased my mother, and tried to clean up my bedroom. Understand that this was no simple task; I am a "collector" in the purest of terms. And as I have informed my mother, I have no intention of reforming this impractical character trait. She understood, but handed me three large garbage bags. I accepted them without argument: they were biodegradable. Environmentally-safe garbage bags in hand, I cautiously opened my door. . . . only to be disappointed that the mess had not magically disappeared. Desks and floors were still coated with a thick layer of birthday cards, college brochures, a hardbound version of *The Complete Works of Shakespeare*, pink tissue paper, the California Academic Decathlon syllabus, unmatched socks, cumbersome textbooks, the last six months of *Time* magazine, and bright purple boots. And I thought that I would need several more large bags.

But as I sorted through what my mother insisted was "mess," I realized that there was very little that deserved to be canned. (The college brochures were the exception). I could hardly be expected to part with the empty toothpaste tube that had accompanied me to Stanford University for a demanding summer session. After all, I deserved material proof that I had spent six weeks studying political systems, government, and speech with the Junior Statesmen Foundation. Nor could I bring myself to give up last year's wrinkled National Forensics League scoring ballots that described me as having "a voice that could stand up in a blast furnace." And how could I be expected to part with last year's varsity girls' soccer game schedule? It only represented the months of perseverance, paperwork, phone calls, and sweat that it took for me to persuade the high school administration that Grant H.S. could not survive without a girls' soccer program. Conspicuously underlined at the bottom of the second page were the two teams slated to play in the Los Angeles City Championship. Grant was one of them. So I set all the papers in a "neat stack" to my left.

Of course the first thing I tripped over upon entering my "sacred temple" was the rejected copy of the Mock Trial team's closing arguments. The case was strewn across my floor, along with scattered notecards, various unmatched pens with no ink, four different highlighting markers also with no ink, and the evaluation sheet from the previous night's competition. It hailed Grant High School as the winning team, promoting it to the semi-final round of Mock Trial competition. I glanced through the case and then stuck the notecards and pens neatly to my right.

As I sat there in the middle of my life, I could not help but notice my Academic Decathlon tee-shirt in a ball in front of my outstretched legs, caked with sweat and adorned with three pins: The first argued that "It is better to light one candle than to curse the darkness," the second pleaded "Save the trees," and the third accused "You must be from the shallow end of the gene pool". Could I be expected to part with such a trophy? All right, so I could have folded it.

I shuffled through estranged newspaper articles and shoes, pursuing headlines and labels along the way. "Colored Glass Helps Dyslexics," read one title. I had to laugh to myself, because the only thing my prescribed "pink" reading glasses had helped me to achieve was sinus headaches. I still preferred to use green plastic overlays to aid me in my reading, a dozen of which I stacked above on a shelf.

But perhaps the most intriguing article I excavated from deep recesses of my room was a poem for South African Women, written in commemoration of the 40,000 women and children who, in August 9, 1956, presented themselves in bodily protest against the "dompass" in the capital of apartheid. The last lines read:

> And who will join this standing up
> and the ones who stood without sweet company
> will sing and sing
> back into the mountains and
> even under the sea—
> we are the ones we have been waiting for

I had managed to part with some miscellaneous xeroxes at that point, but this one I saved, marveling at how well a thought presented at The United Nations on August 9, 1978 could be such an appropriate statement for society today, as a challenge for the youth of tomorrow. As I allowed myself to consider the last line, I was reminded of several milestones of the past years—Glasnost, the Alaskan oil spill, the massacre in Tiananmen Square, Solidarity's victory in Poland, the breaking of the Berlin Wall—and I forced myself to reconsider my place in the world, my purpose, and my potential. Should I strive to become "just another graduate student" and join the ranks of practicing lawyers as a surplus commodity? Is that a fair objective for someone with creativity and tenacity? When those talents are in especially great demand to solve global problems and preserve global resources, is it fair for me to be satisfied with a six figure income? As I sat there in my room, between the green shoelaces and The Republic, I decided that it was not. My generation does not need another high tax bracket consumer. It needs a leader, an achiever, an educator, and a builder of dreams—because there are some things that need to be cleaned up.

Now and then, real-life secondary school tales can be conveyed with great humor. But only now and then:

F.

I've taken many different courses throughout my high school career, but many were just "typical." Last year, however, I took an advanced Biology program. Advanced Bio at my school is a lab-oriented course requiring patience and manual dexterity.

During the year our class dissected four specimens: a fetal pig, a bull frog, a pigeon and a cat. In each specimen we studied only a few systems, but in the cat we studied them all. Each presented special challenges.

People knew I was enrolled in Advance Bio and would cringe when I sat next to them on the bus. It wasn't me—it was my fetal pig. My favorite perfume became "Formalin No. 5". Probably the worst experience I had was with my cat: three dogs chased me home once when my specimen was still under my arm. One girl's dog ate her cat's arms, so another student loaned her his specimen's arms. Another student ended up with two left feet on his skeleton until someone came up with a cat skeleton that had two right feet. One guy used Krazy Glue to hold his cat's arteries together. Granted, these were not a surgeon's techniques, but they did help us survive Advanced Bio.

I'll always remember that course. . . .

And now and then a candidate will get into a topic that conveys a bit more than was perhaps intended:

G.

> The summer of my junior year was the most educational and exciting I have spent. I was employed in New York, in the offices of Penthouse, Ltd. Here I worked with the staff photographer of *Penthouse, Viva,* and *Penthouse Photo World* magazines. Working here I almost gained a professional's knowledge. During the course of the summer I had contact with many famous and influential people. I feel that my knowledge gained from this experience will benefit me as much, if not more, than any formal education I have acquired as of yet, and I can truly say that I will not forget that to which I was exposed.

The application essay (some colleges will ask for more than one) should be done thoughtfully, personally, imaginatively, and with equal shares of seriousness and daring. Your record is your record . . . but the essay can add a refreshing and vital dimension to your college candidacy.

The College Interview: Tell and Sell

"Every candidate should leave here having *enjoyed* the interview; at the same time, every candidate should leave here having been *challenged* by the interview," my boss in the Yale admissions office told me some years ago. Most admissions colleagues at other institutions would perceive the interview similarly: a serious but friendly, informal conversation between college representative and prospective student.

The interview and the application essay create good opportunities for high school seniors to personalize, explain, and perhaps even dramatize their candidacy for college. And because young people today have been trained and encouraged to speak up, to express their feelings and their differences, the interview comes easily for most. It often serves to strengthen the student's chances for admission.

Selective colleges do not accord nearly the weight to the interview as to the actual in-school academic and extracurricular record. But at some private institutions where there are far more superior records than there are places in the class, the interview can make a difference. Bruce Poch, Dean of Admissions at Pomona College (California), says that for 90 percent of the students, the interview simply confirms what is already in the folder, but for the other 10 percent the interview can and does make a significant difference. Doug Thompson, Dean of Admissions at Hamilton (New York), adds that the interview sometimes "just brings a kid's folder to life!"

Most of the selective public institutions (and some of the private ones—Stanford, for example) do not interview at all. On the other hand, a few smaller "public Ivys"—for instance, William and Mary and New College of the University of Southern Florida—do value the interview process.

At the many selective colleges that do interview, the process serves two purposes: (1) to reveal personal strengths of the candidate that perhaps have not been transmitted adequately through other channels, and (2) to answer questions about the institution that the candidate has not found answered satisfactorily through the college literature or the tour.

The interview should not be perceived as a "test." To the contrary, the admissions officer (or faculty member or undergraduate or alumnus/a) will make every effort to create a friendly, relaxed atmosphere so that the applicant can feel as natural as possible. There is tension, of course, but the astute interviewer will seek to defuse the charged atmosphere. Also, the astute interviewer will try to pass the initiative to the candidate as quickly as possible. And the astute candidate will seize that opportunity and run with it.

The applicant should not come to the interview unprepared. Basic information about the college should be mastered before this personal meeting. The viewbook and/or catalogue, the back-home guidance counselor and local alumni, and the pre-interview campus tour can help. Nothing antagonizes an interviewer more than a candidate's pulling out a long list of questions beginning with "Are you coed?" and "What is the size of your student body?" The list approach is particularly annoying if the student is more interested in getting to the next question than in absorbing the answer to the last. Probing and thoughtful questions, of course, *are* appropriate: "Do you envision major campus renovations or expansion in the near future?" "Do classes for freshmen tend to be considerably larger than classes for juniors and seniors?" "Are there tensions on this campus between men and women? Between African Americans and whites?" "What happens here on weekends—do students tend to stay or leave?" "What are the major complaints of students here?" "Is your library crowded?" Questions should be prompted by a yearning to know rather than a yearning to impress: The interviewer can almost always guess the intent, and "staged" inquiries frequently backfire.

For his or her part, the interviewer will ask questions with the intent of simply getting to know the applicant better. True, some interviewers can be Bores Supreme and can only muster discussions of your grades, your scores, your activities, your home, your summers, and why-do-you-want-to-go-to-this-college. But the drab interviewer is an exception. Most would truly like to know the applicant and will work at reaching that goal.

Initial let's-get-relaxed chatter proceeds to more serious discussion if and when the interviewer feels the candidate will be comfortable switching gears, or if the candidate himself turns in a new direction. John Hoy, former dean of admissions at Wesleyan (Connecticut), compiled a helpful, representative list of questions the candidate might be asked at the selective college's interview.° A sampling:

1. Do you have contemporary heroes? historical heroes?
2. If I visited your school for a few days, what would I find is your role in the school community? What would your teachers say were your greatest strengths as a person? as

---

° This list appeared in *Choosing a College* (New York: Dell, 1967).

a student? likewise, what about your shortcomings or weaknesses?
3. What kind of self-development do you wish to see in yourself in the next four years?
4. What do you feel is the most important weak point you would like to overcome in the next four years?
5. What is the most significant contribution you've made to your school?
6. What will be the "good life" for you twenty years from now?
7. Where and when do you find yourself most stimulated intellectually?
8. If our roles were reversed, what would you like to know about me so that you could make an intelligent and fair decision on my application for admission or, better still, on my competence as your interviewer?
9. In a sentence or two what points about yourself would you like to leave with me so that I can present your strongest side to our committee on admissions?
10. What books or articles have made a lasting impression on your way of thinking? Have you read deeply into any one author or field?
11. What events would you deem crucial in your life thus far?
12. What pressures do you feel operating on you in society to conform? Describe ways in which you and your friends "go your own way."
13. Describe some things that you have really become indignant over in the past year.
14. What do you feel sets you apart as an individual in your school?
15. If I could hand you my telephone and let you talk to any one person living, to whom would you like to talk? Why?
16. If I said you had $20,000 and a year to spend between high school and college, how would you spend the money and time?

17. Have you ever thought of not going to college? What would you do?
18. What have you read, seen, or heard about [Oldebrick] College that you don't like? What rumors can I confirm or deny?
19. If you were chosen as the new principal in your high school, what would be your first move?
20. Is there anything you'd like to toss into the interview as a parting comment?

The average college interview is thirty to forty minutes—sometimes shorter, sometimes longer if the two people enjoy talking with each other. Usually the admissions officer will request the candidate to come into his/her office alone for the interview, and sometimes ask the parents to come in for a few minutes at the end to see if they have questions. These last few minutes can be a bit tense if either parent insists that the entire interview be reenacted to make certain all the bases have been covered. (Important as parents are to the college search, the interview should be the candidate's.)

Today, there are any number of "official" interviewers for colleges. The bulk of on-campus interviews at selective colleges are handled by professional admissions officers, but now and then a faculty member will be called in to substitute. And it is popular today to hire a few outstanding undergraduate seniors to interview on campus, particularly in the fall, when admissions officers are away from campus, recruiting nationwide in the secondary schools. Often these "senior interviewers" do the best job: They can convey news of the college in a credible manner, and they are adept at getting the candidate to talk about himself. Also, because becoming a "senior interviewer" is such a campus honor, the undergrads take the job quite seriously, write extensive interview reports, and even follow up on some candidates with encouraging letters. Some of the most satisfied candidates have had college seniors as interviewers, unpopular though this may be with a few parents (particularly fathers), who feel the teenager may not have been exposed to the "power

The College Looks at the Candidate

base." In actuality, all campus interview reports are considered with equal weight, no matter who interviewed.

Alumni interview in their hometowns for nearly all private institutions, and on the whole they do a superb job, considering the fact they are often years out of Alma Mater and miles away. Indeed, keeping alumni interviewers in touch with the changing college is a major challenge for the admissions office. But alumni who volunteer as interviewers usually take the job seriously (with some embarrassing exceptions). They return to campus for seminars, often at their own expense, and spend hours visiting local high schools and candidates' homes to spread the word. For the candidate who lives quite a distance from the college of his or her choice, the alumnus/a (usually) provides a happy and responsible substitute for dealing with the admissions office directly.

Students undoubtedly wonder what goes into the file after an interview has been completed. Interview reports are usually not long, and they rarely repeat all that has been or will be listed in the way of courses and activities on the application. High points of the personal impression are recorded along with any information that the interviewer feels might not otherwise be known to the admissions committee.

A typical report:

Roxanne could be described as a "low-keyed bohemian—or a moderate individualist." This I gather from her gypsy jaunty dress and her description of clashes she has had with the Journalism staff, who, she says, fail to give her articles bylines. She's not afraid to be herself nor to speak her mind freely, though she's not a full-fledged maverick. Roxanne is not highly provocative or scintillating personally, but certainly has a lot going for her academically, having pushed herself in curriculum and in activities (she's ARISTA president, a jock, etc.). I'd say Roxanne is a moderately accomplished, fairly solid applicant, although not quite strong enough in any zone to transcend The Big Middle.

Reference to "jaunty dress" in the above passage surely begs the question of the importance of appearance. Granted, the interview should be a "natural" occasion. At the same time, it is an event. And one usually dresses up to events: interviewers do, and candidates should also. Coats and ties or heels are not necessary, but a comfortable "up" appearance is appropriate and most welcome. The tattered-jean look doesn't quite make it.

In sum, the interview can be enjoyable, informative, and in some cases, highly supportive of the candidate's "case." As many colleges have deemphasized the interview because of logistics, a family should not feel impelled to race from campus to campus. Do, however, investigate the degree to which your top-choice schools value the interview. If the interview seems high on their list, go!

The Extracurricular Whirl

There is one more unfortunate myth afloat that was not mentioned in Chapter 2. It goes something like this: The more activities, clubs, sports, and busy-busy things the candidate can mention on his or her application, the more the college will be impressed. Actually, the opposite is probably closer to the truth.

If a teenager gives priority to learning, in addition to fulfilling his or her responsibilities in the home, there isn't time left for joining everything. A student who takes the more demanding courses and does well in them must often pass up the temptation of high school Americana, boosting all the teams, helping raise money for the drug center, and being in the front lines of club after club. The longer the list of school and community activities, the more suspicious colleges will become that a superficial joiner is at hand, popping from place to place, responsibly involved in very little.

Back in the innocent fifties, when I was working at Yale, we talked about filling the class with "well-rounded men." Yale and its brothers and sisters are still looking for a healthy roster of Category 5 types, but the "well-rounded" theory has been altered somewhat. Now most highly selective colleges are looking for a well-rounded *class*—a class of different types of individuals, some quite lopsided and some involved in a variety of things, but deeply involved. The feeling is that a classful of well-rounded kids who are mirror images of one another would be a dull class indeed.

Often, some of the most mature and accomplished young people are those who have given enormous time to one extracurricular endeavor, at the expense of others. A Yale dean of admissions, Worth David, addressed that point nicely:

> One of the most compelling characteristics that a candidate can bring to the admissions committee is the demonstrated capacity to do something superbly. If it's obvious that a youngster has thrown an enormous amount of energy into some worthwhile activity, that helps his case. It might not necessarily be an activity which is available at Yale. For example, there's the Midwesterner who does a superb job with the 4-H Club. But some kind of demonstration of the willingness and the ability to commit oneself to a worthwhile activity is a very compelling argument for admission.

Today the emphasis in the extracurricular zone is "depth," not "breadth." He plays ball—is he disciplined, improving, *good*? She paints—has she sought the best instruction in the area? Does she show? Is she *promising*?

Don't fret. Obviously, every teenager can't have the One Big Talent. But every student can, at 17, be aware of his or her own strengths and talents and find appropriate outlets. The youth of the seventies left many marks on this nation—one was the healthy notion that teenagers *think, get involved*, and can move responsibly. That legacy makes Betty Boop the cheerleader look a little pale today.

Let's not forget the young person who has to work every waking hour when not in school, and who consequently must leave blank the extracurricular slots on the application. Not only can employment demonstrate extraordinary discipline, it also can stimulate one's ambition to learn. Some of the young people who have had to work rather than join clubs or teams or bands are the most mature around, and admissions committees would like to hear from more of them.

There can be no precise "how to" on impressing the admissions committee with the extracurricular record. What's done is done. Certainly the candidate should not whirl to a few club meetings in the last weeks before filing an application just to be able to list another activity. Depth of involvement is central today—a sense of caring, contributing, and yes, achieving.

On Chasing Recommendations

Some few years ago, parents of a college candidate in Connecticut demanded to see what the high school guidance counselor had written about their son, surmising that a less-than-glowing recommendation had surely been the reason for the boy's rejection by selective Bates College of Maine. That inconspicuous court case ultimately led to the now-famous Buckley Amendment, which became law in 1974. The moral (and political) concept behind the Buckley Amendment made sense at the time and perhaps still does: the right of a student and/or his parents (until the youngster reaches age eighteen) to know what is in the student's file—statistical data, counselors' and teachers' reports, and so on. The amendment ordered high schools and colleges to open their files at the request of an enrolled youngster or the parent unless a waiver had been signed by the family allowing the institution to keep the material confidential.

The night before the Buckley Amendment became law, I remember heading to the Harpswell, Maine, town dump—the most beautiful dump in the world, tucked in a series of Atlantic islands near Bowdoin College—to burn all interview reports, school recommendations, and teacher recommendations of the then-enrolled Bowdoin students for fear that students would storm the dean's office the next day to prepare suit against the counselor or interviewer who had once said "Jane is bright, but a trifle dull." As I entertained the gulls with my frenzied offerings to the fire gods, at more mechanized institutions the shredding machines were hard at work. The schools and colleges eventually learned to cope with the amendment, although they had quite mixed emotions.

Why "mixed emotions"? We all agreed that the students and their parents had, to some responsible degree, "the right to know"—but *everything*? The immediate consequence of the amendment was to curb distinctly what high schools, particularly the public ones, were willing to tell. The fear of libel ran so deep immediately following the enactment of the "The Privacy Act" that counselors and teachers and principals just decided it was safer to keep their mouths shut regarding candidates. "We must let the numbers speak for themselves" was a common response. And that was directly contrary to the way the private colleges—and some selective publics, particularly in reviewing out-of-staters—were accustomed to going about their admissions business.

If one admits "by the numbers" (as some selective public universities, regrettably, must do by law)—judging each candidate by a formula with appropriate weights accorded gradepoint average, class rank, and standardized test scores—there obviously can be little room for the student who does B work in tough courses, for the classic late bloomer whose awful first two years are offset by two fine "come alive" years, for the kid who may flunk math but is a genius in foreign language, for the student whose grades have been affected by bad health or family problems, for the nifty kid (scholar or not) who might turn out to be one of those rare leaders of men. Only personalized recommendations can explain these subtleties and their causes to colleges that care.

It simply would not be fair to say that all schools stopped sending balanced, sensitive, insightful reports on candidates when the Buckley Amendment became law. But many, if not most, watered down their comments considerably in order to water down their risk. On the whole, the prep schools ran less scared than the public high schools. (I don't know why, as the "private" status would be irrelevant, I'm told, in court.)

In short, college admissions officers are told less about the human dimension of the candidate today (and consequently the application essay and interview become all the more important). Here are three rather typical public high school counselor reports on candidates to one Ivy college:

> Constance Jameth is an outstanding high school senior. She is a good student as well as being very active in school and in the community. She is a varsity player on the tennis team. Swimming is her favorite sport and she belongs to the AAU at the local junior college. She competed in the Junior Olympics. She also likes to ski and surf.
>
> Constance is very interested in Art and has won awards for her ability. She plays the piano and works part-time. Other activities at school have been her membership in the Service Club, C.S.F., and Ski Club.
>
> She is a very personable and attractive young lady who has set her goals toward art. She is an independent worker who seems to have lots of self-discipline.

> Possessing superior academic potential, Robert Krakus has performed very well in academic work in high school. He impresses me as a very sincere, dedicated student who has a wide range of interests.
>
> Not only has Robert been a good student academically; he has also been very active in extracurricular activities in the school and community. He was selected by AFS to spend last summer in Paraguay, worked on the yearbook staff, and participated in a tutoring program.
>
> Robert has impressed me as a conscientious student and is a strong candidate for college admission.

> Melinda Jacobs is, in my opinion, a multi-talented young lady who is applying to a number of excellent academic schools. She is capable of academic success in those institutions receiving this recommendation.
>
> This young lady has constantly followed a solid college preparatory course of study, including a number of honors courses.
>
> Feedback from her teachers indicate positive contributing in all of her classes even though in Physics this year she is having some difficulty.
>
> I am highly supportive of Melinda's application to your fine institution.

One can't blame the public school counselors for reporting only the obvious. First, they are enormously overworked. Having 450 students to advise is considered a "small load" these days. College counseling is only a segment of their responsibility: Class scheduling, discipline problems, and career counseling are all part of their job. And budget cuts often mean the elimination of a counselor rather than other school officers or teachers. Some counselors probably welcomed the Buckley Amendment because they felt uneasy making personal judgments: Their heavy student load meant not knowing individual students well. In many ways, the cards are stacked against the public school counselors. So considering the odds, counselors do a good job (some much better than others). The following sensitive and thorough recommendation came from a public high school counselor in an affluent California suburb.

Recommendation for Simon Smith

Simon is one of the most verbal, inquisitive and enthusiastic students I have counseled in my 15+ years at ——————— H.S. He is always there with a question or an observation. In a school of highly verbal youngsters, Simon's voice is always heard above the din. He thrives on competition so has been very content in this intensely competitive environment. His American History AP teacher credits him with being in the top 1–2% of the students he has taught in 25 years! Another AP History teacher comments, "Simon is most perceptive and picks up quickly on the subtleties in lectures and class discussion as the class goes through the readings which include some complex data." His AP English teacher also praises his excellent mind and finds him very willing to put forth and discuss complex ideas. All comment on his high level of intellectual curiosity.

Simon's competitive nature has, on occasion, worked to his disadvantage. If he isn't comfortable, he tends to be his own worst enemy by reacting to everyone and everything. At first he can be difficult to like; however, once he feels that he doesn't have to prove himself, he relaxes and shows his true intellect and wonderful sense of humor. This is the essence of Simon. He is so eager to be liked and accepted, and has such a quick mind that sometimes he gets in the way of himself (please keep this in mind if he comes for an interview). But, indeed, he is a likable and caring youngster, eager to please and succeed.

He has been a devoted member of the Cross Country and Track teams. Whatever he lacks in native ability in this area he makes up for in heart and determination. He also has been a feature sports writer for the school newspaper and this year is the Opinion Editor—so perfect for Simon who has an opinion about everything!

Simon has a sparkle and glow to his personality that enliven any group he joins. At times he may aggravate, but things are never dull when he's around. We support his application to Oldebrick and are certain that, given the opportunity, he will become a productive and memorable member of your new class.

As a result of many school counselors' saying less to the colleges about specific candidates, the colleges have turned to the high school teacher. This is obviously unfair. The teacher is also overworked and underpaid—and here come the colleges asking perspicacious comments on each and every kid. Generally, however, teachers tell us more than counselors—they're uninhibited, they know the students better, they have seen them in the environment the college cares most about, and they write rather well (particularly the English teachers). Admissions officers at the colleges feel guilty asking teachers for student appraisals—but frankly they don't know where else to turn, and most teachers are unbelievably cooperative.

Following is a rather typical teacher's report submitted on the Common Application form (which teachers love, since a single report can be photocopied and sent to as many as 100 cooperating colleges). (*See pages 176–79.*)

I am reluctant to draw a firm line between the public schools and the private schools regarding college recommendations. But I must: the private schools win, hands down. There are obviously some bold exceptions on either side of the boundary: but *most* private school principals, college advisers, and teachers go the extra mile to inform colleges about the candidate beyond the obvious. Yes, some risks are taken and some highly subjective judgments are made, but almost always to the benefit of

I.

School Recommendation for Cassandra Hopewell

Cassie is probably brilliant and certainly exasperating. The brilliance is literary, and Cassie's gifts are dazzling. Intuitive and instinctive, she makes quick leaps of insight. Her mind cannot be described as analytical in its methods, but she achieves results that go far beyond what her methodical contemporaries can manage. Her Class XI English teacher wrote, "Cassie has a genuinely aesthetic sensibility and a creative imagination of awesome proportion." She is already a considerable stylist. Another English teacher comments, "She writes a marvelously baroque style which is truly delightful to read after the usual student prose; it is like coming upon a genuine oriental rug after miles and miles of indoor/outdoor carpeting." Cassie's gifts are not confined to the writing of prose. When she was in Class VIII, she won the Middle School Poetry Prize with an amazingly mature poem entitled "Wondering." Last year, her English teacher and her French teacher both marveled at her multilingual poem, written in imitation of T. S. Eliot. By her own account, in the fall of eleventh grade she had "started about seventeen novels and finished about seven volumes of journals." Much of her literary sophistication is the natural result of wide and constant reading. When Cassie applied to enter our fourth grade she was already reading *Jane Eyre,* and she has kept on at the same rate. She is the only student in years to have read all of Proust.

It is Cassie's attitude and methods that exasperate her teachers. She is a true intellectual for whose mill the world provides grist in abundance, but Cassie limits herself to a narrow group of subjects and will grind at no others. She is, for instance, mathematically gifted, and (rather against her will) she has often been fascinated by math. In the last analysis, however, she seems to have dismissed it as alien to her sensibility if not to her intellect. Even in those subjects to which she is attracted, Cassie shows little staying power. She balks at assignments that demand the patient construction of a thorough argument supported by evidence. As her American History and Literature teacher pointed out, "Her very facility with language oc-

Agnes Scott • Allegheny • American University • Antioch • Bard College • Bates • Beloit • Bennington • Boston College • Boston University Bowdoin • Brandeis • Bucknell • Carleton • Case Western Reserve • University of Chicago • Clark • Coe • Colby • Colby-Sawyer • Colgate Colorado College • Connecticut College • Denison • University of Denver • Dickinson • Drew • Earlham • Eckerd • Elmira • Emory • Fairfield • Fisk Fordham • Franklin and Marshall • Furman • Gettysburg • Goucher • Hamilton • Hampshire • Hartwick • Haverford • Hobart • Hood Kalamazoo • Kenyon • Knox • Lafayette • Lawrence • Lehigh Lewis and Clark • Macalester • Manhattan • Manhattanville • Mills Mount Holyoke • Muhlenberg • Newcomb College • New York University Oberlin • Occidental • Ohio Wesleyan • Pitzer • Pomona • University of Puget Sound • Randolph Macon Woman's College • University of Redlands • Reed Rice • University of Richmond • Ripon • University of Rochester • Rollins • St Lawrence • Salem • Sarah Lawrence • Scripps • Simmons • Skidmore University of the South • Stephens • Stetson • Susquehanna • Texas Christian University • Tulane • Union • Valparaiso • Vanderbilt • Vassar Washington College • Washington University • Washington and Lee • Wesleyan • Wheaton • Wheelock • Whitman • Willamette • William Smith • Williams

COMMON APPLICATION

TEACHER REFERENCE

Student name ____Matthews, Bonnie_____

                 Last   *First*   *Middle*

Address ____323 S. Central Ave., Mason City, Iowa_____

School Now Attending ____North High School_____

The colleges and universities listed above encourage the use of this form. The accompanying instructions tell you how to complete the copy and file with any one or several of the colleges. Please type or print in black ink.

APPLICANT:

Fill in the above information and give this form and a stamped envelope, addressed to each college to which you are applying that requests a Teacher Reference, to a teacher who has taught you an academic subject.

TEACHER:

The student named above is applying for admission to one or more Common Application group colleges. The Admissions Committees find candid evaluations helpful in choosing from among highly qualified candidates. We are primarily interested in whatever you think is important about the applicant's academic and personal qualifications for college. Please submit your references promptly, particularly if the student is applying to a college as an early decision candidate. A photocopy of this reference form, or another reference you may have prepared on behalf of this student is acceptable. You are encouraged to keep the original of this form in your private files for use should the student need additional recommendations. We are grateful for your assistance.

RATINGS

Compared to other students in your school who are applying to selective colleges, check how you would rate the applicant in terms of academic skills and potential:

	No basis	Below Average	Average	Good (above average)	Excellent (top 10%)	Outstanding (top 2-3%)	One of the top few encountered in my career
Creative, original thought					X		
Motivation					X		
Independence, initiative					X		
Intellectual ability					X		
Academic achievement				X			
Written expression of ideas				X	X	X	
Effective class discussion					X		
Disciplined work habits						X	
Potential for growth							
SUMMARY EVALUATION					X		

(Please see reverse side)

EVALUATION

1. What are the first words which come to mind to describe the applicant?

Open, dynamic, insightful, probing, concerned, interested

2. Academic Characteristics:

Bonnie has not always shown her potential in terms of academic grades. Perhaps this is because she has some difficulty expressing herself clearly, especially when she first writes or speaks. Her ideas and originality, however, are gratifying. She is able to make connections between ideas and areas of study - and is able to deal with the figurative in creative ways. She is truly a student and is interested in study and growth.

3. Personal Characteristics:

I can't praise Bonnie highly enough! She is a fine person who is going to make a wonderful contribution in whatever field she enters. She is always willing to work, to reach, to learn. She is full of ideas which are significant. In addition, she is blossoming as a person now, taking in knowledge from her surroundings and making it part of herself.

BACKGROUND INFORMATION

How long have you known the applicant? __3 years__

Note any capacity in which you have known the applicant outside the classroom (advisor, family friend, etc): __

List the courses you have taught, noting for each course the applicant's year in school (10th, 11th, 12th), the level of course difficulty (AP, elective), and the applicant's grade. Sections of English II - B
Sections in English IV - Psychology in Literature B+

Please return to the appropriate admissions office(s) in the envelope(s) provided you by the applicant. (challenging section)

Secondary School ___North High School___

School Address ___1717 Northern Boulevard, Mason City, Iowa___

Name (print) ___Jane Euibler (Mrs.)___

Position ___Instructor of English___

Signature ___Jane Euibler___ Date ___12/3/93___

CONFIDENTIALITY.

We value your comments highly and ask that you complete this form in the knowledge that it may be retained in the student's file should the applicant matriculate at a member college. In accordance with the Family Educational Rights and Privacy Act of 1974, matriculating students do have access to their permanent files which may include forms such as this one. Colleges do not provide access to admissions records to applicants, those students who are rejected, or those students who decline an offer of admission. Again, your comments are important to us and we thank you for your cooperation.

These colleges admit students of any race, sex,* color, national and ethnic origin to all rights, privileges, programs, and activities generally accorded or made available to students at the college. They do not discriminate on the basis of race, sex,* color, handicap, national and ethnic origin in administration of their educational policies, admissions policies, scholarship and loan programs, and athletic and other college administered programs.

*Private undergraduate institutions which have been traditionally and continually single sex are exempted by Title IX.

casionally hampers her ability to deal faithfully and fairly with a text." Her attraction to the bizarre and the peripheral vitiates her ability to confront a task of substance. As her current French teacher observed, "She remains a dilettante, juggling with ideas and titles, unable to analyze a text in depth or to write a complete, balanced essay." But what an inspired dilettante! It will surprise none of us if Cassie becomes a novelist or belletrist of peculiar power.

Just as Cassie has set herself apart from certain subjects, she has removed herself from the usual routines of school life. The punctuality of either her papers or her person is of small concern. She has found our gym requirements irksome, and in fact cut so many gym classes in tenth grade that she failed the course and was surprised to find herself making it up the following year. Startled surprise is Cassie's usual reaction to any reminder of her responsibility, and indeed the concept of personal responsibility does not seem to be part of her philosophical constitution. Vague and dreamy, she is immensely polite and charming, especially to adults, with whom she feels most comfortable. She has had little time for adolescence. Cassie's parents are immensely cultivated people who have made her a part of their very adult life. She loves the ballet and goes as often as possible. In eleventh grade she worked on weekends at the New York City Ballet in a routine but fascinating backstage job. Cassie has traveled widely and with discrimination. In the summer after tenth grade, she studied English art and architecture and Elizabethan literature at Lincoln College, Oxford, and then went on to study French at the Institut de Touraine in Tours. Cassie has a highly personal style which depends only partly on wardrobe, though her fashion sense is as baroque as her prose. Her tenth grade homeroom teacher observed, "Much of her style is a matter of playing roles, but she has instinct and taste as well. When she grows into and out of the attitudes she now assumes like poses, she will be a very formidable person indeed. . . . Underneath a facade of enervated indifference and superiority, Cassie harbors a good heart and kind instincts." Cassie presently inhabits a small world in which these latter qualities are less valued than her great beauty, her style, and her responsiveness to any aesthetic pleasure. We hope the balance may some day be redressed. Our acquaintance with her has been fascinating.

II.

Headmaster's Recommendation on Justice Bayrock

At first glance the muscular young man who stares you right in the eye gives the impression of a tough teenager of his urban milieu. In a way, Justice Bayrock is just that if one allows for perhaps fifty points more IQ, a sensitive insight into himself and his world, and the kind of moral toughness which will, one day, sweep aside the epicene competition.

Indeed, Justice is a first-rate athlete: a varsity basketball and baseball star, accomplished swimmer, skier, etc. These are important to Justice, yet clearly subordinate to a more profound competitive sport of which he is increasingly aware: survival—moral, intellectual, and aesthetic—in a muddled society.

He brings rare skills to the business of survival. A natural mathematician and apt science student, Justice clearly intends to somehow put his talents at the service of an eventual career (economics? business? law?). A leader by instinct and training, his counselor positions have prepared him to deal with constant demands with dignity and authority.

There is, however, an emergent Justice who is less predictable. This is the sensitive observer of an urban milieu. The romantic buff of Black music, the catholic reader balancing science fiction against the philosophical flow of García Márquez, is no longer the uncomplicated, bright athlete/leader.

Justice is the most exciting kind of student one offers to college. He has absolute character, loyalty, and guts. He adds to that a growing sensitivity enhanced by a truly powerful intelligence. He is open and offers himself body and mind to his community. Vassar is the kind of environment which can reward the virility and energy which will make this young man be heard from in years to come.

III.

School's Recommendation for John Downing III

_____ School very rarely accepts students after the 10th grade year, long after close friendships have been made and academic skills necessary to compete in a high-powered intellectual environment have been ingrained. Because John Downing felt so unchallenged by his previous schooling, he literally uprooted himself and talked his way into being admitted to _____ at the beginning of his junior year. The only child of quintessentially middle-class parents, John had led a sheltered, highly conventional existence.

John has written far more graphically and eloquently than can we about the great awakening he experienced at _____ , but suffice it to say that this is a very different young man from the naive one that came to us last fall. It is to John's credit that he aspired to something more than a humdrum existence and he has taken maximum advantage of the educational and creative opportunities at _____ . Exposing himself to a wide variety of new ideas, lifestyles, and priorities, John was encouraged to think and be his own man for the first time. As a result, he has unleashed his profound sense of the absurd and begun to develop his ample abilities (SAT: Verbal 670, Math 630).

John has paid the price for daring to open up his mind. His parents, particularly his father, claim that he has changed so much that they do not recognize him. His father feels threatened by John's increasingly liberal attitude and father and son barely communicate. John's mother realized that most of the changes that have occurred with John will ultimately be for the good, but she too finds it difficult to adjust to her son's orientation. Although John has found special satisfaction and interest in the theatre, he is firmly committed to the pursuit of an enriched and balanced liberal arts education. His solid grade point average becomes all the more impressive in light of the voluminous number of credits he accrued in an effort to make up for lost time. He has done his best work in English and Social Science.

John has become greatly enamored of English culture, almost to the point of being an Anglophile. His mannerisms and comportment could easily lead to being deemed an affectation, were it not for John's basic honesty and openness. A veritable aficionado of the English theatre, John has shared his expertise with the entire _____ community.

Last year he assumed a leading role in *The Real Inspector Hound* and this past fall directed an extremely well-received production of *Billy Liar*. "John's direction was remarkable in its humor and in its ability to create reality on stage," says ———, resident director of theatre operations, who has presided over a series of award-winning productions. This spring he is undertaking a major independent project directing two of his classmates in *Sleuth*.

John also tried his hand at scriptwriting with an original play entitled *You Can't Have Chairs in the Audience*. It was patterned after the highly successful contemporary black comedy of Tom Stoppard and Joe Orton. "John has a good grasp of the English speech and manners as demonstrated by the dialogue," says his teacher. "John's wit is charming and his imagination stimulating. When he releases his unusual capabilities into more refined patterns, he will become an outstanding student. It has been a distinct pleasure to see John discover a decided talent for writing. He must continue to polish up his techniques as a writer of expository essays but he possesses great imagination and inventiveness which should be nurtured."

In sum, we are happy to have shaken up John Downing's world in a positive way. Although slightly offbeat at times, John has a firm grasp on where he is headed. Having responded so well to the academic and personal demands of a competitive liberal arts secondary school environment, John is looking for a similar experience in college. This is one young man who does not take education for granted. He knows the difference between being a student and merely going to school, and we feel confident that he will take maximum advantage of a quality college experience. He has added zest and life to our community, and we recommend him with affection.

Some schools, public and private, do an end run around the Buckley Amendment by showing the student a draft of his or her recommendation before it is sent to colleges. Ironically—but predictably, it seems to me—the student often feels the school authority has gilded the lily and asks for a more balanced, believable report. Kids today are candid and will often be disappointed with the counselor who is playing safe with the new law. Would that every school might incorporate this technique. It seems to work to the benefit of all parties.

With the complications today in reporting on students—the law, finding time when other responsibilities call, questioning whether one knows the student well enough to write a personal appraisal—it is a wonder we get as many good recommendations as we do. The college admissions office is grateful for them—and clearly the candidate who comes alive in the folder has an advantage over others.

Now and then, however, the recommending parties get carried away and we are challenged to defoliate the green prose or are treated to sheer comic relief. As a breather, let's consider a few recent examples:

> She can be trusted to not only exploit college like a stripminer, but to replace every bit of topsoil—fertilized as well.

> An able, yet somewhat inscrutable product of intellectually oriented and academically distinguished parents, Monty has quietly and resolutely carved out an interesting act of scholarly interests and personal pursuits. . . . His reluctance to become his own advocate may cause him to get lost in the shuffle of your high-powered applicant pool. But secure in his own abilities and eager to expose himself to a wide variety of experiences, Monty is slowly coming to the conclusion that it is decidedly in the best interests of the entire community for him to heighten his profile. Thus, his accomplishments at college will undoubtedly transcend his rather mediocre high school achievements.

> Other students may be brighter but I know no one but Jimmy who is clean to the bone.

> Joyce was driven to our school by the gnawings of hunger. She felt the offerings of her previous school could not satisfy the demands of her voracious academic appetite.

> As literary editor of the school magazine in her junior year, she salvaged it from distinction.

> He has been active—instrumentally so—in the losing campaign of a candidate for Congress.

> His parents are twice divorced and Alex lives with his mothers.

> Although Jennifer is under considerable pressure from her family to achieve high grades, she has resisted this pressure with a high degree of success.

If June didn't have so much difficulty with tests and quizzes, her average would be an "A."

Margaret is a student who has demonstrated her intentions to me.*

As stated or implied in other sections of this book, the student must bear considerable responsibility for all segments of his or her college application, and not just turn over sections to others (counselors and teachers), uncaring. A concerned student should ask what the major points of the recommendation will be, and whether or not the final report is to be shared. Often students can offer valuable suggestions for balancing recommendations, and those asked to recommend are usually grateful.

Also, it is within the realm of common sense, not to mention good manners, to ask if a particular teacher feels comfortable writing a sound recommendation for a student and whether he has the time and is willing. This is not in the regular line of duty for a teacher, particularly in the public school system, and should be considered no small favor, if it is done well. (By the way, some of the most convincing teachers' reports come from those who teach the most demanding courses, not from those popular ones who hand out the highest grades.)

Finally, a word about "other recommendations"—the ones from outside the school, particularly those unsolicited by the college.

Certainly a student's employer can say a great deal about the candidate—and usually employers say it well. This is a particularly important ingredient in the application when the student has not been involved in school affairs. But the line stops there.

Rarely does the friend of the family (alumnus/a of the college included) add much but pressure to a candidate's folder by sending a "friendly, unsolicited" recommendation. These letters

---

* Reprinted in part from an article by Mr. Moll in the *Wall Street Journal*, April 16, 1978.

are almost always bare-boned summaries of what a student has done in and out of the classroom (we know all this), a celebration of the parents' importance to the community, and a "warm endorsement" of so-and-so, about whom the endorser generally knows very little. Lawyers and senators and rabbis and chief committeewomen don't add an ounce of punch to a candidate's folder, because nine times out of ten they simply don't know the candidate well enough to comment. There are exceptions, of course, but I don't recall more than a handful in three decades.

4.

Sell, Sell, Sell: Why Colleges *and* Students Must Flaunt Themselves

THE COLLEGE

Where Have All the Students Gone?

In the mid-eighties, the Alumni Association chairman of the Committee on Undergraduate Admissions said to a throng of Old Blues and other assembled Yale compatriots: "This whole issue of admissions takes on greater importance when you realize that there are now thousands of vacancies in American colleges, that the number of good schools is increasing, that many former 'cow colleges' are now distinguished universities, and that the number of high school graduates is declining. That spells competition. Anyone who assumes that Yale is somehow buoyed effortlessly on its reputation, or is immune to the pressures of the marketplace, had better take another look. Special efforts will have to be made to reach out and identify the first-class minds in this country and to interest them in Yale. It will have to be much more than a casual business of sitting back and waiting for the lucky to arrive somehow in New Haven."

If Yale was uneasy about the future, consider what unrest loomed elsewhere. And for good reason. When this book appeared in its first incarnations—in the late seventies and early eighties—colleges were hearing ominous demographic warnings regarding the probability of a severe decline in student numbers (at least of the traditional age group) due to earlier low birth rates, and to a lesser degree, the possibility of pricing families "out of the market" in an uncertain economy.

Humphrey Doermann, a former director of admissions at Harvard, became one of the respected doomsayers. Here are excerpts of his "The Future Market for College Education," presented at a College Board symposium in 1976:

> Following a century of expansion, higher education in the United States is about to enter at least a 15-year period of either no growth or shrinkage. . . . The number of high school graduates each year will begin to shrink: 15 percent by 1984, and 22+ percent by 1990. . . . The general pressures of steady or declining enrollment probably will place individual colleges and systems of colleges under strains they were not designed for. The principal casualty is most likely to be the capacity of these institutions to adapt and to preserve vitality. . . .
>
> During the 100 years prior to 1970, degree enrollment in colleges in the United States doubled approximately every 14 or 15 years. During the 1950s and 1960s the rate of expansion was even faster. Never has there been a long period of enrollment decline. Brief declines occurred only during the two world wars, the Korean War, and in 1933–34. Expectations, planning processes, federal and state budgeting mechanisms, and the administration of colleges and college systems have until recently all been built with an assumption of continued growth in enrollment. . . . Whether we now believe the no-growth projections, the sharp-decline projections, or something in between, colleges appear to face a decade or two of unprecedented stress, competition, and perhaps retrenchment.

Doermann, gazing into the crystal ball for the near future, issued predictions of economic consequence, too:

1. The number of students prosperous enough to pay full tuition at private colleges and academically able enough to do satisfactory work at most of them will be a relatively small portion of the total high school graduate population. The many colleges that

plan to expand by enrolling more students of this kind will not succeed; the applicant pool is too small.
2. Colleges that attempt to raise tuition faster than family incomes rise and colleges wishing to raise dramatically the measured verbal aptitude of their entering students are likely to find these moves unexpectedly difficult unless they are also willing to decrease enrollment, or somehow are able to broaden and strengthen their applicant pool.

In short, Humphrey Doermann and his dry demographic prognosticator friends proved to be accurate on a number of counts. As the nation headed toward 1990, the teenage body count declined severely—as much as 25 percent during the eighties in some states. Also, careerism became the cry, and many young people (with their parents) wondered if the traditional liberal arts colleges' program fit the new rush for meaningful jobs. And the economy began souring. Even so, private and public colleges continued raising tuition and fees at a much steeper pace than the annual inflation rate warranted. As a result of these combined factors, most of the expensive private colleges saw a severe fall-out in their applicant pools, and were forced as a group to settle for an even smaller percentage (around 20 percent) of a declining national number of college attendees. The public institutions, guilty of outrageous price increases also, remained the more viable option in uncertain economic declines. But *all* institutions were suddenly forced to hustle for students, just as the gentleman at Yale had warned his alums.

And some of the hustling grew ugly. With most institutions thinking the traditional-age population decline and the faltering economy would affect everyone but themselves (only a few wise institutions planned ahead for retrenchment, like savvy Franklin and Marshall College of Pennsylvania), the admissions offices moved from an era of Tell to an era of Sell, big-time. No longer was there a collegial gentility in collecting a freshman class. There was suddenly a tweedy form of warfare among college admissions officers to produce ever-slicker brochures, ever-more-costly videos, and ever-more-streamlined computerization to point the institution toward primary, secondary, and tertiary markets that could be subjected to unsolicited "personalized" mailings (signed by machine), telemarketing, and even home visits. And awarding scholarship on the basis of need, as had been the way in American higher education for decades, fell in many quarters to the no-need or "merit" scholarship (or, as some would say, "bribe"). There was creativity and aggression all around in attracting new students.

One stern warning from Doermann, in retrospect, merits repeating two decades later:

> A college's ability to adapt intelligently, quickly, and surefootedly probably will determine its quality and even its survival during the next 15 years to a far greater degree than was true during the past 30 years. . . . If colleges manage only to compete aggressively with each other for a larger share of a shrinking pool, the total system will be in disarray 15 years from now.

And, in the mid-nineties, disarray abounds. Some colleges have closed; others have wisely merged; and many, many institutions have been reduced in student body size while wishing it otherwise. All have laid off faculty, let much of the physical plant wait until another day for repair or replacement, lopped off full programs that have questionable appeal (some with long-standing respectability, such as the study of foreign languages), and have searched for and introduced whatever programs have new sex appeal (more often than not related to specific careers, like Physical Therapy or Dental Hygiene).

The admissions officers, suddenly treated like football coaches by their superiors ("Win a bigger and better class, or you may well be out of here"), have, on the whole, kept smiling while pushing. Their salaries are up, because getting a class has become life or death to some institutions, unlike the good old days of the sixties, when you invited a class and everyone just came. And they attend seminar after seminar on marketing and "product design." Each institution has sought unique "positioning" in the marketplace—but how many "positions" can there be? Hundreds of small colleges sound painfully similar in pushing "personalized" education with every possible new dressing on the old staple, "liberal arts." It must be said, however, that some have succeeded with their institutional redesign and aggressive marketing plans; but the majority just struggle on.

As push has promoted shove, questionable tactics and professional respectability have become issues within the college admissions world. One highly respected director—Richard Haines of Lafayette College in Easton, Pennsylvania—sent the following missive to secondary counselors before he moved out of the admissions profession altogether to sell running shoes (a relationship between his old work and his new?):

> A college, someone said a century and a half ago, is a "community of scholars engaged in the search for truth." Colleges still say that about themselves. How, then, can colleges justify the deceptive and misleading tactics so often now associated with their recruitment activities?
>
> It should surprise no one that students sometimes make poor college choices, considering the dazed state which must result when an adolescent mind collides with the powerful barrage of information and misinformation penned by publicists and poured forth by admissions officers. If it were accurate information alone, evaluation would be difficult. The intrusion of a vast store of misinformation makes the task of selection almost impossible.
>
> Some colleges have planted a veritable forest of fraud. Growing in it are such hardy perennials as glittering generalities, gross exaggerations and outdated statistics, which flourish alongside new varieties such as trumped-up majors and "special programs" that sprout but never bloom. A recruiter will guide any willing student through the forest to the "one" college which merits all the superlatives he can command.
>
> Disraeli said, "There are three kinds of lies: lies, damned lies, and statistics." Colleges are adept at the use of all three. Let me cite a current example of each. A lie: the brochure boasts that "admission to the College is competitive," while less readily available information reveals that 96% of all applicants are accepted. A damned lie (damned because it implicates others) is a statement in a two-year college catalogue reading: "The following are some of the institu-

tions to which graduates have transferred within the past few years," followed by a carefully culled list including Lafayette, which has no record of any transfers from that institution during the past decade. A statistic: an admissions officer's statement that "95% of our medical school applicants were placed last year," with no mention of the step-by-step screening process which weeds out well over half of the pre-meds before applications can be filed.

There will be honest mistakes made by every admissions officer. Colleges are so complex and conditions change so rapidly that no one can know everything about one institution. I'm concerned, though, about the *dishonest* mistakes, those made with intent to deceive. We need to discover them and eliminate them, in the interest of informed choices by students, and also to preserve the integrity of higher education as a whole.

Meanwhile, counselors, students, and parents should challenge suspicious statements emanating from colleges, remembering Artemus Ward's warning that "It ain't so much the things we don't know that get us into trouble. It's the things we know that ain't so."

The majority of private colleges, going about their recruitment business earnestly and honestly, are dismayed that a relatively small band of hungry institutions can cloud the ethical image for all. One salutary result of this scare was the formation of the "Ethics Committee" (more formally entitled the Admissions Practices and Procedures Committee) of the National Association of College Admissions Counselors, a huge and influential professional organization that brings together admissions officers and guidance counselors for nationwide discussion and service. This committee authored, and annually revises, an important document entitled "Statement of Principles of Good Practice" (see Appendix, p. 225), a Ten Commandment–type tablet that colleges and secondary schools can emulate. The statement was made "law" by the organization. There is also a no-nonsense monitoring system to check abuses.

Thanks largely to regional Ethics Committees—divisions of the national ACAC framework—the "Statement of Principles of Good Practice" has had some clout. Some local committees

—the one in New England, for example—have issued severe warnings to colleges that abuse the guidelines stated in "Principles." One target has been the institution that admits a student early and demands a hefty deposit before the student has heard from other institutions (the most selective colleges inform by early April). The "Principles" states: A college must permit the candidate to choose without penalty (deposit) among offers of admission until he has heard from all colleges to which the candidate has applied, or until May 1." Secondary school counselors, college admissions personnel, and candidates can report abuses in the recruitment and enrollment process to their regional Ethics Committee and be assured of complete confidentiality.

The declining birthrate, the questionable value of the liberal arts–oriented baccalaureate degree in the current job market, and the high cost of higher education will obviously have an increasingly profound effect on the manner in which selective colleges conduct their admissions operations. Some results are already obvious: the dazzling advertising campaigns, the wealth now of no-need scholarships, the gala parties for admitted-but-not-yet-enrolled students, the hiring of professionals to accelerate the hoopla and make it more productive. Colleges, including the most selective, are pondering the future with concern. But they *must* sell.

Buyer, beware.

THE STUDENT

We've come full circle now, touching on all key components of the undergraduate application process. It is time to remind the candidate and parents of the "basic concepts" listed when this exercise began. Hopefully, they mean even more now:

1. Many prestigious colleges in America today are *not* highly selective; if they feel you can survive their program, you'll be admitted. High price, a declining number of college-age Americans, and

apprehension regarding the worth of a bachelor's degree in the job marketplace have created this phenomenon.

2. Unfortunately, many colleges and universities pose as being more selective than they really are. They feel good students will not be attracted to them if they do not create an aura of selectivity at the front gate. But as a result of the hidden anxiety that the upcoming class may not be filled with the quantity and quality of students hoped for, the admissions office tends to *over*state the qualities of the institution. So students and families must analyze a private college as carefully as they would analyze an automobile before buying it. Probing questions must be asked to confirm what is advertised and to check tone, performance, and justification of price. "Test rides" must be made by visiting classes, libraries, Union buildings, campus art galleries, athletic facilities, laboratories, and dorms. Hunches must be confirmed by talking with those who earlier decided in favor of the product.

3. A *few* public and private undergraduate institutions in America today are as highly selective as they ever have been, and a handful are even more selective. But it is rare that a college enjoys the luxury of admitting one out of two of their candidates, and not more than a half dozen colleges nationwide admit one out of five applicants. Aspiring kids and parents flock in droves to the latter little inner circle, hoping to get a bit of the juicy and seemingly irresistible prestige. Even though fame-of-a-name is not always consistent with an elite college's quality, the hordes keep applying, not realizing (or caring?) that the academic program may be as good or better at a place considerably more accessible.

4. Nothing speaks louder than a strong high school record in the college admissions game. "Other considerations" are almost always secondary in importance to the degree of difficulty of a candidate's courseload, grades, class rank, recommendations from teachers and school officials, standardized test scores, and the depth of extracurricular involvement.

5. Given the (rare) highly selective college situation, and given an average candidate in that college's admissions competition, "other considerations" can indeed enter the picture, some of which the candidate can capitalize on. Who is admitted from the muddy middle of a selective college's applicant pool is partly a matter of chance, and the applicant has some control over "positioning" himself. (Also, alas, one applicant's ability to pay the full cost without financial aid may well be relevant when two candidates seem equally attractive.)

Sell, Sell, Sell

Given the gloomy demographic and economic realities that affect colleges today, high school juniors and seniors might be tempted to relax, knowing that colleges and universities will hustle to seek them out and admit them. Granted, college admissions has changed from the seller's market of the sixties to the buyer's market of today. But *remember*, a few colleges have never been more difficult to enter: Amherst and Virginia and Brown and Harvard and Berkeley and Yale and Stanford and Cooper Union and Williams and Duke and Georgetown and a handful of others. The very small openings at their front gates may widen with time, but for the moment the great majority of young people who want to get in are left standing outside.

It is human nature perhaps for the candidate and the family to try for whatever is most difficult to get. As long as one realizes that hardest-to-procure is not necessarily best, and not necessarily life versus death, then why *not* play the college admissions game? A strategy of good moves to attempt to win the most difficult victory can only serve to put one in a better position for scoring "down" a few notches (where the education and environment may be as good as or better than up top). So nothing is lost—indeed, a great deal is gained. Candor, introspection, imagination, energy, time, relaxation: all these are prerequisites to "playing the game" well.

Perhaps a few good tips have been passed along to candidates in these chapters. Here now are the thoughts of some colleagues when asked, "What quick advice would you give a college candidate regarding 'selling' him/herself to the college of his/her choice?":

Amherst (Massachusetts): Relax and be totally candid. Know plenty about the college, and know even more about yourself.

Beloit (Wisconsin): Be realistic.

Boston University (Massachusetts): Do your homework.

Bowdoin (Maine): You personable ones: arrange an interview! You with an edge, a special ability or a significant hobby: define these well to the admissions office!

Brandeis (Massachusetts): Shut off the TV. Read. Relax.

Case/Western Reserve (Ohio): Look carefully before you leap. View college selection as a major life decision.

Colgate (New York): 1. If you have a clear first choice, apply early decision. 2. Don't be so modest as to shield accomplishments. 3. Visit the campuses. 4. Present a strong record.

Denison (Ohio): Be yourself, and blow your horn.

Duke (North Carolina): Remember that the "sales job" doesn't start with the application process. And the "selling" is not directly to us, but through teachers and counselors to us. They can best measure and capture you.

Earlham (Indiana): Be open and forthright. Know the college well, and say why you are as appropriate a choice for them as they are for you. Address your weaknesses as well as your strengths.

Franklin and Marshall (Pennsylvania): Visit the college. Prepare a neat, clean, and concise application. Tell a college if it is clearly your first choice.

Hampshire (Massachusetts): Demonstrate energy, honesty, and a sense of humor. Show a high "aspiration index" regarding college. Don't allow yourself to be propped up by counselors or parents.

Harvard (Massachusetts): Through the application, the interview, etc., develop your strong points. Too often applicants just don't tell colleges enough about their exceptional accomplishments. But don't *fake* them. Be clever, but don't cross the fine line between clever and gimmicky.

Kenyon (Ohio): Present what you are with pride.

Knox (Illinois): Be honest, but warn the admissions officers first: this will help prevent trauma and shock.

Lafayette (Pennsylvania): 1. Seize the initiative. Don't let Mommy or Daddy take it from you. 2. Be neither too modest nor too boastful. Rather, be factual and thorough. 3. Don't be afraid to be yourself. You want to get into a college which is appropriate for you, not for someone you're pretending to be.

Mount Holyoke (Massachusetts): Read.

Sell, Sell, Sell

Pomona (California): Do a competent, complete job on the application itself. Solicit recommendations *only* from those who know you well.

Princeton (New Jersey): A demonstration of energy is the key—in things academic, in things nonacademic. Beware, most of all, of being glib.

St. Lawrence (New York): There is no quick fix. The die is cast by the time the application is filed.

Scripps (California): Think of good questions. Ask them. Laugh in the interview. Do all the basic stuff: dress right and don't chew gum (unless you're an artist). Have thoughts about what you want, what you like, and what you are pretty sure of. Show some spunk. And write the application thoughtfully, properly, and with flair.

Stanford (California): Be yourself. Don't *try* to be what you think Stanford *wants* you to be. Where are the natural Huck Finns in our applicant pool?

Tulane (Louisiana): Tell everything, good and bad. If the bad is revealed, an admissions officer might suggest senior-year strategy to enhance your chances of admission.

College admissions, as hinted throughout this book, is not an exact science. Happily, formulas do not reign supreme in deciding whether John and/or Jane will be admitted to Oldebrick. Instead, people with biases and quirks and bad days and good days are (rather humbly, and very earnestly) "judging" other people, hoping to find the best possible match between institution and student. An uncomfortable task.

The Director of Admissions of Trinity College, Connecticut, expressed the human dimension from his side of the desk nicely:

We don't define the shape of our ideal candidate, as if there were such a phenomenon, but instead try to stress the importance of selecting those who seem most ready to identify themselves as they really are. . . .

Thus, the objective of the admissions policy is not most importantly defined in terms of good grades, of high College Board scores, of all-state tackle nominations or class presidencies, but by the selection of persons embodying the outward marks of an inner determination to live at their fullest capacities. It is all very, very subjective.

The Duke viewbook says something similar a bit differently:

> Intelligence, imagination, creativity, a disciplined approach to study—these are just some of the qualities which members of the admissions committee look for in selecting a class for Duke. Beyond that, they seek men and women who are eager to face future challenges in life; people who believe that what they do will make a difference. That does not mean that you have to be a Renaissance man or woman to have a chance for admission. More than anything else, what Duke looks for in its students is potential—the potential to take full advantage of an unusual environment in which undergraduates work closely with fellow students and professors in exploring complex issues and challenging problems.

Absolutely every young person has some attribute worthy of Duke's or Michigan's notice. Regrettably, too many feel that if Duke or Michigan *doesn't* notice, it's all over. The college admissions decision can be harsh, often because it is the first judgment of finality handed to a teenager.

But no harm trying to "play the game" to claim a spot in the prestigious winner's circle. If you play, try your hardest. Do remember, however: There are deeper seas to conquer than a place in next year's freshman class at Oldebrick.

APPENDIX 1

When Evaluating an Independent Counselor

In choosing an independent college counselor or educational consultant, parents and student should ask a number of questions about the qualifications of the counselor. The following are suggested questions that will help you to know more about the experience and expertise of the counselor:

- Do you have a brochure that explains your services and experience?
- What are your qualifications? Have you worked in a school as a college counselor or for a college or university as an admissions officer? How much experience did you have in that setting and how recent is the experience?
- How long have you been an independent college counselor?
- What academic degrees do you have? Do you have professional training as a college counselor? What institutes and workshops have you attended and when?
- What professional organizations do you belong to as a college counselor?
    ——National Association of College Admission Counselors (NACAC)

――Independent Educational Consultants Association (IECA)
――American Counseling Association (ACA)
――Other

- What professional meetings do you regularly attend?
- Do you visit college campuses? How many do you visit a year? Which high schools have you visited recently?
- Do you communicate regularly with the school counselors of your clients?
- What services do you offer? What resources do you have? Do you advise both on the college application process and on financial aid?
- What do your services cost? Do you have a sliding scale depending on the ability of your client to pay?
- What kind of follow-up study do you do with former clients and do you publish a profile?
- Can you give me names of satisfied clients with whom I might talk?

Two national associations grant membership specifically to independent college counseling consultants based on set criteria. If you have questions about those criteria and what to look for in an independent college counselor, contact the following nonprofit organizations:

National Association of College Admission Counselors
1800 Diagonal Road, Suite 430
Alexandria, VA 22314
(703)836-2222

The Independent Educational
  Consultants Association
P.O. Box 125
Forestdale, MA 02644
(617)477-2127

APPENDIX II

Financial Aid Guide: Caltech, 1993–94*

FINANCING A COLLEGE EDUCATION

A quality education is an investment that will provide lifelong personal and monetary returns. Because of rising educational costs, however, paying for such an investment has become a major expense and a complex task.

The California Institute of Technology has a long history of providing educational opportunities to qualified students regardless of their families' economic circumstances. We are strongly committed to assisting all admitted students in meeting their demonstrated financial need. In addition to providing assistance through the traditional need-based aid programs, Caltech offers information on payment plans and other financial options.

What follows outlines some of these options which are available to families for financing a Caltech education. With the exception of the subsidized Stafford Loan, most of the options described are available independent of the "need" concept as-

---

* We are grateful to David Levy of the California Institute of Technology for sharing Caltech's "Financial Aid Guide." This guide is typical of what many selective private and public colleges circulate, particularly those which award financial aid largely on the basis of a family's financial *need*.

sociated with the traditional financial aid programs offered by Caltech.

Need-Based Aid

The first consideration when determining how to finance a students's education is his or her possible eligibility for need-based financial aid. To begin this process, let's start with some questions and answers provided by Caltech:

Q. *Can our family afford a college like the California Institute of Technology?*

A. Caltech is committed to providing sufficient aid to allow every admitted student to enroll. Federal financial aid is awarded to students who demonstrate financial need, as defined by the standard national formula, Federal Methodology. The Institute is strongly committed to meeting fully the demonstrated financial need of students whose families cannot afford the total cost of a Caltech education. In the 1992–93 school year two-thirds of the undergraduate student body received assistance through the Caltech Financial Aid Office. The Caltech Financial Aid Office administers and coordinates federal, state, private, and institutional funds for grants, scholarships, low-interest loans, and part-time jobs.

Q. *What is demonstrated financial need?*

A. Financial need is the difference between the annual cost of attending Caltech and the amount the student and parents can reasonably be expected to contribute toward that cost. Caltech's estimate of a family's ability to contribute is determined annually in accordance with policies established nationally by the U.S. Department of Education and the College Scholarship Service. These policies and procedures take into account normal college expenses and the financial resources of the student and family.

Q. *Is there a point at which a family's income is too high to be eligible for financial aid?*

A. No. There is no automatic cutoff at a certain level of income. A number of factors such as family size, number of family members in college, and taxes paid are used in determining the amount the family can reasonably be expected to contribute toward Caltech's costs. The Caltech Financial Aid Office carefully reviews individual family circumstances; all students and families who feel that aid is necessary should apply.

Q. *Will our savings and other assets be considered?*

A. Family assets, such as stocks and bonds, net business worth, and savings are taken into account in determining Caltech's expected family contribution toward a student's education. The Federal Methodology formula provides an allowance for retirement needs in computing this contribution.

Q. *Will applying for financial aid affect a student's chances for admission to Caltech?*

A. No. Applications for admission are evaluated entirely separately from requests for financial aid. No applicant will be denied admission on the basis of limited financial resources.

Q. *When will we be told whether we have qualified for aid?*

A. In most cases, Caltech notifies students of conditional financial aid decisions at the time of admission. Official awards are made upon receipt of all necessary documentation, such as tax returns, and will reflect the student's verified financial need. Every effort is made to maintain consistency with the amounts of aid listed on the conditional financial aid award decision. However, in reviewing documentation submitted, adjustments may be appropriate, and an official award may consequently be different than a conditional award.

Determination of Financial Need

The basic formula for determining the amount of financial need at Caltech is:

College Expenses
less the family contribution (parents and student)
less all other financial resources
equals the amount of demonstrated financial need.

College Expenses

The following are estimates of the costs associated with attendance at Caltech for the 1993–94 academic year:

Tuition	$15,900
Fees	210
Room and Board	4,815
Meals not covered by the Board Contract	1,320
Books and Supplies	700
Personal Expenses	1,350
Total*	$24,295

* Does not include an alowance for two round trips from home to Caltech.

Expected Family Contribution

Caltech's estimate of a family's ability to contribute is determined on a yearly basis from the information provided on the Free Application for Federal Student Aid (FAFSA) and the Financial Aid Form (FAF). The information is analyzed using the nationally approved need analysis system called Federal Methodology. Federal Methodology views families as the primary source of financial support for undergraduate education and is designed to evaluate families' resources in a consistent and equitable manner. The determination of the family contribution may take into account factors such as family size, number of children in college, income, assets, taxes, and medical expenses.

The Institute also subscribes to the principle that families at the higher end of the financial scale should contribute proportionately more than those at the lower end. The general principles of Federal Methodology can be summarized as follows:

- Parents have an obligation to finance the education of their children to the extent they are able.
- A family's combined income and assets produce a comprehensive measure of the family's financial strength and ability to contribute toward educational costs.
- Factors such as family size, extraordinary expenses, age of parents, and other considerations are weighed in relation to income and asset information in order to measure a family's true ability to pay for an education.
- Students have a responsibility to help pay for their own education and, as primary beneficiaries of that education, should contribute a proportionately greater share of their income and assets than should their parents.

The student portion of the family contribution comes from an assessment of resources. Each student is expected to contribute toward his or her educational costs from employment earnings. The minimum earnings contributions expected by Caltech are based on academic class level. The expected minimum contribution amounts for the 1993–94 academic year are as follows:

Freshman	$1,200
Sophomore	$1,300
Junior	$1,400
Senior	$1,500

Students are also expected to contribute, each year, 35 percent of their cash, savings, investments, trust funds, and other assets up to the annual cost of a Caltech education.

Revisions to an award are always possible, because personal financial circumstances are subject to change. Further, financial aid may be increased for legitimate educational expenses not covered in the standard financial aid budget.

Changes in a family's financial situation subsequent to the applications for aid being filed can also affect the award. Students should contact the Caltech Financial Aid Office if they think they might, for any reason, qualify for additional aid. They must also report to the Financial Aid Office any additional resources, such as earnings from a job during the academic year, outside scholarships, or gifts. If these additional resources reduce or offset a student's financial need, the award will be adjusted.

Outside scholarships acquired by students are considered to be a resource available during the academic year. In general, the amount of each outside merit award will be used to replace a like amount of the self-help (work and/or loan) portion of the financial aid award. If the amount of the outside award exceeds the self-help portion, the excess amount will replace Caltech grant eligibility.

How to Apply for Financial Aid

Early Decision Admission Candidates should file an *Early Decision Financial Aid Form* with Caltech no later than December 1 of the year the student is applying for aid. If this Early Version FAF is postmarked by the December deadline, a conditional estimate of financial aid eligibility will be issued with the admissions offer. Before an official award can be offered, the application procedures for freshman admission candidates must also be completed.

Freshman Admission Candidates Who Are United States Citizens or Permanent Residents: By completing the Financial Aid Information Card included with the Caltech Freshman Admissions Application, freshman admission candidates will automatically be sent a Free Application for Federal Student Aid (FAFSA) and a College Scholarship Service (CSS) Financial Aid Form (FAF) after December 15 of the year the student is applying. Students applying for financial aid must complete and submit both of these forms to CSS between January 1 and February 1 in the year in which they are applying for priority consideration. After receipt of the FAFSA and FAF, the Financial Aid Office will determine a student's eligibility for financial aid. Conditional awards will be issued with offers of admission. Awards then will become official after student and parent tax returns and all other requested documents are received by the Financial Aid Office and any necessary award adjustments are made.

Types of Aid Available

Once financial need has been determined, that need will be met either by a single type of aid or by a combination of grants or scholarships, student employment, and low-interest loans. Such a combination makes up a financial aid "package."

Grants and scholarships, which include those provided both through Caltech and by the federal and state governments, do not have to be repaid. Loans are a sound means of meeting a portion of current educational expenses by borrowing against future earnings. Loans, of course, must be repaid. Employment wages comprise money earned during the academic year either on or off campus. Employment opportunities exist for students who must work to help meet their educational costs.

Grants and scholarships are typically disbursed to the student's account, one-third at the beginning of each term. Federal Perkins Loans and Caltech Loans are also disbursed to the account in thirds, after a promissory note is signed (usually at registration). Wages for on-campus employment are paid as earned, by check, through the Caltech payroll system.

Caltech Grants and Scholarships

Caltech Grants and "name" scholarships are awarded from an institutional fund or endowment specially established for the purpose of helping undergraduates meet their demonstrated financial need. The amount of the award depends entirely on financial need.

"Name" scholarships are awarded to undergraduates from gifts to the Institute given for scholarship purposes, and are named by or for the donor. All aid applicants who meet the specifications of the donor are considered for a "name" scholarship. No special application need be filed.

Federal and State Grants

The Federal Pell Grant Program is for undergraduate students who have not yet completed a baccalaureate degree. Beginning July 1, 1993, eligible students may receive Federal Pell Grants for the period of time necessary to complete a first undergraduate baccalaureate degree.

The Pell Grant program is intended to be the "floor" of the student's financial aid package. This is usually the first program for which a student's eligibility is determined because many other federal aid programs require that a student's Pell Grant eligibility be taken into consideration prior to determining eligibility for other aid. Application for a Pell Grant is made by using the Free Application for Federal Student Aid (FAFSA). Applicants will receive a Student Aid Report (SAR) directly from the FAFSA processor. Upon receipt of the SAR, students should submit all pages of the SAR to the Financial Aid Office, which will determine the amount of the award. The exact amount of the student's award will be determined based upon the cost of attendance, the Expected Family Contribution, and the student's enrollment status (in 1993–94, Pell Grant awards ranged up to $2,300).

The Federal Supplemental Educational Opportunity Grants (SEOG) Program provides grant funds for undergraduate students who have not completed their first baccalaureate degree and who are financially in need of this grant to enable them to pursue their education. Awards of SEOG funds must be made first to students who show exceptional financial need (defined as those students with the lowest federal expected family contribution at the Institute). Priority for SEOG funds must be given to Pell Grant recipients. No additional application is required. These grants are contingent upon federal appropriations. The minimum annual SEOG award is $100, and the maximum annual award is $4,000.

Most states also have their own system of financial aid (for example, in California *Cal Grants* are awarded to California residents by the California Student Aid Commission. All students who are eligible to apply are required to do so each year at the time they apply for assistance). This needs to be investigated by students and families applying for aid in the particular state in which they reside.

Self-Help: Employment and Loans

A self-help award is a combination of loans and employment opportunities students may take advantage of during the year to help meet school expenses. Students often can choose how much of their self-help they wish to earn and how much they wish to borrow.

The amount of self-help expected of a student is established yearly by the Institute. For the 1993–94 academic year, a freshman typically received $5,200 in self-help funds, with remaining need being met with grant money.

Employment

The Federal Work-Study Program provides jobs for undergraduates as well as graduate and professional students who are in need of such earnings to meet a portion of their educational expenses. Jobs may be located on campus or off campus. The employer may be Caltech; a federal, state, or local public agency; or a private nonprofit organization; or a private for-profit organization if the job is academically relevant. Work-Study employees are paid at least the federal minimum wage rate. Freshmen must receive permission to work from the Dean of Students before accepting their first work assignment. Federal Work-Study is made a part of a freshman's financial package for the second and third terms only.

The maximum amount of Federal Work-Study wages that students may earn is determined by financial need. To locate a job, the student may contact the campus Career Development Center and may check the student newspaper.

Loans

Federal Perkins Loans are awarded by the Institute to students with demonstrated financial need. Funds are obtained from the federal government and from former Caltech students who are in the process of repaying their loans. No interest is charged on the loan while a student maintains at least a half-time academic load. Repayment begins nine months after leaving school or dropping below half-time status. Interest is then charged at a rate of 5 percent on the unpaid balance. Perkins Loans are limited to a total of $3,000 annually during undergraduate study, a total of $15,000 for all years of undergraduate study, and a maximum of $30,000 for the entire undergraduate and graduate career. Students may be allowed up to ten years to repay based upon the amount they have borrowed. Information concerning deferment, repayment, postponement, and cancellation will be provided on each borrower's loan promissory note and in a disclosure statement given to students prior to disbursements of the loan.

Caltech Loans are made from funds provided by many sources, and are used to supplement the Institute's Perkins Loan funds. Generally, no interest is charged and no repayment of principal is required while a student maintains a continuous course of study as an undergraduate at Caltech. Repayment begins nine months after leaving school or dropping below half-time status. Interest is then charged at a rate of 5 percent on the unpaid balance until the loan has been repaid in full. As with Perkins Loans, if the student transfers to another institution or attends graduate school, here or at another institution, no payments need to be made on the principal or interest as long as half-time attendance is maintained at the other institution. More specific information is provided to each borrower on the promissory note and in a disclosure statement given to students prior to disbursements of the loan. (Most individual institutions have this type of loan.)

Federal Family Education Loans

The Federal Stafford Loan Program is the largest source of low-interest loans administered by the Department of Education. These loans are available to both undergraduate and graduate students. Caltech uses these loans primarily to offset a student's unusual expenses, and thus they may not be initially included in a student's aid package. Both subsidized and unsubsidized Stafford loans are available to students. The federal government "subsidizes" a loan by paying the interest while the student is in school, during the grace period, and during periods of deferment. For an unsubsidized loan, the government does not provide the subsidy; therefore, interest on the loan accrues during those periods. Another difference between these two loans is that the calculated family contribution is taken into consideration when determining a student's need for a subsidized loan. To determine eligibility for an unsubsidized loan, the family contribution is not considered. Other than these two differences, the provisions of the Stafford Loan Program apply to both subsidized and unsubsidized Stafford Loans (i.e., loan limits, deferment provisions, etc.).

A separate application is required for Federal Stafford Loans. Applications can be obtained from participating commercial lenders or from the Financial Aid Office. In most cases, the student completes the Stafford Loan application and sends it to Caltech for certification of enrollment, cost of attendance, expected family contribution, and documentation of other financial aid awarded. Caltech generally then forwards the application directly to the lender indicated by the student; however, it may also be given back to the student, so that she/he can take it to a particular lender.

Before Caltech can certify the loan application, a determination of the student's eligibility for a Pell Grant must be made. In order to make this determination, the applicant must complete a Free Application for Federal Student Aid and submit the resultant Student Aid Report (SAR) to the Caltech Financial Aid Office. The SAR contains the official expected family contribution figure of the student. Subsidized Stafford Loans may not be used to substitute for that expected family contribution; however, unsubsidized Stafford Loans may be used in this capacity. Before a student can apply for an unsubsidized Stafford Loan, eligibility for a subsidized loan will be determined. Unsubsidized Stafford Loan borrowers are not required to demonstrate need in order to be eligible. However, if the student is eligible for a subsidized Stafford Loan, he or she will be awarded that loan first, and this award will be taken into consideration when determining eligibility for the unsubsidized Stafford Loan. The amount borrowed under the subsidized and unsubsidized loans combined may not exceed the annual/aggregate loan limits, or the total cost of education.

The maximum annual amounts that may be borrowed are: $2,625 for the first year of undergraduate study; $3,500 for the second year of undergraduate study; and $5,500 per year for the remaining years of undergraduate study. The aggregate loan amount is $23,000 for undergraduates.

All loans must be disbursed in at least two installments. Further, loan checks for first time, first year undergraduate borrowers may not be released to the student until she/he has been enrolled in her/his program of study for at least thirty days.

At the time of this writing the maximum interest rate for new borrowers is 9%. However, the actual rate is variable, and is determined annually according to a formula linked to the 91-day Treasury bill rate. You should check the rate applicable in the year you are applying for this loan by calling the Financial Aid Offices of the institutions to which you are applying or checking with a lender.

The Federal government's costs in the Stafford Loan program stem from: (1) the payment of interest benefits on behalf of qualified borrowers; (2) payment of a "special allowance" to lenders to encourage their participation in a low-interest loan program; and (3) payment of default, death, disability, bankruptcy claims, and administrative costs to guaranty agencies.

To offset the federal government's cost of the program, the lender is authorized to charge the borrower an up-front origination fee of up to 5% of the principal amount of the loan. This origination fee is used to offset some of the federal costs to the program and was enacted in 1981 when interest costs were exceptionally high. In addition to the 5% origination fee, borrowers also pay an insurance premium which by law cannot exceed 3% of the principal amount of the loan.

Repayment begins six months after graduation or termination of enrollment on at least a half-time basis. Students may be allowed up to ten years to repay, based upon the amount they have borrowed, with a minimum annual repayment of $600 ($50 per month). This $600 amount would include any required repayments under the Supplemental Loan for Students (SLS) Program. Specific information on repayment and deferment are included in the loan promissory note and in the loan disclosure statement provided to student borrowers.

The Federal Supplemental Loans for Students (SLS) Program is a source of loan funds available to independent undergraduate students and to graduate and professional students.

SLS Loans are limited to the difference between the student's cost of attendance and other financial aid, and may replace the expected family contribution. A student's eligibility for a Pell Grant and Stafford Loan must be determined before any SLS loan can be certified. The amounts of Pell Grant and Stafford Loan for which the student would be eligible must be considered in determining the amount of the SLS loan, whether or not he/she actually applies for those programs. More detailed information on the SLS loan may be obtained by contacting the financial aid office at any school to which you plan to apply. Your college counselor or the school's College Center may also have this information.

Federal PLUS (Parent) Loan Program. Under the Federal

PLUS Program, parents of dependent undergraduate students may borrow up to the difference between costs of attendance and all other financial aid, per dependent student. PLUS loans may also be used to replace the expected family contribution. There is no cumulative maximum limit that can be borrowed under the PLUS Program. PLUS loan checks are copayable to the parent and the school.

Interest rates on PLUS loans are variable, linked to 52-week Treasury bill rates, but may not exceed 10%. There is no federal interest subsidy on PLUS loans. However, the lender is authorized to charge the borrower an up-front origination fee of up to 5% to offset the federal government's cost of the program.

Unless the parent borrower qualifies for one of the deferments under the Stafford Loan Program, repayment of principal and interest must begin 60 days after disbursement. Parent borrowers who qualify for deferment may pay interest only, beginning 60 days after disbursement, unless interest is capitalized (i.e., deferred and added to the loan principal).

Applications for PLUS loans are available from lenders, as well as from the Caltech Financial Aid Office. Applications must be certified by the Financial Aid Office.

Other Resources

Student Employment is generally available to all students regardless of whether they apply for financial aid. The Caltech Career Development Office will be happy to assist students in finding part-time jobs. Income earned during the academic year may affect the award of students receiving financial aid, so students should notify the Financial Aid Office when they begin employment.

The Summer Undergraduate Research Fellowships Program (SURF) is a unique opportunity for Caltech undergraduates to obtain practical research experience, working directly with Caltech faculty members or JPL staff scientists.

A number of both local and national organizations offer *outside scholarships* to students throughout the year, regardless of need (see bibliography on p. 220). Also available are a number of departmentally awarded scholarships.

Army and Air Force Reserve Officers' Training Corps (ROTC) scholarships are available through arrangements with neighboring universities.

Lines of Credit

ExtraCredit Loan is a privately sponsored loan option available to credit-worthy applicants under The College Board's College Credit program. ExtraCredit is designed to bridge the gap between college costs and family resources. To be eligible, applicants must be U.S. Citizens or permanent residents and be the parent or legal guardian of the student for whom the loan will be used.

The minimum loan amount is $2,000 and up to 100% of college expenses can be borrowed. The inception interest rate from June 1993 to May 1994 will be 7.25%. After that date the rate will vary quarterly at 4.5 percentage points above the 13 week Treasury bill rate rounded to the nearest quarter. There is a one-time only nonrefundable $45 application fee. There are no guarantee, insurance, or origination fees. Repayment begins immediately with 10 to 15 years to repay. For an ExtraCredit application call (800) 874-9390.

Academic Credit Line (ACL)—Academic Management Services (AMS) offers an unsecured revolving line of credit designed to help families manage extra education expenses. AMS offers the following features: (1) A line of credit up to $25,000; (2) No origination or guarantee fee, the annual fee of $25 is waived the first year; (3) A one-time application with loan approval within 72 hours in most cases (telephone applications are available); (4) Lower Payment Option (LPO) of interest only for up to two, four, or six years; (5) Interest rate of prime rate plus 4 percent. For more information, write AMS, P.O. Box 14668,

East Providence, Rhode Island 02914-9852, or call (800) 722-1300.

Educational Line of Credit is offered by Chemical Banking Corporation. The Educational Line of Credit is a loan in the form of a credit line that can be drawn upon over the years to meet student educational expenses. Any parent or legal guardian of a financially dependent student may qualify. The credit line can be set up to provide from $5,000 to $40,000 through up to five years of education. The total outstanding balance is protected by credit life insurance at no extra charge.

The interest rate (APR) is variable and is established quarterly, based on the prime rate plus 4.5 percent. There is no application fee or origination fee. The minimum monthly payment is 1/84th of the outstanding balance plus interest.

For more information, write to: The Educational Financing Group, 57 Regional Drive, Concord, New Hampshire 03301-9846, or call (800) 258-3640.

Supplemental Loan Plans

A Better Loan for Education (ABLE), offered by the Knight Tuition Payment Plans, is a long-term unsecured loan plan which allows credit-worthy applicants to repay one year of education cost over 15 years. The annual percentage rate is adjusted quarterly to 2.5% above the prime rate, as published in the *Wall Street Journal*.

There are no origination or guarantee fees. The nonrefundable application fee is $55. For more information contact: Knight Tuition Payment Plans, 855 Boylston Street, Boston, MA 02116, or call (800) 225-6783.

The *TERI Supplemental Loan Program* is privately guaranteed by The Education Resources Institute of Boston, Massachusetts. Loan capital is currently provided by approximately 20 private lenders. TERI offers annual loans from $2,000 to $20,000 to credit-worthy families. The student and parent or legal guardians are co-borrowers. At least one applicant must be a U.S. Citizen or permanent resident.

The variable interest rate is tied to the lender's base or prime rate plus 2 percent. Although the rate is variable, the monthly payment will be fixed throughout the term of the loan. The total number of payments may increase or decrease depending on fluctuations in the interest rate during the loan period. Effective May 1, 1991, a guarantee fee of 5 percent of the total loan amount will be deducted at the time of disbursement. Borrowers may take up to 20 years to repay.

For more information on participating lenders and lender-specific policies, contact TERI at 330 Stuart Street, Suite 500, Boston, MA 02116, or call (800) 255-8374.

EXCEL Education Loans—Credit-worthy applicants at any income level, who are U.S. Citizens or U.S. permanent residents, may be eligible for EXCEL Education loans. EXCEL offers loan amounts ranging from $2,000 to the cost of attendance less financial aid. Borrowers can choose between two interest-rate options, and may choose to defer principal payments while the undergraduate or graduate student is enrolled, or to pay fixed monthly payments of principal and interest. Repayment periods range from 4 to 20 years, depending on the amount borrowed.

For more information or an EXCEL application, write to Nellie Mae, EXCEL Department, 50 Braintree Hill Park, Suite 300, Braintree, MA 02184, or call (800) 634-9308 or (617) 849-3447.

Payment Plans

The following organizations offer financial payment plans to help with the costs of education at various colleges and universities nationwide:

1. Academic Management Services, Inc., P.O. Box 14668, East Providence, Rhode Island 02914, (800) 635-0120,

offers a plan for paying educational costs on a ten-month basis beginning July 1. The annual fee is $50, and Life Benefit Coverage is provided at no charge.

2. The Knight Insured Tuition Payment Plan, 855 Boylston Street, Boston, Massachusetts 02116, (617) 267-1500 or (800) 225-6783, offers a monthly payment program to cover multiple years of educational expenses. Plans may be arranged for one or more years of education. Insurance coverage is optional at additional cost. The initial fee is $55, with no annual fee for a multiple-year plan.

3. The Tuition Plan of New England, Inc., 57 Regional Drive, Concord, New Hampshire 03301-9846, (800) 343-0911, offers the Educational Financing Manager (EFM), which allows participants to cover educational costs over nine monthly installments. Life insurance covering the balance of the budgeted amount is provided at no additional cost. The annual participation fee is $45.

4. The Education Resources Institute (TERI), 330 Stuart Street, Suite 500, Boston, Massachusetts 02116-5237, (800) 255-8374, offers a Tuition Payment Plan for paying educational costs on a nine-month basis. The annual application fee is $45.

The above information was received from financing sources concerning available programs and is believed to be accurate and current as of the date of this publication. However, this information does not constitute an offer of endorsement by Caltech or by the writer of any particular program; and, accordingly, readers should inquire directly for complete details regarding the individual programs described above.

° ° °

Sample Financial Aid Packages*

The following sample financial aid packages are not actual awards, but examples of the kinds of packages that colleges award.

Student 1: Family income = $40,000,
4 in family, 1 in college.
Expected Family Contribution (EFC) = $1,800

	Pkg. #1	Pkg. #2
Cost of Attendance	$ 9,000	$16,000
Family Contribution	1,800	1,800
Financial Need	$ 7,200	$14,200
Sample Package:		
Pell Grant	$ 650	$ 650
SEOG	1,000	2,000
State Grant	800	800
Institutional Grant	1,000	3,875
CWS	1,750	2,250
Perkins Loan	2,000	2,000
Stafford Loan	0	2,625
Total Financial Aid Offered:	7,200	14,200
Unmet Need	$ 0	$ 0

Student 2: Family income = $80,000,
5 in family, 2 in college.
Expected Family Contribution (EFC) = $8,500/student

	Pkg. #1	Pkg. #2
Cost of Attendance	$11,500	$23,000
Family Contribution	8,500	8,500
Financial Need	3,000	14,500

* From Bart Astor of the *College Planning Quarterly*.

Sample Financial Aid Packages (cont.)

	Sample Package:		
Pell Grant/SEOG		0	0
State Grant		0	0
Institutional Grant		0	6,000
CWS		1,500	2,250
Perkins Loan		1,500	2,000
Stafford Loan		0	2,625
Total Financial Aid Offered		$ 3,000	$12,875
Unmet Need		0	$ 1,625

FINANCIAL AID BIBLIOGRAPHY

The A's and B's of Academic Scholarships. Deborah L. Klein. Octameron Associates, P.O. Box 2748, Alexandria, VA 22301.

The College Cost Book. College Board Publications, Box 886, New York, NY 10101.

College Planning Quarterly. Bart Astor and Associates, P.O. Box 844, South Orange, NJ 07079 (800-457-1492).

Don't Miss Out! (The Ambitious Student's Guide to Financial Aid.) Anna Leider, Octameron Associates, P.O. Box 2748, Alexandria, VA 22301.

Winning Money for College: The High School Student's Guide to Scholarship Contests. Alan Deutschman, Peterson's Guides, Princeton, NJ 08543.

APPENDIX III

Representative Responses to Moll's *Harper's* Article, "The College Admissions Game"*

1. *At time of publication:*

From the headmistress of the Nightingale-Bamford School, N.Y.C.:

> Your article in *Harper's* was being handed out wholesale to parents until the Bryn Mawr Director of Admissions told me that it might soon be part of a book; better they should wait and read the whole thing!

From the dean of admissions, Amherst College, Massachusetts:

> My *Harper's* finally arrived yesterday. What a great article! I'm certain that a few of our counterparts will squirm when they read it, but what you said needed to be said and I'm glad you took the time and trouble to put such straight talk down on paper.
>
> I basically agree with your thesis although Amherst doesn't get very excited about your Category 5.

From the college adviser at Phillips Exeter, New Hampshire:

* March 1978.

Well, naturally, I read your *Harper's* article. I thought it was fine and accurate. In fact, I have recommended it to all our parents in my column of the Exeter Parents Newsletter. As you may know, your article was quoted extensively last Sunday in the *Boston Globe*.

From an officer of the Public Interest Economics Foundation, Washington, D.C.:

Thanks for the lucid, myth-shattering article in *Harper's*. We plan to circulate large numbers of copies, particularly to Washington's local contingent of hysterics.

From the college counselor of the Fieldston School, N.Y.C.:

I found your article in *Harper's* to be the most accurate and useful document available to guidance counselors in many a year. I've referred it to all 11th graders and their parents and have also alerted our seniors who are waiting impatiently to receive much painful news from those "impossible" colleges.

From the Associate Dean of Admissions at Colgate University, Hamilton, N.Y.:

I have just finished reading your *Harper's* article and can find fault with you in only one way: why should you be able to capably put into print those sentiments which I at times have difficulty simply conceptualizing? So much for the praise; now back to the "categorical" decision making.

From the college counselor at the Breck School in Minnesota:

Thanks for saying in *Harper's* what should have been said long ago. You have not only enlightened your reader with marvelous insight, but have given students a ray of hope to cling to. My own experience has shown that applicants don't really mind being rejected if they can see some rationale behind the process. Your article gave them a sound explanation.

From the Director of Admissions at Oberlin College, Ohio:

Your *Harper's* article does a great job of telling it like it is! As usual, you're right on target.

2. A questionnaire was circulated to over 100 admissions directors of private colleges following publication of the article. The question: "Do you agree with the basic thesis of Moll's *Harper's* article?" The response: a categorical "yes" from such colleges as Bates (Maine), Beloit (Wisconsin), Boston College ("Bravo!"), Bucknell (Pennsylvania), Colby-Sawyer (New Hampshire), Franklin and Marshall (Pennsylvania), Furman (South Carolina), Hampshire (Massachusetts), Lafayette (Pennsylvania), Manhattan (New York), Manhattanville, (New York), Ohio Wesleyan, Ripon (Wisconsin), St. Lawrence (New York), Stephens (Missouri), Susquehanna (Pennsylvania). Other respondents had reservations:

Brandeis (Massachusetts):

> For the most part, yes. Some schools, I suspect, are more engaged in this type of admission than others. The other very interesting question is: who decides how big each interest group's "share of the pie" is?—in reality, are not the groups then in direct competition for seats in the new class?

Earlham (Indiana):

> Not being in the position of the Ivies, we feel a bit removed from the issue. Earlham has not been in a position during recent years to be more than mildly selective. We are saved by students who self-select us for special reasons and we tell our prospective students just that.

Knox (Illinois):

> Surely what you say is true for the most selective colleges in the country. But this has little bearing on the majority of private institutions, and will have less as we move into the eighties and nineties.

Lewis and Clark (Oregon):

> I don't doubt your thesis for the most selective colleges. But it hardly applies to the institutions in our area. Aren't you really talking about a very small number of colleges?

Mount Holyoke (Massachusetts):

> Not completely. Your analysis may lead to the idea that *everyone* is "boxed." There is no uniform standard for making a decision, since much of the process depends on personal judgment and experience with previous classes. Selection is an art, not a science, and although special talents, legacies, geography and other factors may play a part, there is no uniform method of weighting.

University of Richmond (Virginia):

> With our volume of applications, I don't feel the candidates fall into categories as neatly as you have described them.

APPENDIX IV

Statement of Principles of Good Practice

For Members of the National Association of College Admission Counselors

STATEMENT OF STUDENTS' RIGHTS AND RESPONSIBILITIES IN THE COLLEGE ADMISSION PROCESS

Revised July 1992

An outgrowth of the *Statement of Principles of Good Practice*, the Students' Rights Statement makes clear to entering college students those "rights" which are only alluded to by the Principles of Good Practice. It also spells out the responsibilities students have in the admission process.

When You Apply to Colleges and Universities You Have Rights

Before You Apply:

- You have the right to receive full information from colleges and universities about their admission, financial aid, scholarship, and housing policies. If you consider applying under an early decision plan you have the right to complete information from the college about its process and policy.

When You Are Offered Admission:

- You have the right to wait to respond to an offer of admission and/or financial aid until May 1.
- Colleges that request commitments to offers of admission, financial assistance, and/or housing prior to May 1, must clearly offer you the opportunity to request (in writing) an extension until May 1. They must grant you this extension and your request may not jeopardize your status for housing and/or financial aid. (This right does not apply to candidates admitted under an early decision program.)

If You Are Placed on a Wait List or Alternate List:

- The letter that notifies you of that placement should provide a history that describes the number of students on the wait list, the number offered admission, and the availability of financial aid and housing.
- Colleges may require neither a deposit nor a written commitment as a condition of remaining on a wait list.
- Colleges are expected to notify you of the resolution of your wait list status by August 1 at the latest.

When You Apply to Colleges and Universities You Have Responsibilities

Before You Apply:

- You have a responsibility to research and understand the policies and procedures of each college or university regarding application fees, financial aid, scholarships, and housing. You should also be sure that you understand the policies of each college or university regarding deposits that you may be required to make before you enroll.

As You Apply:

- You must complete all material that is required for application, and submit your application on or before the published deadlines. You should be the sole author of your applications.
- You should seek the assistance of your high school counselor early and throughout the application period. Follow the process recommended by your high school for filing college applications.
- It is your responsibility to arrange, if apropriate, for visits to and/or interviews at colleges of your choice.

After You Receive Your Admission Decisions:

- You must notify each college or university which accepts you whether you are accepting or rejecting its offer. You should make these notifications as soon as you have made a final decision as to the college that you wish to attend, but no later than May 1.
- You may confirm your intention to enroll and, if required, submit a deposit to only one college or university. The exception to this arises if you are put on a wait list by a college or university and are later admitted to that institution. You may accept the offer and send a deposit. However, you must immediately notify a college or university at which you previously indicated your intention to enroll.
- If you are accepted under an early decision plan, you must promptly withdraw the applications submitted to other colleges and universities and make no additional applications. If you are an early decision candidate and are seeking financial aid, you need not withdraw other applications until you have received notification about financial aid.

If you think that your rights have been denied, you should contact the college or university immediately to request additional information or the extension of a reply date. In addition, you should ask your counselor to notify the president of the state or regional affiliate of the National Association of College Admission Counselors. If you need further assistance, send a copy of any correspondence you have had with the college or university and a copy of your letter of admission to: Executive Director, NACAC, 1631 Prince Street, Alexandria, VA 22314-2818.

APPENDIX V

The Lighter Side

We on one side of the admissions desk realize that candidates who sit on the other side compare notes and chatter and giggle among themselves about all the unexpected, somewhat zany things that happen along the pathway of "getting into college." Well, we on the "authoritative" side of the desk smile at a few things that happen en route also. Here are a few tidbits that Directors of Admissions have consented to divulge:

Bowdoin (Maine):

> I interviewed a superb candidate at a College Day in a hotel room. As the forty-minute interview drew to a close, I happened to mention the word "Bowdoin," and the kid jumped up with alarm.... He had intended to see the Williams College representative in the next room.

Bucknell (Pennsylvania):

> Leaning back in my chair during an interview to achieve that perfect projection of the casual and interested air, the rollers on my chair took off, and I did a reverse somersault. The candidate was obviously stunned. His face seemed to say: "Wow, I wonder what this guy does for encores?"

Colgate (New York):

About to interview two boys at one of the nation's most prestigious prep schools, I asked the college adviser about the first boy's credentials. "He ranks 150 out of 150," was the response. "What about the second boy?" I asked. "He's tied with the other."

Franklin and Marshall (Pennsylvania):

What *should* I have done when the young man I was interviewing grew so nervous that he wet his pants? But perhaps that incident was only the runner-up. One time I called a young man to tell him that he had won a special scholarship. His mother answered the phone and I said: "Hello, this is the Director of Admissions of Franklin and Marshall College. Is your son there?" She said, "No." I said, "Well, I'm calling to tell him about a special scholarship he has won." And she said: "For heaven's sakes, George, I told you *never* to call me at home!" I repeated my story, and she still thought it was George pulling her leg, and said, "Please hang up. I can see my husband coming up the walk now." I hung up and wrote a letter.

Furman (South Carolina):

A young man completed the "Sex" blank on our application by saying: "Once, in Charlotte, North Carolina." A young woman, in completing the question which asks about the "state of your health," put "Georgia."

Lafayette (Pennsylvania):

Interviewer: "And why do you think that Lafayette might be a good college for you?"
Candidate: "Well, I don't want to go to a real big college or a real small college. I just want a mediocre college like Lafayette."

Manhattan (New York):

At a New York City Fair, I tried to hand a young lady an application. She said: "Oh, no thank you. I've already applicated."

The Lighter Side

Ripon (Wisconsin):

> One girl told me she was the accompanist for the a capella choir. Best prize: A young man wrote on his application that he first heard about Ripon by reading its name on the wall of the Men's Room in the Boston Public Library.

St. Lawrence (New York):

> I met a nun at a conference representing another college, who said: "What I like about most of you men in admissions is that you're young enough to be sexy, but too old to be dangerous." Also, I remember the guidance counselor's report which arrived saying: "Prepared in copulation with the principal."

Scripps (California):

> The cosmic giggle hasn't happened to me yet. But the possibilities haunt me.

Stanford (California):

> Several quips from recommendations linger in my mind: The teacher (of typing) who wrote, "Barbara has the fastest hands in the class"; the counselor who wrote, "John's only weakness is his lack of potential." And we're still mystified by the principal who wrote, "Burt is in the top third quarter of his class."

Tulane (Louisiana):

> A conversation with a high Math, low Verbal applicant for Engineering:
> Counselor: "Are you a good student?"
> Applicant: "I don't do too good in English."
> Counselor: "I don't do too *well* in English."
> Applicant: "Me neither."

FOR THE BEST IN PAPERBACKS, LOOK FOR THE

In every corner of the world, on every subject under the sun, Penguin represents quality and variety—the very best in publishing today.

For complete information about books available from Penguin—including Pelicans, Puffins, Peregrines, and Penguin Classics—and how to order them, write to us at the appropriate address below. Please note that for copyright reasons the selection of books varies from country to country.

In the United Kingdom: For a complete list of books available from Penguin in the U.K., please write to *Dept E.P., Penguin Books Ltd, Harmondsworth, Middlesex, UB7 0DA.*

In the United States: For a complete list of books available from Penguin in the U.S., please write to *Consumer Sales, Penguin USA, P.O. Box 999— Dept. 17109, Bergenfield, New Jersey 07621-0120.* VISA and MasterCard holders call 1-800-253-6476 to order all Penguin titles.

In Canada: For a complete list of books available from Penguin in Canada, please write to *Penguin Books Canada Ltd, 10 Alcorn Avenue, Suite 300, Toronto, Ontario, Canada M4V 3B2.*

In Australia: For a complete list of books available from Penguin in Australia, please write to the *Marketing Department, Penguin Books Ltd, P.O. Box 257, Ringwood, Victoria 3134.*

In New Zealand: For a complete list of books available from Penguin in New Zealand, please write to the *Marketing Department, Penguin Books (NZ) Ltd, Private Bag, Takapuna, Auckland 9.*

In India: For a complete list of books available from Penguin, please write to *Penguin Overseas Ltd, 706 Eros Apartments, 56 Nehru Place, New Delhi, 110019.*

In Holland: For a complete list of books available from Penguin in Holland, please write to *Penguin Books Nederland B.V., Postbus 195, NL-1380AD Weesp, Netherlands.*

In Germany: For a complete list of books available from Penguin, please write to *Penguin Books Ltd, Friedrichstrasse 10-12, D-6000 Frankfurt Main 1, Federal Republic of Germany.*

In Spain: For a complete list of books available from Penguin in Spain, please write to *Longman, Penguin España, Calle San Nicolas 15, E-28013 Madrid, Spain.*

In Japan: For a complete list of books available from Penguin in Japan, please write to *Longman Penguin Japan Co Ltd, Yamaguchi Building, 2-12-9 Kanda Jimbocho, Chiyoda-Ku, Tokyo 101, Japan.*

FOR THE BEST IN PAPERBACKS, LOOK FOR THE

Whether you're trying to get into college or are there already, let Penguin Books be your personal guidance counselor:

☐ **ACING COLLEGE**
Joshua Halberstam, Ph.D.

Studying is not enough to guarantee As! This book shows you the secrets of how professors determine grades and how to play the games that will help you get top marks. *ISBN: 0-14-013998-2*

☐ **COLLEGE LIFE**
Ellen Rosenberg

Practical advice and straight talk about the real stuff of everyday college life, including being away from home, roommates, academic expectations, alcohol and drugs, and dating and sex.
ISBN: 0-14-014484-6

☐ **LOOKING BEYOND THE IVY LEAGUE**
Finding the College That's Right For You
Loren Pope

A college counselor to students and parents for more than 35 years guides you through the labyrinthine college selection process.
ISBN: 0-14-012209-5

You can find all these books at your local bookstore, or use this handy coupon for ordering:
Penguin Books By Mail
Dept. BA Box 999
Bergenfield, NJ 07621-0999

Please send me the above title(s). I am enclosing _____
(please add sales tax if appropriate and $1.50 to cover postage and handling). Send check or money order—no CODs. Please allow four weeks for shipping. We cannot ship to post office boxes or addresses outside the USA. *Prices subject to change without notice.*

Ms./Mrs./Mr. _____

Address _____

City/State _____ Zip _____